Just The facts101 Textbook Key Facts

Japan Immigration Laws and Regulations Handbook: Strategic Information and Basic Laws

by Cram101
Textbook NOT Included

Table of Contents

Index: Answers

Just The Facts101

Exam Prep for

Japan Immigration Laws and
Regulations Handbook: Strategic
Information and Basic Laws

Just The Facts101 Exam Prep is your link from
the textbook and lecture to your exams.

**Just The Facts101 Exam Preps are unauthorized and comprehensive reviews
of your textbooks.**

All material provided by CTI Publications (c) 2019

Textbook publishers and textbook authors do not participate in or contribute to these reviews.

Just The Facts101 Exam Prep

eAIN 438687

Foundations of Business

A business, also known as an enterprise, agency or a firm, is an entity involved in the provision of goods and/or services to consumers. Businesses are prevalent in capitalist economies, where most of them are privately owned and provide goods and services to customers in exchange for other goods, services, or money.

:: International trade ::

In finance, an _____ is the rate at which one currency will be exchanged for another. It is also regarded as the value of one country's currency in relation to another currency. For example, an interbank _____ of 114 Japanese yen to the United States dollar means that ¥114 will be exchanged for each US$1 or that US$1 will be exchanged for each ¥114. In this case it is said that the price of a dollar in relation to yen is ¥114, or equivalently that the price of a yen in relation to dollars is $1/114.

Exam Probability: **Medium**

1. *Answer choices:*

(see index for correct answer)

- a. Agreement on Technical Barriers to Trade
- b. Swiss Formula
- c. Exchange rate
- d. Global financial system

Guidance: level 1

:: Packaging ::

In work place, _____ or job _____ means good ranking with the hypothesized conception of requirements of a role. There are two types of job _____ s: contextual and task. Task _____ is related to cognitive ability while contextual _____ is dependent upon personality. Task _____ are behavioral roles that are recognized in job descriptions and by remuneration systems, they are directly related to organizational _____, whereas, contextual _____ are value based and additional behavioral roles that are not recognized in job descriptions and covered by compensation; they are extra roles that are indirectly related to organizational _____. Citizenship _____ like contextual _____ means a set of individual activity/contribution that supports the organizational culture.

Exam Probability: **Low**

2. *Answer choices:*

(see index for correct answer)

- a. Optical disc packaging
- b. Shake well
- c. Performance
- d. Active packaging

Guidance: level 1

:: ::

Culture is the social behavior and norms found in human societies. Culture is considered a central concept in anthropology, encompassing the range of phenomena that are transmitted through social learning in human societies. _____ universals are found in all human societies; these include expressive forms like art, music, dance, ritual, religion, and technologies like tool usage, cooking, shelter, and clothing. The concept of material culture covers the physical expressions of culture, such as technology, architecture and art, whereas the immaterial aspects of culture such as principles of social organization , mythology, philosophy, literature , and science comprise the intangible _____ heritage of a society.

Exam Probability: **Low**

3. *Answer choices:*

(see index for correct answer)

- a. surface-level diversity
- b. hierarchical
- c. similarity-attraction theory
- d. functional perspective

Guidance: level 1

:: ::

_____ is a means of protection from financial loss. It is a form of risk management, primarily used to hedge against the risk of a contingent or uncertain loss

4. *Answer choices:*

(see index for correct answer)

- a. imperative
- b. information systems assessment
- c. Insurance
- d. interpersonal communication

Guidance: level 1

:: Public relations ::

_____ is the public visibility or awareness for any product, service or company. It may also refer to the movement of information from its source to the general public, often but not always via the media. The subjects of _____ include people , goods and services, organizations, and works of art or entertainment.

Exam Probability: **Medium**

5. *Answer choices:*

(see index for correct answer)

- a. International
- b. European Public Relations Education and Research Association

- c. Spin
- d. Lawfare

Guidance: level 1

:: Telecommunication theory ::

In reliability theory and reliability engineering, the term _____ has the following meanings.

Exam Probability: **High**

6. *Answer choices:*

(see index for correct answer)

- a. Modulation order
- b. Center frequency
- c. Routing and wavelength assignment
- d. Bandwidth

Guidance: level 1

:: Generally Accepted Accounting Principles ::

In business and accounting, _____ is an entity's income minus cost of goods sold, expenses and taxes for an accounting period. It is computed as the residual of all revenues and gains over all expenses and losses for the period, and has also been defined as the net increase in shareholders' equity that results from a company's operations. In the context of the presentation of financial statements, the IFRS Foundation defines _____ as synonymous with profit and loss. The difference between revenue and the cost of making a product or providing a service, before deducting overheads, payroll, taxation, and interest payments. This is different from operating income .

Exam Probability: **High**

7. *Answer choices:*

(see index for correct answer)

- a. Consolidation
- b. Earnings before interest, taxes, depreciation, and amortization
- c. Net income
- d. Completed-contract method

Guidance: level 1

:: Market research ::

A _____ is a small, but demographically diverse group of people and whose reactions are studied especially in market research or political analysis in guided or open discussions about a new product or something else to determine the reactions that can be expected from a larger population. It is a form of qualitative research consisting of interviews in which a group of people are asked about their perceptions, opinions, beliefs, and attitudes towards a product, service, concept, advertisement, idea, or packaging. Questions are asked in an interactive group setting where participants are free to talk with other group members. During this process, the researcher either takes notes or records the vital points he or she is getting from the group. Researchers should select members of the _____ carefully for effective and authoritative responses.

Exam Probability: **Low**

8. *Answer choices:*

(see index for correct answer)

- a. Mendelsohn Affluent Survey
- b. News ratings in Australia
- c. Mall-intercept personal interview
- d. New economic order

Guidance: level 1

:: Export and import control ::

" _____ " means the Government Service which is responsible for the administration of _____ law and the collection of duties and taxes and which also has the responsibility for the application of other laws and regulations relating to the importation, exportation, movement or storage of goods.

Exam Probability: **Medium**

9. *Answer choices:*

(see index for correct answer)

- a. GOST R Conformity Declaration
- b. International Traffic in Arms Regulations
- c. Export Management and Compliance Program
- d. Customs

Guidance: level 1

:: Service industries ::

_____ are the economic services provided by the finance industry, which encompasses a broad range of businesses that manage money, including credit unions, banks, credit-card companies, insurance companies, accountancy companies, consumer-finance companies, stock brokerages, investment funds, individual managers and some government-sponsored enterprises. _____ companies are present in all economically developed geographic locations and tend to cluster in local, national, regional and international financial centers such as London, New York City, and Tokyo.

10. *Answer choices:*

(see index for correct answer)

- a. Excel Insurance Solutions
- b. Maid service
- c. Financial services
- d. Tourism

Guidance: level 1

:: Marketing ::

A _____ is an overall experience of a customer that distinguishes an organization or product from its rivals in the eyes of the customer. _____ s are used in business, marketing, and advertising. Name _____ s are sometimes distinguished from generic or store _____ s.

11. *Answer choices:*

(see index for correct answer)

- a. Performance-based advertising
- b. Chaotics
- c. Customer newsletter service

- d. Jobbing house

Guidance: level 1

:: Debt ::

_____ is when something, usually money, is owed by one party, the borrower or _____ or, to a second party, the lender or creditor. _____ is a deferred payment, or series of payments, that is owed in the future, which is what differentiates it from an immediate purchase. The _____ may be owed by sovereign state or country, local government, company, or an individual. Commercial _____ is generally subject to contractual terms regarding the amount and timing of repayments of principal and interest. Loans, bonds, notes, and mortgages are all types of _____ . The term can also be used metaphorically to cover moral obligations and other interactions not based on economic value. For example, in Western cultures, a person who has been helped by a second person is sometimes said to owe a " _____ of gratitude" to the second person.

Exam Probability: **Medium**

12. *Answer choices:*

(see index for correct answer)

- a. Museum of Foreign Debt
- b. Cessio bonorum
- c. Arrears
- d. Debt

Guidance: level 1

:: Marketing analytics ::

_____ is a long-term, forward-looking approach to planning with the fundamental goal of achieving a sustainable competitive advantage. Strategic planning involves an analysis of the company's strategic initial situation prior to the formulation, evaluation and selection of market-oriented competitive position that contributes to the company's goals and marketing objectives.

Exam Probability: **Low**

13. *Answer choices:*

(see index for correct answer)

- a. Return on marketing investment
- b. Marketing operations management
- c. Marketing strategy
- d. Market share analysis

Guidance: level 1

:: Bribery ::

_____ is the act of giving or receiving something of value in exchange for some kind of influence or action in return, that the recipient would otherwise not offer. _____ is defined by Black's Law Dictionary as the offering, giving, receiving, or soliciting of any item of value to influence the actions of an official or other person in charge of a public or legal duty. Essentially, _____ is offering to do something for someone for the expressed purpose of receiving something in exchange. Gifts of money or other items of value which are otherwise available to everyone on an equivalent basis, and not for dishonest purposes, is not _____ . Offering a discount or a refund to all purchasers is a legal rebate and is not _____ . For example, it is legal for an employee of a Public Utilities Commission involved in electric rate regulation to accept a rebate on electric service that reduces their cost for electricity, when the rebate is available to other residential electric customers. Giving the rebate to influence them to look favorably on the electric utility's rate increase applications, however, would be considered _____ .

Exam Probability: **Low**

14. *Answer choices:*

(see index for correct answer)

- a. Cunningham scandal
- b. Bribery
- c. Global Corruption Barometer
- d. Holyland Case

Guidance: level 1

:: Organizational structure ::

An _____ defines how activities such as task allocation, coordination, and supervision are directed toward the achievement of organizational aims.

Exam Probability: **Medium**

15. *Answer choices:*

(see index for correct answer)

- a. Organizational structure
- b. The Starfish and the Spider
- c. Unorganisation
- d. Blessed Unrest

Guidance: level 1

:: Business ::

The seller, or the provider of the goods or services, completes a sale in response to an acquisition, appropriation, requisition or a direct interaction with the buyer at the point of sale. There is a passing of title of the item, and the settlement of a price, in which agreement is reached on a price for which transfer of ownership of the item will occur. The seller, not the purchaser typically executes the sale and it may be completed prior to the obligation of payment. In the case of indirect interaction, a person who sells goods or service on behalf of the owner is known as a salesman or saleswoman or salesperson, but this often refers to someone _____ goods in a store/shop, in which case other terms are also common, including salesclerk, shop assistant, and retail clerk.

16. *Answer choices:*

(see index for correct answer)

- a. Selling
- b. Uncorporation
- c. First party leads
- d. Absentee business owner

Guidance: level 1

:: Decision theory ::

A _____ is a deliberate system of principles to guide decisions and achieve rational outcomes. A _____ is a statement of intent, and is implemented as a procedure or protocol. Policies are generally adopted by a governance body within an organization. Policies can assist in both subjective and objective decision making. Policies to assist in subjective decision making usually assist senior management with decisions that must be based on the relative merits of a number of factors, and as a result are often hard to test objectively, e.g. work-life balance _____ . In contrast policies to assist in objective decision making are usually operational in nature and can be objectively tested, e.g. password _____ .

17. *Answer choices:*

(see index for correct answer)

- a. Minimax
- b. Inference engine
- c. Expected value of perfect information
- d. Policy

:: Social security ::

_____ is "any government system that provides monetary assistance to people with an inadequate or no income." In the United States, this is usually called welfare or a social safety net, especially when talking about Canada and European countries.

Exam Probability: **Medium**

18. *Answer choices:*

(see index for correct answer)

- a. Child benefit
- b. Total Social Security Accounts
- c. Social security in Turkey
- d. Social security

:: Production and manufacturing ::

_____ is a set of techniques and tools for process improvement. Though as a shortened form it may be found written as 6S, it should not be confused with the methodology known as 6S .

Exam Probability: **Medium**

19. *Answer choices:*

(see index for correct answer)

- a. Reverse engineering
- b. Pegging report
- c. Low rate initial production
- d. MAPICS

Guidance: level 1

:: Investment ::

In finance, the benefit from an _____ is called a return. The return may consist of a gain realised from the sale of property or an _____ , unrealised capital appreciation , or _____ income such as dividends, interest, rental income etc., or a combination of capital gain and income. The return may also include currency gains or losses due to changes in foreign currency exchange rates.

20. *Answer choices:*

(see index for correct answer)

- a. Investment goods
- b. Juniperus Capital
- c. Asset price inflation
- d. Investing online

Guidance: level 1

:: Financial risk ::

_____ is a type of risk faced by investors, corporations, and governments that political decisions, events, or conditions will significantly affect the profitability of a business actor or the expected value of a given economic action. _____ can be understood and managed with reasoned foresight and investment.

21. *Answer choices:*

(see index for correct answer)

- a. Tracking error
- b. Consistent pricing process

- c. Political risk
- d. Equity risk

Guidance: level 1

:: Budgets ::

A _____ is a financial plan for a defined period, often one year. It may also include planned sales volumes and revenues, resource quantities, costs and expenses, assets, liabilities and cash flows. Companies, governments, families and other organizations use it to express strategic plans of activities or events in measurable terms.

Exam Probability: **Low**

22. *Answer choices:*

(see index for correct answer)

- a. Performance-based budgeting
- b. Budget
- c. Operating budget
- d. Link budget

Guidance: level 1

:: Supply chain management ::

_____ is the process of finding and agreeing to terms, and acquiring goods, services, or works from an external source, often via a tendering or competitive bidding process. _____ is used to ensure the buyer receives goods, services, or works at the best possible price when aspects such as quality, quantity, time, and location are compared. Corporations and public bodies often define processes intended to promote fair and open competition for their business while minimizing risks such as exposure to fraud and collusion.

Exam Probability: **Medium**

23. *Answer choices:*

(see index for correct answer)

- a. competitive bidding
- b. Global supply-chain finance
- c. Vendor-managed inventory
- d. Entry visibility

Guidance: level 1

:: E-commerce ::

_____ is the activity of buying or selling of products on online services or over the Internet. Electronic commerce draws on technologies such as mobile commerce, electronic funds transfer, supply chain management, Internet marketing, online transaction processing, electronic data interchange , inventory management systems, and automated data collection systems.

24. *Answer choices:*

(see index for correct answer)

- a. Pay at the pump
- b. Soldsie
- c. Switchwise
- d. Playism

Guidance: level 1

:: Television commercials ::

_____ is a phenomenon whereby something new and somehow valuable is formed. The created item may be intangible or a physical object .

25. *Answer choices:*

(see index for correct answer)

- a. Blipvert
- b. Creativity
- c. Blue Velvet
- d. Frozen Peas

:: Credit cards ::

A _____ is a payment card issued to users to enable the cardholder to pay a merchant for goods and services based on the cardholder's promise to the card issuer to pay them for the amounts plus the other agreed charges. The card issuer creates a revolving account and grants a line of credit to the cardholder, from which the cardholder can borrow money for payment to a merchant or as a cash advance.

Exam Probability: **Medium**

26. *Answer choices:*

(see index for correct answer)

- a. Kisan Credit Card
- b. MPP Global Solutions
- c. Credit card
- d. Payments as a service

:: Business models ::

A _____ is "an autonomous association of persons united voluntarily to meet their common economic, social, and cultural needs and aspirations through a jointly-owned and democratically-controlled enterprise". _____ s may include.

Exam Probability: **High**

27. *Answer choices:*

(see index for correct answer)

- a. Praenumeration
- b. Cooperative
- c. Business model pattern
- d. European Cooperative Society

Guidance: level 1

:: Data collection ::

A _____ is an utterance which typically functions as a request for information. _____ s can thus be understood as a kind of illocutionary act in the field of pragmatics or as special kinds of propositions in frameworks of formal semantics such as alternative semantics or inquisitive semantics. The information requested is expected to be provided in the form of an answer.

_____ s are often conflated with interrogatives, which are the grammatical forms typically used to achieve them. Rhetorical _____ s, for example, are interrogative in form but may not be considered true _____ s as they are not expected to be answered. Conversely, non-interrogative grammatical structures may be considered _____ s as in the case of the imperative sentence "tell me your name".

Exam Probability: **Medium**

28. *Answer choices:*

(see index for correct answer)

- a. Flow tracer
- b. Biopac student lab
- c. Question
- d. Crude Oil Data Exchange

Guidance: level 1

:: Analysis ::

_____ is the process of breaking a complex topic or substance into smaller parts in order to gain a better understanding of it. The technique has been applied in the study of mathematics and logic since before Aristotle, though _____ as a formal concept is a relatively recent development.

29. *Answer choices:*

(see index for correct answer)

- a. DESTEP
- b. Rational analysis
- c. Dialogical analysis
- d. Analysis

Guidance: level 1

:: ::

Business is the activity of making one's living or making money by producing or buying and selling products . Simply put, it is "any activity or enterprise entered into for profit. It does not mean it is a company, a corporation, partnership, or have any such formal organization, but it can range from a street peddler to General Motors."

30. *Answer choices:*

(see index for correct answer)

- a. corporate values
- b. Firm
- c. functional perspective
- d. empathy

Guidance: level 1

:: Marketing ::

_____ is based on a marketing concept which can be adopted by an organization as a strategy for business expansion. Where implemented, a franchisor licenses its know-how, procedures, intellectual property, use of its business model, brand, and rights to sell its branded products and services to a franchisee. In return the franchisee pays certain fees and agrees to comply with certain obligations, typically set out in a Franchise Agreement.

Exam Probability: **Medium**

31. *Answer choices:*

(see index for correct answer)

- a. Party plan
- b. Marketing warfare strategies
- c. Franchising
- d. Fourth screen

:: Marketing techniques ::

_____ is the activity of dividing a broad consumer or business market, normally consisting of existing and potential customers, into sub-groups of consumers based on some type of shared characteristics. In dividing or segmenting markets, researchers typically look for common characteristics such as shared needs, common interests, similar lifestyles or even similar demographic profiles. The overall aim of segmentation is to identify high yield segments – that is, those segments that are likely to be the most profitable or that have growth potential – so that these can be selected for special attention .

Exam Probability: **Medium**

32. *Answer choices:*

(see index for correct answer)

- a. Virtual event
- b. Campaign plan
- c. Not sold in stores
- d. Market segmentation

:: Costs ::

In microeconomic theory, the _____ , or alternative cost, of making a particular choice is the value of the most valuable choice out of those that were not taken. In other words, opportunity that will require sacrifices.

Exam Probability: **Medium**

33. *Answer choices:*

(see index for correct answer)

- a. Opportunity cost
- b. Manufacturing cost
- c. Joint cost
- d. Quality costs

Guidance: level 1

:: Debt ::

_____ is the trust which allows one party to provide money or resources to another party wherein the second party does not reimburse the first party immediately , but promises either to repay or return those resources at a later date. In other words, _____ is a method of making reciprocity formal, legally enforceable, and extensible to a large group of unrelated people.

Exam Probability: **Low**

34. *Answer choices:*

(see index for correct answer)

- a. Credit
- b. Debtors Anonymous
- c. Museum of Foreign Debt
- d. Default

Guidance: level 1

:: Accounting terminology ::

_____ is a legally enforceable claim for payment held by a business for goods supplied and/or services rendered that customers/clients have ordered but not paid for. These are generally in the form of invoices raised by a business and delivered to the customer for payment within an agreed time frame.

_____ is shown in a balance sheet as an asset. It is one of a series of accounting transactions dealing with the billing of a customer for goods and services that the customer has ordered. These may be distinguished from notes receivable, which are debts created through formal legal instruments called promissory notes.

Exam Probability: **Low**

35. *Answer choices:*

(see index for correct answer)

- a. Absorption costing
- b. Accounts receivable

- c. Internal auditing
- d. Fair value accounting

Guidance: level 1

:: Manufacturing ::

A _____ is an object used to extend the ability of an individual to modify features of the surrounding environment. Although many animals use simple _____ s, only human beings, whose use of stone _____ s dates back hundreds of millennia, use _____ s to make other _____ s. The set of _____ s needed to perform different tasks that are part of the same activity is called gear or equipment.

Exam Probability: **Medium**

36. *Answer choices:*

(see index for correct answer)

- a. Tool
- b. B2MML
- c. Sewing
- d. Ashery

Guidance: level 1

:: Management ::

_____ is a process by which entities review the quality of all factors involved in production. ISO 9000 defines _____ as "A part of quality management focused on fulfilling quality requirements".

37. *Answer choices:*

(see index for correct answer)

- a. Operations research
- b. Quality control
- c. Business workflow analysis
- d. Top development

Guidance: level 1

:: Customs duties ::

A _____ is a tax on imports or exports between sovereign states. It is a form of regulation of foreign trade and a policy that taxes foreign products to encourage or safeguard domestic industry. _____ s are the simplest and oldest instrument of trade policy. Traditionally, states have used them as a source of income. Now, they are among the most widely used instruments of protection, along with import and export quotas.

38. *Answer choices:*

(see index for correct answer)

- a. Import Surtaxes
- b. Tariff
- c. Court of Exchequer
- d. Canada Corn Act

Guidance: level 1

:: ::

An _____ is a contingent motivator. Traditional _____ s are extrinsic motivators which reward actions to yield a desired outcome. The effectiveness of traditional _____ s has changed as the needs of Western society have evolved. While the traditional _____ model is effective when there is a defined procedure and goal for a task, Western society started to require a higher volume of critical thinkers, so the traditional model became less effective. Institutions are now following a trend in implementing strategies that rely on intrinsic motivations rather than the extrinsic motivations that the traditional _____ s foster.

Exam Probability: **Low**

39. *Answer choices:*

(see index for correct answer)

- a. open system
- b. deep-level diversity

- c. personal values
- d. Incentive

Guidance: level 1

:: Statistical terminology ::

_____ is the magnitude or dimensions of a thing. _____ can be measured as length, width, height, diameter, perimeter, area, volume, or mass.

Exam Probability: **High**

40. *Answer choices:*
(see index for correct answer)

- a. Burstiness
- b. Univariate
- c. Size
- d. Endogeneity

Guidance: level 1

:: Statistical terminology ::

_____ es can be learned implicitly within cultural contexts. People may develop _____ es toward or against an individual, an ethnic group, a sexual or gender identity, a nation, a religion, a social class, a political party, theoretical paradigms and ideologies within academic domains, or a species. _____ ed means one-sided, lacking a neutral viewpoint, or not having an open mind. _____ can come in many forms and is related to prejudice and intuition.

41. *Answer choices:*

- a. Bias
- b. Natural process variation
- c. Standardised mortality rate
- d. Probability distribution function

Guidance: level 1

:: Project management ::

Contemporary business and science treat as a _____ any undertaking, carried out individually or collaboratively and possibly involving research or design, that is carefully planned to achieve a particular aim.

42. *Answer choices:*

(see index for correct answer)

- a. Value of work done
- b. Cost estimate
- c. Theory X and Theory Y
- d. Resource allocation

Guidance: level 1

:: Macroeconomics ::

_____ is the increase in the inflation-adjusted market value of the goods and services produced by an economy over time. It is conventionally measured as the percent rate of increase in real gross domestic product, or real GDP.

Exam Probability: **Medium**

43. *Answer choices:*

(see index for correct answer)

- a. Internal balance
- b. New neoclassical synthesis
- c. Economic growth
- d. Ordoliberalism

:: Regression analysis ::

A _____ often refers to a set of documented requirements to be satisfied by a material, design, product, or service. A _____ is often a type of technical standard.

Exam Probability: **Low**

44. *Answer choices:*

(see index for correct answer)

- a. Specification
- b. Residual sum of squares
- c. Component analysis
- d. Principal component regression

:: Income ::

_____ is a ratio between the net profit and cost of investment resulting from an investment of some resources. A high ROI means the investment`s gains favorably to its cost. As a performance measure, ROI is used to evaluate the efficiency of an investment or to compare the efficiencies of several different investments. In purely economic terms, it is one way of relating profits to capital invested. _____ is a performance measure used by businesses to identify the efficiency of an investment or number of different investments.

Exam Probability: **Medium**

45. *Answer choices:*

(see index for correct answer)

- a. Gratuity
- b. Real income
- c. Meetup fee
- d. Return on investment

Guidance: level 1

:: Management ::

A _____ describes the rationale of how an organization creates, delivers, and captures value, in economic, social, cultural or other contexts. The process of _____ construction and modification is also called _____ innovation and forms a part of business strategy.

46. *Answer choices:*

(see index for correct answer)

- a. Certified Energy Manager
- b. Completed Staff Work
- c. Business model
- d. Integrative thinking

Guidance: level 1

:: Consumer theory ::

_____ is the quantity of a good that consumers are willing and able to purchase at various prices during a given period of time.

Exam Probability: **Medium**

47. *Answer choices:*

(see index for correct answer)

- a. Engel curve
- b. Compensated demand
- c. Demand
- d. Hicksian demand function

:: Employment ::

_____ is a relationship between two parties, usually based on a contract where work is paid for, where one party, which may be a corporation, for profit, not-for-profit organization, co-operative or other entity is the employer and the other is the employee. Employees work in return for payment, which may be in the form of an hourly wage, by piecework or an annual salary, depending on the type of work an employee does or which sector she or he is working in. Employees in some fields or sectors may receive gratuities, bonus payment or stock options. In some types of _____ , employees may receive benefits in addition to payment. Benefits can include health insurance, housing, disability insurance or use of a gym. _____ is typically governed by _____ laws, regulations or legal contracts.

Exam Probability: **Low**

48. *Answer choices:*

(see index for correct answer)

- a. Intra-company transfer
- b. Employment
- c. Executive Order 10925
- d. Job Services Australia

:: Globalization-related theories ::

_____ is the process in which a nation is being improved in the sector of the economic, political, and social well-being of its people. The term has been used frequently by economists, politicians, and others in the 20th and 21st centuries. The concept, however, has been in existence in the West for centuries. "Modernization, "westernization", and especially "industrialization" are other terms often used while discussing _____ . _____ has a direct relationship with the environment and environmental issues. _____ is very often confused with industrial development, even in some academic sources.

Exam Probability: **Medium**

49. *Answer choices:*

(see index for correct answer)

- a. postmodernism
- b. Economic Development
- c. Capitalism

Guidance: level 1

:: ::

_____ is the study and management of exchange relationships. _____ is the business process of creating relationships with and satisfying customers. With its focus on the customer, _____ is one of the premier components of business management.

Exam Probability: **Low**

50. *Answer choices:*

(see index for correct answer)

- a. deep-level diversity
- b. Marketing
- c. similarity-attraction theory
- d. surface-level diversity

Guidance: level 1

:: Project management ::

Some scenarios associate "this kind of planning" with learning "life skills". _____ s are necessary, or at least useful, in situations where individuals need to know what time they must be at a specific location to receive a specific service, and where people need to accomplish a set of goals within a set time period.

Exam Probability: **Medium**

51. *Answer choices:*

- a. Changes clause
- b. Schedule
- c. Point of total assumption
- d. Team performance management

Guidance: level 1

:: Logistics ::

_____ is generally the detailed organization and implementation of a complex operation. In a general business sense, _____ is the management of the flow of things between the point of origin and the point of consumption in order to meet requirements of customers or corporations. The resources managed in _____ may include tangible goods such as materials, equipment, and supplies, as well as food and other consumable items. The _____ of physical items usually involves the integration of information flow, materials handling, production, packaging, inventory, transportation, warehousing, and often security.

Exam Probability: **Medium**

52. *Answer choices:*

- a. Logistics Support System
- b. DASH7

- c. Logistics
- d. Short shipment

Guidance: level 1

:: Stock market ::

A shareholder is an individual or institution that legally owns one or more shares of stock in a public or private corporation. _____ may be referred to as members of a corporation. Legally, a person is not a shareholder in a corporation until their name and other details are entered in the corporation's register of _____ or members.

Exam Probability: **Low**

53. *Answer choices:*

(see index for correct answer)

- a. Shareholders
- b. NorCom
- c. Mark Twain effect
- d. Pattern day trader

Guidance: level 1

:: Information science ::

_____ is the resolution of uncertainty; it is that which answers the question of "what an entity is" and thus defines both its essence and nature of its characteristics. _____ relates to both data and knowledge, as data is meaningful _____ representing values attributed to parameters, and knowledge signifies understanding of a concept. _____ is uncoupled from an observer, which is an entity that can access _____ and thus discern what it specifies; _____ exists beyond an event horizon for example. In the case of knowledge, the _____ itself requires a cognitive observer to be obtained.

Exam Probability: **Low**

54. *Answer choices:*

(see index for correct answer)

- a. Information
- b. Information architecture
- c. Toy problem
- d. SIRCA

Guidance: level 1

:: Management ::

In business, a _____ is the attribute that allows an organization to outperform its competitors. A _____ may include access to natural resources, such as high-grade ores or a low-cost power source, highly skilled labor, geographic location, high entry barriers, and access to new technology.

55. *Answer choices:*

(see index for correct answer)

- a. Crisis management
- b. Executive development
- c. Fredmund Malik
- d. Law practice management

Guidance: level 1

:: Stock market ::

The _____ of a corporation is all of the shares into which ownership of the corporation is divided. In American English, the shares are commonly known as "_____ s". A single share of the _____ represents fractional ownership of the corporation in proportion to the total number of shares. This typically entitles the _____ holder to that fraction of the company's earnings, proceeds from liquidation of assets , or voting power, often dividing these up in proportion to the amount of money each _____ holder has invested. Not all _____ is necessarily equal, as certain classes of _____ may be issued for example without voting rights, with enhanced voting rights, or with a certain priority to receive profits or liquidation proceeds before or after other classes of shareholders.

Exam Probability: **Low**

56. *Answer choices:*

(see index for correct answer)

- a. Investor relations
- b. Underweight
- c. Alpha generation platform
- d. Profit warning

Guidance: level 1

:: ::

_____ is the collection of mechanisms, processes and relations by which corporations are controlled and operated. Governance structures and principles identify the distribution of rights and responsibilities among different participants in the corporation and include the rules and procedures for making decisions in corporate affairs. _____ is necessary because of the possibility of conflicts of interests between stakeholders, primarily between shareholders and upper management or among shareholders.

Exam Probability: **Low**

57. *Answer choices:*

(see index for correct answer)

- a. empathy
- b. levels of analysis
- c. surface-level diversity
- d. co-culture

:: ::

A _____ is any person who contracts to acquire an asset in return for some form of consideration.

Exam Probability: **Medium**

58. *Answer choices:*

(see index for correct answer)

- a. Buyer
- b. similarity-attraction theory
- c. personal values
- d. cultural

:: Financial markets ::

A _____ is a financial market in which long-term debt or equity-backed securities are bought and sold. _____ s channel the wealth of savers to those who can put it to long-term productive use, such as companies or governments making long-term investments. Financial regulators like the Bank of England and the U.S. Securities and Exchange Commission oversee _____ s to protect investors against fraud, among other duties.

Exam Probability: **Medium**

59. *Answer choices:*

(see index for correct answer)

- a. Market data
- b. Head fake
- c. Crossing network
- d. Capital market

Guidance: level 1

Management

Management is the administration of an organization, whether it is a business, a not-for-profit organization, or government body. Management includes the activities of setting the strategy of an organization and coordinating the efforts of its employees (or of volunteers) to accomplish its objectives through the application of available resources, such as financial, natural, technological, and human resources.

:: ::

Business is the activity of making one's living or making money by producing or buying and selling products . Simply put, it is "any activity or enterprise entered into for profit. It does not mean it is a company, a corporation, partnership, or have any such formal organization, but it can range from a street peddler to General Motors."

1. *Answer choices:*

(see index for correct answer)

- a. hierarchical perspective
- b. open system
- c. co-culture
- d. Firm

Guidance: level 1

:: Stochastic processes ::

_____ is a system of rules that are created and enforced through social or governmental institutions to regulate behavior. It has been defined both as "the Science of Justice" and "the Art of Justice". _____ is a system that regulates and ensures that individuals or a community adhere to the will of the state. State-enforced _____ s can be made by a collective legislature or by a single legislator, resulting in statutes, by the executive through decrees and regulations, or established by judges through precedent, normally in common _____ jurisdictions. Private individuals can create legally binding contracts, including arbitration agreements that may elect to accept alternative arbitration to the normal court process. The formation of _____ s themselves may be influenced by a constitution, written or tacit, and the rights encoded therein. The _____ shapes politics, economics, history and society in various ways and serves as a mediator of relations between people.

2. *Answer choices:*

(see index for correct answer)

- a. Markov process
- b. Innovation
- c. Gaussian process
- d. Wiener process

Guidance: level 1

:: ::

_____ is the stock of habits, knowledge, social and personality attributes embodied in the ability to perform labor so as to produce economic value.

Exam Probability: **High**

3. *Answer choices:*

(see index for correct answer)

- a. open system
- b. imperative
- c. personal values
- d. co-culture

Guidance: level 1

:: Industrial Revolution ::

The _____ , now also known as the First _____ , was the transition to new manufacturing processes in Europe and the US, in the period from about 1760 to sometime between 1820 and 1840. This transition included going from hand production methods to machines, new chemical manufacturing and iron production processes, the increasing use of steam power and water power, the development of machine tools and the rise of the mechanized factory system. The _____ also led to an unprecedented rise in the rate of population growth.

Exam Probability: **High**

4. *Answer choices:*
(see index for correct answer)

- a. Mill town
- b. Surplus women
- c. Pinsley Mill
- d. Industrial Revolution

Guidance: level 1

:: Export and import control ::

" _____ " means the Government Service which is responsible for the administration of _____ law and the collection of duties and taxes and which also has the responsibility for the application of other laws and regulations relating to the importation, exportation, movement or storage of goods.

Exam Probability: **Medium**

5. *Answer choices:*

(see index for correct answer)

- a. Import parity price
- b. International Traffic in Arms Regulations
- c. Export Control Classification Number
- d. Customs

Guidance: level 1

:: Marketing techniques ::

In industry, product lifecycle management is the process of managing the entire lifecycle of a product from inception, through engineering design and manufacture, to service and disposal of manufactured products. PLM integrates people, data, processes and business systems and provides a product information backbone for companies and their extended enterprise.

Exam Probability: **Medium**

6. *Answer choices:*

(see index for correct answer)

- a. As seen on TV
- b. Product life cycle
- c. Elevator pitch
- d. Angel dusting

Guidance: level 1

:: ::

The _____ is a political and economic union of 28 member states that are located primarily in Europe. It has an area of 4,475,757 km2 and an estimated population of about 513 million. The EU has developed an internal single market through a standardised system of laws that apply in all member states in those matters, and only those matters, where members have agreed to act as one. EU policies aim to ensure the free movement of people, goods, services and capital within the internal market, enact legislation in justice and home affairs and maintain common policies on trade, agriculture, fisheries and regional development. For travel within the Schengen Area, passport controls have been abolished. A monetary union was established in 1999 and came into full force in 2002 and is composed of 19 EU member states which use the euro currency.

Exam Probability: **High**

7. *Answer choices:*

(see index for correct answer)

- a. process perspective
- b. similarity-attraction theory
- c. empathy
- d. European Union

Guidance: level 1

:: Survey methodology ::

An _____ is a conversation where questions are asked and answers are given. In common parlance, the word " _____ " refers to a one-on-one conversation between an _____ er and an _____ ee. The _____ er asks questions to which the _____ ee responds, usually so information may be transferred from _____ ee to _____ er . Sometimes, information can be transferred in both directions. It is a communication, unlike a speech, which produces a one-way flow of information.

Exam Probability: **High**

8. *Answer choices:*
(see index for correct answer)

- a. Survey research
- b. Scale analysis
- c. National Health Interview Survey
- d. Data editing

Guidance: level 1

:: ::

In production, research, retail, and accounting, a _____ is the value of money that has been used up to produce something or deliver a service, and hence is not available for use anymore. In business, the _____ may be one of acquisition, in which case the amount of money expended to acquire it is counted as _____ . In this case, money is the input that is gone in order to acquire the thing. This acquisition _____ may be the sum of the _____ of production as incurred by the original producer, and further _____ s of transaction as incurred by the acquirer over and above the price paid to the producer. Usually, the price also includes a mark-up for profit over the _____ of production.

Exam Probability: **Medium**

9. *Answer choices:*

(see index for correct answer)

- a. hierarchical perspective
- b. imperative
- c. Cost
- d. deep-level diversity

Guidance: level 1

:: ::

The _____ officer or just _____ , is the most senior corporate, executive, or administrative officer in charge of managing an organization especially an independent legal entity such as a company or nonprofit institution. CEOs lead a range of organizations, including public and private corporations, non-profit organizations and even some government organizations . The CEO of a corporation or company typically reports to the board of directors and is charged with maximizing the value of the entity, which may include maximizing the share price, market share, revenues or another element. In the non-profit and government sector, CEOs typically aim at achieving outcomes related to the organization's mission, such as reducing poverty, increasing literacy, etc.

Exam Probability: **Low**

10. *Answer choices:*

(see index for correct answer)

- a. Chief executive
- b. hierarchical
- c. surface-level diversity
- d. interpersonal communication

Guidance: level 1

:: Management ::

In business, a _____ is the attribute that allows an organization to outperform its competitors. A _____ may include access to natural resources, such as high-grade ores or a low-cost power source, highly skilled labor, geographic location, high entry barriers, and access to new technology.

Exam Probability: **High**

11. *Answer choices:*

(see index for correct answer)

- a. Competitive advantage
- b. Total security management
- c. Smiling curve
- d. Energy monitoring and targeting

Guidance: level 1

:: Monopoly (economics) ::

A _____ is a form of intellectual property that gives its owner the legal right to exclude others from making, using, selling, and importing an invention for a limited period of years, in exchange for publishing an enabling public disclosure of the invention. In most countries _____ rights fall under civil law and the _____ holder needs to sue someone infringing the _____ in order to enforce his or her rights. In some industries _____ s are an essential form of competitive advantage; in others they are irrelevant.

12. *Answer choices:*

(see index for correct answer)

- a. Patent portfolio
- b. Quasi-rent
- c. Coercive monopoly
- d. Network effect

Guidance: level 1

:: Marketing ::

_____ or stock control can be broadly defined as "the activity of checking a shop's stock." However, a more focused definition takes into account the more science-based, methodical practice of not only verifying a business` inventory but also focusing on the many related facets of inventory management "within an organisation to meet the demand placed upon that business economically." Other facets of _____ include supply chain management, production control, financial flexibility, and customer satisfaction. At the root of _____ , however, is the _____ problem, which involves determining when to order, how much to order, and the logistics of those decisions.

Exam Probability: **Low**

13. *Answer choices:*

(see index for correct answer)

- a. Cult brand
- b. Inventory control
- c. Business-to-employee
- d. Franchise fee

Guidance: level 1

:: Elementary mathematics ::

_____ is a numerical measurement of how far apart objects are. In physics or everyday usage, _____ may refer to a physical length or an estimation based on other criteria . In most cases, " _____ from A to B" is interchangeable with " _____ from B to A". In mathematics, a _____ function or metric is a generalization of the concept of physical _____ . A metric is a function that behaves according to a specific set of rules, and is a way of describing what it means for elements of some space to be "close to" or "far away from" each other.

Exam Probability: **High**

14. *Answer choices:*

(see index for correct answer)

- a. Algebraic operation
- b. Functional notation
- c. Distance
- d. Term

:: Management ::

_____ is a process by which entities review the quality of all factors involved in production. ISO 9000 defines _____ as "A part of quality management focused on fulfilling quality requirements".

Exam Probability: **High**

15. *Answer choices:*

(see index for correct answer)

- a. Data Item Descriptions
- b. Quality control
- c. Supervisory board
- d. Knowledge ecosystem

:: ::

_____ refers to the confirmation of certain characteristics of an object, person, or organization. This confirmation is often, but not always, provided by some form of external review, education, assessment, or audit. Accreditation is a specific organization's process of _____ . According to the National Council on Measurement in Education, a _____ test is a credentialing test used to determine whether individuals are knowledgeable enough in a given occupational area to be labeled "competent to practice" in that area.

Exam Probability: **Medium**

16. *Answer choices:*

(see index for correct answer)

- a. Sarbanes-Oxley act of 2002
- b. information systems assessment
- c. Certification
- d. hierarchical

Guidance: level 1

:: Data collection ::

A _____ is an utterance which typically functions as a request for information. _____ s can thus be understood as a kind of illocutionary act in the field of pragmatics or as special kinds of propositions in frameworks of formal semantics such as alternative semantics or inquisitive semantics. The information requested is expected to be provided in the form of an answer. _____ s are often conflated with interrogatives, which are the grammatical forms typically used to achieve them. Rhetorical _____ s, for example, are interrogative in form but may not be considered true _____ s as they are not expected to be answered. Conversely, non-interrogative grammatical structures may be considered _____ s as in the case of the imperative sentence "tell me your name".

Exam Probability: **High**

17. *Answer choices:*

(see index for correct answer)

- a. Biopac student lab
- b. General Social Survey
- c. Relational data mining
- d. Question

Guidance: level 1

:: ::

_____ is a means of protection from financial loss. It is a form of risk management, primarily used to hedge against the risk of a contingent or uncertain loss

18. *Answer choices:*

(see index for correct answer)

- a. Insurance
- b. levels of analysis
- c. process perspective
- d. Character

Guidance: level 1

:: Employment discrimination ::

A _____ is a metaphor used to represent an invisible barrier that keeps a given demographic from rising beyond a certain level in a hierarchy.

Exam Probability: **Medium**

19. *Answer choices:*

(see index for correct answer)

- a. Employment discrimination law in the European Union
- b. Marriage bars
- c. LGBT employment discrimination in the United States
- d. Employment Non-Discrimination Act

:: Project management ::

A _____ is a professional in the field of project management. _____ s have the responsibility of the planning, procurement and execution of a project, in any undertaking that has a defined scope, defined start and a defined finish; regardless of industry. _____ s are first point of contact for any issues or discrepancies arising from within the heads of various departments in an organization before the problem escalates to higher authorities. Project management is the responsibility of a _____ . This individual seldom participates directly in the activities that produce the end result, but rather strives to maintain the progress, mutual interaction and tasks of various parties in such a way that reduces the risk of overall failure, maximizes benefits, and minimizes costs.

Exam Probability: **High**

20. *Answer choices:*

(see index for correct answer)

- a. Cost database
- b. NetPoint
- c. Project manager
- d. Task

:: Human resource management ::

_____ expands the capacity of individuals to perform in leadership roles within organizations. Leadership roles are those that facilitate execution of a company's strategy through building alignment, winning mindshare and growing the capabilities of others. Leadership roles may be formal, with the corresponding authority to make decisions and take responsibility, or they may be informal roles with little official authority .

Exam Probability: **Medium**

21. *Answer choices:*

(see index for correct answer)

- a. Organizational orientations
- b. ROWE
- c. Human resource management
- d. Focal Point Review

Guidance: level 1

:: Goods ::

In most contexts, the concept of _____ denotes the conduct that should be preferred when posed with a choice between possible actions. _____ is generally considered to be the opposite of evil, and is of interest in the study of morality, ethics, religion and philosophy. The specific meaning and etymology of the term and its associated translations among ancient and contemporary languages show substantial variation in its inflection and meaning depending on circumstances of place, history, religious, or philosophical context.

Exam Probability: **Low**

22. *Answer choices:*

(see index for correct answer)

- a. Good
- b. excludable
- c. Public good
- d. Experience good

Guidance: level 1

:: ::

A _____ is a fund into which a sum of money is added during an employee's employment years, and from which payments are drawn to support the person's retirement from work in the form of periodic payments. A _____ may be a "defined benefit plan" where a fixed sum is paid regularly to a person, or a "defined contribution plan" under which a fixed sum is invested and then becomes available at retirement age. _____ s should not be confused with severance pay; the former is usually paid in regular installments for life after retirement, while the latter is typically paid as a fixed amount after involuntary termination of employment prior to retirement.

Exam Probability: **High**

23. *Answer choices:*

(see index for correct answer)

- a. Pension
- b. open system
- c. hierarchical perspective
- d. surface-level diversity

Guidance: level 1

:: Business law ::

A _____ is a group of people who jointly supervise the activities of an organization, which can be either a for-profit business, nonprofit organization, or a government agency. Such a board's powers, duties, and responsibilities are determined by government regulations and the organization's own constitution and bylaws. These authorities may specify the number of members of the board, how they are to be chosen, and how often they are to meet.

Exam Probability: **Low**

24. *Answer choices:*

(see index for correct answer)

- a. Ordinary course of business
- b. Equity of redemption
- c. Ease of doing business index
- d. Output contract

Guidance: level 1

:: Management ::

The _____ is a strategy performance management tool – a semi-standard structured report, that can be used by managers to keep track of the execution of activities by the staff within their control and to monitor the consequences arising from these actions.

Exam Probability: **Low**

- a. Provectus IT Inc
- b. Event to knowledge
- c. Balanced scorecard
- d. Lead scoring

Guidance: level 1

:: ::

_____ is the process of making predictions of the future based on past and present data and most commonly by analysis of trends. A commonplace example might be estimation of some variable of interest at some specified future date. Prediction is a similar, but more general term. Both might refer to formal statistical methods employing time series, cross-sectional or longitudinal data, or alternatively to less formal judgmental methods. Usage can differ between areas of application: for example, in hydrology the terms "forecast" and "_____" are sometimes reserved for estimates of values at certain specific future times, while the term "prediction" is used for more general estimates, such as the number of times floods will occur over a long period.

Exam Probability: **Medium**

- a. functional perspective

- b. levels of analysis
- c. Forecasting
- d. corporate values

Guidance: level 1

:: E-commerce ::

_____ is the activity of buying or selling of products on online services or over the Internet. Electronic commerce draws on technologies such as mobile commerce, electronic funds transfer, supply chain management, Internet marketing, online transaction processing, electronic data interchange , inventory management systems, and automated data collection systems.

Exam Probability: **Low**

27. *Answer choices:*
(see index for correct answer)

- a. Value-added network
- b. Sears Israel
- c. E-commerce
- d. Typhoid adware

Guidance: level 1

:: Management ::

In organizational studies, _____ is the efficient and effective
development of an organization's resources when they are needed. Such resources
may include financial resources, inventory, human skills, production resources,
or information technology and natural resources.

Exam Probability: **High**

28. *Answer choices:*

(see index for correct answer)

- a. Resource management
- b. Managerial Psychology
- c. Event management
- d. Kata

Guidance: level 1

:: ::

_____ , in its broadest context, includes both the attainment of that which is just and the philosophical discussion of that which is just. The concept of _____ is based on numerous fields, and many differing viewpoints and perspectives including the concepts of moral correctness based on ethics, rationality, law, religion, equity and fairness. Often, the general discussion of _____ is divided into the realm of social _____ as found in philosophy, theology and religion, and, procedural _____ as found in the study and application of the law.

Exam Probability: **High**

29. *Answer choices:*

(see index for correct answer)

- a. cultural
- b. Justice
- c. information systems assessment
- d. empathy

Guidance: level 1

:: Production and manufacturing ::

An _____ is a manufacturing process in which parts are added as the semi-finished assembly moves from workstation to workstation where the parts are added in sequence until the final assembly is produced. By mechanically moving the parts to the assembly work and moving the semi-finished assembly from work station to work station, a finished product can be assembled faster and with less labor than by having workers carry parts to a stationary piece for assembly.

Exam Probability: **High**

30. *Answer choices:*

(see index for correct answer)

- a. Assembly line
- b. Expediting
- c. Total quality management
- d. Piece work

Guidance: level 1

:: Product management ::

_____ s, also known as Shewhart charts or process-behavior charts, are a statistical process control tool used to determine if a manufacturing or business process is in a state of control.

Exam Probability: **High**

31. *Answer choices:*

(see index for correct answer)

- a. Control chart
- b. Dwinell-Wright Company
- c. Product family engineering
- d. Service life

Guidance: level 1

:: ::

_____ is the capacity of consciously making sense of things, establishing and verifying facts, applying logic, and changing or justifying practices, institutions, and beliefs based on new or existing information. It is closely associated with such characteristically human activities as philosophy, science, language, mathematics and art, and is normally considered to be a distinguishing ability possessed by humans. _____ , or an aspect of it, is sometimes referred to as rationality.

Exam Probability: **Medium**

32. *Answer choices:*

(see index for correct answer)

- a. levels of analysis
- b. surface-level diversity
- c. Sarbanes-Oxley act of 2002

- d. cultural

Guidance: level 1

:: Employment compensation ::

_____ refers to various incentive plans introduced by businesses that provide direct or indirect payments to employees that depend on company's profitability in addition to employees' regular salary and bonuses. In publicly traded companies these plans typically amount to allocation of shares to employees. One of the earliest pioneers of _____ was Englishman Theodore Cooke Taylor, who is known to have introduced the practice in his woollen mills during the late 1800s .

Exam Probability: **Low**

33. *Answer choices:*
(see index for correct answer)

- a. Open compensation plan
- b. Living wage
- c. Compensation of employees
- d. Profit sharing

Guidance: level 1

:: Quality management ::

_____ ensures that an organization, product or service is consistent. It has four main components: quality planning, quality assurance, quality control and quality improvement. _____ is focused not only on product and service quality, but also on the means to achieve it. _____ , therefore, uses quality assurance and control of processes as well as products to achieve more consistent quality. What a customer wants and is willing to pay for it determines quality. It is written or unwritten commitment to a known or unknown consumer in the market . Thus, quality can be defined as fitness for intended use or, in other words, how well the product performs its intended function

Exam Probability: **Medium**

34. *Answer choices:*

(see index for correct answer)

- a. Bureau Veritas
- b. Dana Ulery
- c. EFQM
- d. China Quality Course

Guidance: level 1

:: Security compliance ::

A _____ is a communicated intent to inflict harm or loss on another person. A _____ is considered an act of coercion. _____ s are widely observed in animal behavior, particularly in a ritualized form, chiefly in order to avoid the unnecessary physical violence that can lead to physical damage or the death of both conflicting parties.

35. *Answer choices:*

(see index for correct answer)

- a. Vulnerability management
- b. Information assurance vulnerability alert
- c. 201 CMR 17.00
- d. Threat

Guidance: level 1

:: ::

_____ refers to the overall process of attracting, shortlisting, selecting and appointing suitable candidates for jobs within an organization. _____ can also refer to processes involved in choosing individuals for unpaid roles. Managers, human resource generalists and _____ specialists may be tasked with carrying out _____ , but in some cases public-sector employment agencies, commercial _____ agencies, or specialist search consultancies are used to undertake parts of the process. Internet-based technologies which support all aspects of _____ have become widespread.

Exam Probability: **Medium**

36. *Answer choices:*

(see index for correct answer)

- a. corporate values
- b. information systems assessment
- c. Recruitment
- d. open system

Guidance: level 1

:: ::

_____ consists of using generic or ad hoc methods in an orderly manner to find solutions to problems. Some of the problem-solving techniques developed and used in philosophy, artificial intelligence, computer science, engineering, mathematics, or medicine are related to mental problem-solving techniques studied in psychology.

Exam Probability: **Medium**

37. *Answer choices:*
(see index for correct answer)

- a. Problem solving
- b. empathy
- c. Character
- d. surface-level diversity

Guidance: level 1

:: Corporate governance ::

An _____ is generally a person responsible for running an organization, although the exact nature of the role varies depending on the organization. In many militaries, an _____ , or "XO," is the second-in-command, reporting to the commanding officer. The XO is typically responsible for the management of day-to-day activities, freeing the commander to concentrate on strategy and planning the unit's next move.

Exam Probability: **Low**

38. *Answer choices:*

(see index for correct answer)

- a. Chartered Secretaries Australia
- b. Executive officer
- c. Nursing management
- d. Headquarters

Guidance: level 1

:: Behavior modification ::

In psychotherapy and mental health, _____ has a positive sense of empowering individuals, or a negative sense of encouraging dysfunctional behavior.

39. *Answer choices:*

(see index for correct answer)

- a. behavioural change
- b. Enabling

Guidance: level 1

:: Labor rights ::

A _____ is a wrong or hardship suffered, real or supposed, which forms legitimate grounds of complaint. In the past, the word meant the infliction or cause of hardship.

Exam Probability: **High**

40. *Answer choices:*

(see index for correct answer)

- a. China Labor Watch
- b. China Labour Bulletin
- c. Right to work
- d. The Hyatt 100

Guidance: level 1

:: Human resource management ::

_____ is the strategic approach to the effective management of people in an organization so that they help the business to gain a competitive advantage. It is designed to maximize employee performance in service of an employer's strategic objectives. HR is primarily concerned with the management of people within organizations, focusing on policies and on systems. HR departments are responsible for overseeing employee-benefits design, employee recruitment, training and development, performance appraisal, and Reward management . HR also concerns itself with organizational change and industrial relations, that is, the balancing of organizational practices with requirements arising from collective bargaining and from governmental laws.

Exam Probability: **Low**

41. *Answer choices:*

(see index for correct answer)

- a. Upward communication
- b. Technical performance measure
- c. Professional employer organization
- d. Human resource management

Guidance: level 1

:: Project management ::

In political science, an _____ is a means by which a petition signed by a certain minimum number of registered voters can force a government to choose to either enact a law or hold a public vote in parliament in what is called indirect _____, or under direct _____, the proposition is immediately put to a plebiscite or referendum, in what is called a Popular initiated Referendum or citizen-initiated referendum).

Exam Probability: **High**

42. *Answer choices:*

(see index for correct answer)

- a. Initiative
- b. Risk register
- c. Executive sponsor
- d. Small-scale project management

Guidance: level 1

:: ::

_____ s and acquisitions are transactions in which the ownership of companies, other business organizations, or their operating units are transferred or consolidated with other entities. As an aspect of strategic management, M&A can allow enterprises to grow or downsize, and change the nature of their business or competitive position.

Exam Probability: **Low**

43. *Answer choices:*

(see index for correct answer)

- a. Merger
- b. cultural
- c. surface-level diversity
- d. open system

Guidance: level 1

:: Business ::

The seller, or the provider of the goods or services, completes a sale in response to an acquisition, appropriation, requisition or a direct interaction with the buyer at the point of sale. There is a passing of title of the item, and the settlement of a price, in which agreement is reached on a price for which transfer of ownership of the item will occur. The seller, not the purchaser typically executes the sale and it may be completed prior to the obligation of payment. In the case of indirect interaction, a person who sells goods or service on behalf of the owner is known as a _____ man or _____ woman or _____ person, but this often refers to someone selling goods in a store/shop, in which case other terms are also common, including _____ clerk, shop assistant, and retail clerk.

Exam Probability: **High**

44. *Answer choices:*

(see index for correct answer)

- a. Sales
- b. Global Social Venture Competition
- c. Winklevoss Capital Management
- d. Vladislav Doronin

Guidance: level 1

:: Strategic management ::

_____ is a strategic planning technique used to help a person or organization identify strengths, weaknesses, opportunities, and threats related to business competition or project planning. It is intended to specify the objectives of the business venture or project and identify the internal and external factors that are favorable and unfavorable to achieving those objectives. Users of a _____ often ask and answer questions to generate meaningful information for each category to make the tool useful and identify their competitive advantage. SWOT has been described as the tried-and-true tool of strategic analysis.

Exam Probability: **Medium**

45. *Answer choices:*

(see index for correct answer)

- a. Training package
- b. Rule of three
- c. First-mover advantage
- d. Predictable surprise

:: Marketing ::

A _____ is an overall experience of a customer that distinguishes an organization or product from its rivals in the eyes of the customer. _____ s are used in business, marketing, and advertising. Name _____ s are sometimes distinguished from generic or store _____ s.

Exam Probability: **Medium**

46. *Answer choices:*

(see index for correct answer)

- a. Brand
- b. Joint product pricing
- c. Instant rebate
- d. Customer acquisition management

:: Occupations ::

An _____ is a person who has a position of authority in a hierarchical organization. The term derives from the late Latin from officiarius, meaning "official".

Exam Probability: **Low**

47. *Answer choices:*

(see index for correct answer)

- a. Mountain guide
- b. Clerk of the course
- c. Market entry consultant
- d. Officer

Guidance: level 1

:: Majority–minority relations ::

_____ , also known as reservation in India and Nepal, positive discrimination / action in the United Kingdom, and employment equity in Canada and South Africa, is the policy of promoting the education and employment of members of groups that are known to have previously suffered from discrimination. Historically and internationally, support for _____ has sought to achieve goals such as bridging inequalities in employment and pay, increasing access to education, promoting diversity, and redressing apparent past wrongs, harms, or hindrances.

Exam Probability: **Low**

48. *Answer choices:*

(see index for correct answer)

- a. positive discrimination
- b. cultural dissonance
- c. Affirmative action

Guidance: level 1

:: Management ::

A _____ describes the rationale of how an organization creates, delivers, and captures value, in economic, social, cultural or other contexts. The process of _____ construction and modification is also called _____ innovation and forms a part of business strategy.

Exam Probability: **Medium**

49. *Answer choices:*

(see index for correct answer)

- a. Pareto analysis
- b. Logistics management
- c. Business model
- d. Vorstand

Guidance: level 1

:: Workplace ::

A _____ , also referred to as a performance review, performance evaluation, development discussion, or employee appraisal is a method by which the job performance of an employee is documented and evaluated. _____ s are a part of career development and consist of regular reviews of employee performance within organizations.

Exam Probability: **Medium**

50. *Answer choices:*

(see index for correct answer)

- a. Performance appraisal
- b. Workplace violence
- c. Workplace conflict
- d. Emotions in the workplace

Guidance: level 1

:: Statistical terminology ::

_____ is the ability to avoid wasting materials, energy, efforts, money, and time in doing something or in producing a desired result. In a more general sense, it is the ability to do things well, successfully, and without waste. In more mathematical or scientific terms, it is a measure of the extent to which input is well used for an intended task or function . It often specifically comprises the capability of a specific application of effort to produce a specific outcome with a minimum amount or quantity of waste, expense, or unnecessary effort. _____ refers to very different inputs and outputs in different fields and industries.

51. *Answer choices:*

(see index for correct answer)

- a. Degrees of freedom
- b. Efficiency
- c. Skewness risk
- d. Probable error

Guidance: level 1

:: Management ::

_____ is the practice of initiating, planning, executing, controlling, and closing the work of a team to achieve specific goals and meet specific success criteria at the specified time.

52. *Answer choices:*

(see index for correct answer)

- a. Flat organization
- b. Project management
- c. Telescopic observations strategic framework
- d. Public sector consulting

Guidance: level 1

:: Management ::

_____ is a set of activities that ensure goals are met in an effective and efficient manner. _____ can focus on the performance of an organization, a department, an employee, or the processes in place to manage particular tasks. _____ standards are generally organized and disseminated by senior leadership at an organization, and by task owners.

Exam Probability: **Medium**

53. *Answer choices:*

(see index for correct answer)

- a. Submission management
- b. Process capability

- c. PDCA
- d. Performance management

Guidance: level 1

:: Packaging ::

In work place, _____ or job _____ means good ranking with the hypothesized conception of requirements of a role. There are two types of job _____ s: contextual and task. Task _____ is related to cognitive ability while contextual _____ is dependent upon personality. Task _____ are behavioral roles that are recognized in job descriptions and by remuneration systems, they are directly related to organizational _____ , whereas, contextual _____ are value based and additional behavioral roles that are not recognized in job descriptions and covered by compensation; they are extra roles that are indirectly related to organizational _____ . Citizenship _____ like contextual _____ means a set of individual activity/contribution that supports the organizational culture.

Exam Probability: **High**

54. *Answer choices:*

(see index for correct answer)

- a. Active packaging
- b. Living hinge
- c. Performance
- d. Wrap rage

:: Human resource management ::

_____ involves improving the effectiveness of organizations and the individuals and teams within them. Training may be viewed as related to immediate changes in organizational effectiveness via organized instruction, while development is related to the progress of longer-term organizational and employee goals. While _____ technically have differing definitions, the two are oftentimes used interchangeably and/or together. _____ has historically been a topic within applied psychology but has within the last two decades become closely associated with human resources management, talent management, human resources development, instructional design, human factors, and knowledge management.

Exam Probability: **Low**

55. *Answer choices:*

(see index for correct answer)

- a. Training and development
- b. Leadership development
- c. Joint Personnel Administration
- d. Workplace mentoring

:: ::

An _____ in international trade is a good or service produced in one country that is bought by someone in another country. The seller of such goods and services is an _____ er; the foreign buyer is an importer.

Exam Probability: **Medium**

56. *Answer choices:*

(see index for correct answer)

- a. surface-level diversity
- b. similarity-attraction theory
- c. personal values
- d. Export

Guidance: level 1

:: Belief ::

_____ is the study of general and fundamental questions about existence, knowledge, values, reason, mind, and language. Such questions are often posed as problems to be studied or resolved. The term was probably coined by Pythagoras . Philosophical methods include questioning, critical discussion, rational argument, and systematic presentation. Classic philosophical questions include: Is it possible to know anything and to prove it What is most real Philosophers also pose more practical and concrete questions such as: Is there a best way to live Is it better to be just or unjust Do humans have free will

Exam Probability: **High**

57. *Answer choices:*

- a. Disquotational principle
- b. Faith
- c. Philosophy
- d. Transubstantiation

Guidance: level 1

:: Income ::

In business and accounting, net income is an entity's income minus cost of goods sold, expenses and taxes for an accounting period. It is computed as the residual of all revenues and gains over all expenses and losses for the period, and has also been defined as the net increase in shareholders' equity that results from a company's operations. In the context of the presentation of financial statements, the IFRS Foundation defines net income as synonymous with profit and loss. The difference between revenue and the cost of making a product or providing a service, before deducting overheads, payroll, taxation, and interest payments. This is different from operating income .

Exam Probability: **High**

58. *Answer choices:*

- a. Trinity study
- b. Aggregate expenditure

- c. Bottom line
- d. Creative real estate investing

Guidance: level 1

:: Human resource management ::

_____ is a family of procedures to identify the content of a job in terms of activities involved and attributes or job requirements needed to perform the activities. _____ provides information of organizations which helps to determine which employees are best fit for specific jobs. Through _____ , the analyst needs to understand what the important tasks of the job are, how they are carried out, and the necessary human qualities needed to complete the job successfully.

Exam Probability: **Medium**

59. *Answer choices:*

(see index for correct answer)

- a. Experticity
- b. Job analysis
- c. Corporate Equality Index
- d. Compensation and benefits

Guidance: level 1

Business law

Corporate law (also known as business law) is the body of law governing the rights, relations, and conduct of persons, companies, organizations and businesses. It refers to the legal practice relating to, or the theory of corporations. Corporate law often describes the law relating to matters which derive directly from the life-cycle of a corporation. It thus encompasses the formation, funding, governance, and death of a corporation.

:: Legal doctrines and principles ::

In the common law of torts, _____ loquitur is a doctrine that infers negligence from the very nature of an accident or injury in the absence of direct evidence on how any defendant behaved. Although modern formulations differ by jurisdiction, common law originally stated that the accident must satisfy the necessary elements of negligence: duty, breach of duty, causation, and injury. In _____ loquitur, the elements of duty of care, breach, and causation are inferred from an injury that does not ordinarily occur without negligence.

Exam Probability: **Medium**

1. *Answer choices:*

(see index for correct answer)

- a. Res ipsa loquitur
- b. Caveat emptor
- c. negligence
- d. Res ipsa

Guidance: level 1

:: Legal reasoning ::

_____ is a Latin expression meaning on its first encounter or at first sight. The literal translation would be "at first face" or "at first appearance", from the feminine forms of primus and facies , both in the ablative case. In modern, colloquial and conversational English, a common translation would be "on the face of it". The term _____ is used in modern legal English to signify that upon initial examination, sufficient corroborating evidence appears to exist to support a case. In common law jurisdictions, _____ denotes evidence that, unless rebutted, would be sufficient to prove a particular proposition or fact. The term is used similarly in academic philosophy. Most legal proceedings, in most jurisdictions, require a _____ case to exist, following which proceedings may then commence to test it, and create a ruling.

Exam Probability: **Low**

2. *Answer choices:*

(see index for correct answer)

- a. Reasonable man
- b. Probable cause
- c. deliberation

Guidance: level 1

:: Abuse of the legal system ::

_____ occurs when a person is restricted in their personal movement within any area without justification or consent. Actual physical restraint is not necessary for _____ to occur. A _____ claim may be made based upon private acts, or upon wrongful governmental detention. For detention by the police, proof of _____ provides a basis to obtain a writ of habeas corpus.

Exam Probability: **Low**

3. *Answer choices:*

(see index for correct answer)

- a. False imprisonment
- b. Obstruction of Justice
- c. Forum shopping

Guidance: level 1

:: Contract law ::

_____ is a legal cause of action and a type of civil wrong, in which a binding agreement or bargained-for exchange is not honored by one or more of the parties to the contract by non-performance or interference with the other party's performance. Breach occurs when a party to a contract fails to fulfill its obligation as described in the contract, or communicates an intent to fail the obligation or otherwise appears not to be able to perform its obligation under the contract. Where there is _____ , the resulting damages will have to be paid by the party breaching the contract to the aggrieved party.

Exam Probability: **High**

4. *Answer choices:*

(see index for correct answer)

- a. Partial integration
- b. Impossibility
- c. Breach of contract
- d. Unjust enrichment

Guidance: level 1

:: Employment discrimination ::

_____ is a form of discrimination based on race, gender, religion, national origin, physical or mental disability, age, sexual orientation, and gender identity by employers. Earnings differentials or occupational differentiation—where differences in pay come from differences in qualifications or responsibilities—should not be confused with _____. Discrimination can be intended and involve disparate treatment of a group or be unintended, yet create disparate impact for a group.

Exam Probability: **Low**

5. *Answer choices:*

(see index for correct answer)

- a. MacBride Principles
- b. Glass ceiling
- c. Employment discrimination
- d. Employment Non-Discrimination Act

Guidance: level 1

:: Law ::

_____ is a body of law which defines the role, powers, and structure of different entities within a state, namely, the executive, the parliament or legislature, and the judiciary; as well as the basic rights of citizens and, in federal countries such as the United States and Canada, the relationship between the central government and state, provincial, or territorial governments.

6. *Answer choices:*

(see index for correct answer)

- a. Legal case
- b. Constitutional law

Guidance: level 1

:: Contract law ::

An _____ is a contract that has not yet been fully performed or fully executed. It is a contract in which both sides still have important performance remaining. However, an obligation to pay money, even if such obligation is material, does not usually make a contract executory. An obligation is material if a breach of contract would result from the failure to satisfy the obligation. A contract that has been fully performed by one party but not by the other party is not an _____ .

7. *Answer choices:*

(see index for correct answer)

- a. Shrink wrap contract
- b. Implied authority
- c. The Rise and Fall of Freedom of Contract

- d. Fundamental breach

Guidance: level 1

:: ::

A _____ can mean the holder of a license, orin U.S. tort law, a _____ is a person who is on the property of another, despite the fact that the property is not open to the general public, because the owner of the property has allowed the _____ to enter. The status of a visitor as a _____ defines the legal rights of the visitor if they are injured due to the negligence of the property possessor .

Exam Probability: **High**

8. *Answer choices:*

(see index for correct answer)

- a. imperative
- b. functional perspective
- c. Licensee
- d. process perspective

Guidance: level 1

:: Contract law ::

_____ is a doctrine in contract law that describes terms that are so extremely unjust, or overwhelmingly one-sided in favor of the party who has the superior bargaining power, that they are contrary to good conscience. Typically, an unconscionable contract is held to be unenforceable because no reasonable or informed person would otherwise agree to it. The perpetrator of the conduct is not allowed to benefit, because the consideration offered is lacking, or is so obviously inadequate, that to enforce the contract would be unfair to the party seeking to escape the contract.

Exam Probability: **Medium**

9. *Answer choices:*

(see index for correct answer)

- a. Capacity
- b. Fundamental breach
- c. Performance Based Contracting
- d. Non-repudiation

Guidance: level 1

:: ::

_____ refers to a business or organization attempting to acquire goods or services to accomplish its goals. Although there are several organizations that attempt to set standards in the _____ process, processes can vary greatly between organizations. Typically the word " _____ " is not used interchangeably with the word "procurement", since procurement typically includes expediting, supplier quality, and transportation and logistics in addition to _____ .

Exam Probability: **Low**

10. *Answer choices:*

(see index for correct answer)

- a. Purchasing
- b. Sarbanes-Oxley act of 2002
- c. deep-level diversity
- d. co-culture

Guidance: level 1

:: Finance ::

A _____ , in the law of the United States, is a contract that governs the relationship between the parties to a kind of financial transaction known as a secured transaction. In a secured transaction, the Grantor assigns, grants and pledges to the grantee a security interest in personal property which is referred to as the collateral. Examples of typical collateral are shares of stock, livestock, and vehicles. A _____ is not used to transfer any interest in real property , only personal property. The document used by lenders to obtain a lien on real property is a mortgage or deed of trust.

Exam Probability: **Medium**

11. *Answer choices:*

(see index for correct answer)

- a. Security agreement
- b. Par value
- c. Financial forecast
- d. Manning rule

Guidance: level 1

:: United States federal public corruption crime ::

Mail fraud and _____ are federal crimes in the United States that involve mailing or electronically transmitting something associated with fraud. Jurisdiction is claimed by the federal government if the illegal activity crosses interstate or international borders.

12. *Answer choices:*

(see index for correct answer)

- a. RICO Act
- b. Racketeer Influenced and Corrupt Organizations Act

Guidance: level 1

:: ::

Competition arises whenever at least two parties strive for a goal which cannot be shared: where one's gain is the other's loss .

Exam Probability: **High**

13. *Answer choices:*

(see index for correct answer)

- a. Competitor
- b. Character
- c. open system
- d. personal values

Guidance: level 1

The Sherman Antitrust Act of 1890 was a United States antitrust law that regulates competition among enterprises, which was passed by Congress under the presidency of Benjamin Harrison.

Exam Probability: **Low**

14. *Answer choices:*

(see index for correct answer)

- a. interpersonal communication
- b. Character
- c. empathy
- d. Sherman Act

Guidance: level 1

:: Business law ::

An _____ is a clause in a contract that requires the parties to resolve their disputes through an arbitration process. Although such a clause may or may not specify that arbitration occur within a specific jurisdiction, it always binds the parties to a type of resolution outside the courts, and is therefore considered a kind of forum selection clause.

15. *Answer choices:*

(see index for correct answer)

- a. Contract failure
- b. Arbitration clause
- c. Country of origin
- d. Duty of fair representation

Guidance: level 1

:: Contract law ::

A _____ , unlike a void contract, is a valid contract which may be either affirmed or rejected at the option of one of the parties. At most, one party to the contract is bound. The unbound party may repudiate the contract, at which time the contract becomes void.

16. *Answer choices:*

(see index for correct answer)

- a. Cover
- b. Option contract
- c. Cohabitation agreement

- d. Voidable contract

Guidance: level 1

:: Decision theory ::

Within economics the concept of _____ is used to model worth or value, but its usage has evolved significantly over time. The term was introduced initially as a measure of pleasure or satisfaction within the theory of utilitarianism by moral philosophers such as Jeremy Bentham and John Stuart Mill. But the term has been adapted and reapplied within neoclassical economics, which dominates modern economic theory, as a _____ function that represents a consumer's preference ordering over a choice set. As such, it is devoid of its original interpretation as a measurement of the pleasure or satisfaction obtained by the consumer from that choice.

Exam Probability: **Medium**

17. *Answer choices:*

(see index for correct answer)

- a. Omission bias
- b. Utility
- c. Quantum cognition
- d. Institutionalism

Guidance: level 1

:: ::

A _____ is a sworn body of people convened to render an impartial verdict officially submitted to them by a court, or to set a penalty or judgment. Modern juries tend to be found in courts to ascertain the guilt or lack thereof in a crime. In Anglophone jurisdictions, the verdict may be guilty or not guilty . The old institution of grand juries still exists in some places, particularly the United States, to investigate whether enough evidence of a crime exists to bring someone to trial.

Exam Probability: **Low**

18. *Answer choices:*

(see index for correct answer)

- a. deep-level diversity
- b. Jury
- c. information systems assessment
- d. corporate values

Guidance: level 1

:: Contract law ::

In jurisprudence, _____ is an equitable doctrine that involves one person taking advantage of a position of power over another person. This inequity in power between the parties can vitiate one party's consent as they are unable to freely exercise their independent will.

19. *Answer choices:*

(see index for correct answer)

- a. Unsolicited goods
- b. Baseball business rules
- c. Undue influence
- d. Option contract

Guidance: level 1

:: ::

_____ is a process under which executive or legislative actions are subject to review by the judiciary. A court with authority for _____ may invalidate laws, acts and governmental actions that are incompatible with a higher authority: an executive decision may be invalidated for being unlawful or a statute may be invalidated for violating the terms of a constitution. _____ is one of the checks and balances in the separation of powers: the power of the judiciary to supervise the legislative and executive branches when the latter exceed their authority. The doctrine varies between jurisdictions, so the procedure and scope of _____ may differ between and within countries.

Exam Probability: **Low**

20. *Answer choices:*

(see index for correct answer)

- a. functional perspective
- b. Judicial review
- c. information systems assessment
- d. open system

Guidance: level 1

:: Contract law ::

An _____ , or simply option, is defined as "a promise which meets the requirements for the formation of a contract and limits the promisor's power to revoke an offer."

Exam Probability: **Medium**

21. *Answer choices:*
(see index for correct answer)

- a. English clause
- b. South African contract law
- c. Terms of service
- d. Option contract

Guidance: level 1

:: Commercial item transport and distribution ::

A _____ is a commitment or expectation to perform some action in general or if certain circumstances arise. A _____ may arise from a system of ethics or morality, especially in an honor culture. Many duties are created by law, sometimes including a codified punishment or liability for non-performance. Performing one's _____ may require some sacrifice of self-interest.

Exam Probability: **Medium**

22. *Answer choices:*

(see index for correct answer)

- a. Skid mount
- b. Duty
- c. Food distribution
- d. Transshipment

Guidance: level 1

:: Legal doctrines and principles ::

The _____ rule is a rule in the Anglo-American common law that governs what kinds of evidence parties to a contract dispute can introduce when trying to determine the specific terms of a contract. The rule also prevents parties who have reduced their agreement to a final written document from later introducing other evidence, such as the content of oral discussions from earlier in the negotiation process, as evidence of a different intent as to the terms of the contract. The rule provides that "extrinsic evidence is inadmissible to vary a written contract". The term "parol" derives from the Anglo-Norman French parol or parole, meaning "word of mouth" or "verbal", and in medieval times referred to oral pleadings in a court case.

Exam Probability: **Low**

23. *Answer choices:*
(see index for correct answer)

- a. Proximate cause
- b. unconscionable contract
- c. Mutual assent
- d. negligence

Guidance: level 1

:: Business law ::

A _____ is a document guaranteeing the payment of a specific amount of money, either on demand, or at a set time, with the payer usually named on the document. More specifically, it is a document contemplated by or consisting of a contract, which promises the payment of money without condition, which may be paid either on demand or at a future date. The term can have different meanings, depending on what law is being applied and what country and context it is used in.

Exam Probability: **Low**

24. *Answer choices:*

(see index for correct answer)

- a. Bulk transfer
- b. Closed shop
- c. Equity of redemption
- d. Refusal to deal

Guidance: level 1

:: ::

In law, an _____ is the process in which cases are reviewed, where parties request a formal change to an official decision. _____ s function both as a process for error correction as well as a process of clarifying and interpreting law. Although appellate courts have existed for thousands of years, common law countries did not incorporate an affirmative right to _____ into their jurisprudence until the 19th century.

25. *Answer choices:*

(see index for correct answer)

- a. Sarbanes-Oxley act of 2002
- b. hierarchical
- c. interpersonal communication
- d. Character

Guidance: level 1

:: Contract law ::

_____ is a legal process for collecting a monetary judgment on behalf of a plaintiff from a defendant. _____ allows the plaintiff to take the money or property of the debtor from the person or institution that holds that property . A similar legal mechanism called execution allows the seizure of money or property held directly by the debtor.

Exam Probability: **High**

26. *Answer choices:*

(see index for correct answer)

- a. Implied authority
- b. Contract

- c. Parent company guarantee
- d. Time is of the essence

Guidance: level 1

:: Contract law ::

_____ , also called an anticipatory breach, is a term in the law of contracts that describes a declaration by the promising party to a contract that he or she does not intend to live up to his or her obligations under the contract.

Exam Probability: **High**

27. *Answer choices:*

(see index for correct answer)

- a. Anticipatory repudiation
- b. Quantum meruit
- c. Reciprocal obligation
- d. Fair Food Program

Guidance: level 1

:: Legal terms ::

_____ is the set of laws that governs how members of a society are to behave. It is contrasted with procedural law, which is the set of procedures for making, administering, and enforcing _____ . _____ defines rights and responsibilities in civil law, and crimes and punishments in criminal law. It may be codified in statutes or exist through precedent in common law.

Exam Probability: **Low**

28. *Answer choices:*

(see index for correct answer)

- a. Patent of precedence
- b. Holding
- c. Plain meaning
- d. Bodily harm

Guidance: level 1

:: ::

A lawsuit is a proceeding by a party or parties against another in the civil court of law. The archaic term "suit in law" is found in only a small number of laws still in effect today. The term "lawsuit" is used in reference to a civil action brought in a court of law in which a plaintiff, a party who claims to have incurred loss as a result of a defendant`s actions, demands a legal or equitable remedy. The defendant is required to respond to the plaintiff`s complaint. If the plaintiff is successful, judgment is in the plaintiff`s favor, and a variety of court orders may be issued to enforce a right, award damages, or impose a temporary or permanent injunction to prevent an act or compel an act. A declaratory judgment may be issued to prevent future legal disputes.

Exam Probability: **Low**

29. *Answer choices:*

(see index for correct answer)

- a. information systems assessment
- b. empathy
- c. Litigation
- d. process perspective

Guidance: level 1

:: ::

A contract is a legally-binding agreement which recognises and governs the rights and duties of the parties to the agreement. A contract is legally enforceable because it meets the requirements and approval of the law. An agreement typically involves the exchange of goods, services, money, or promises of any of those. In the event of breach of contract, the law awards the injured party access to legal remedies such as damages and cancellation.

Exam Probability: **Medium**

30. *Answer choices:*

(see index for correct answer)

- a. Contract law
- b. similarity-attraction theory
- c. open system
- d. imperative

Guidance: level 1

:: Fraud ::

The _____ refers to the requirement that certain kinds of contracts be memorialized in writing, signed by the party to be charged, with sufficient content to evidence the contract.

Exam Probability: **High**

31. *Answer choices:*

(see index for correct answer)

- a. Clothing scam companies
- b. Deceptive advertising
- c. Statute of frauds
- d. 2010 Medicaid fraud

Guidance: level 1

:: Business law ::

A _____ is a form of partnership similar to a general partnership except that while a general partnership must have at least two general partners , a _____ must have at least one GP and at least one limited partner.

Exam Probability: **Medium**

32. *Answer choices:*

(see index for correct answer)

- a. Unfair Commercial Practices Directive
- b. Managed service company
- c. Limited partnership
- d. Financial Security Law of France

Guidance: level 1

An _____ is a contingent motivator. Traditional _____ s are extrinsic motivators which reward actions to yield a desired outcome. The effectiveness of traditional _____ s has changed as the needs of Western society have evolved. While the traditional _____ model is effective when there is a defined procedure and goal for a task, Western society started to require a higher volume of critical thinkers, so the traditional model became less effective. Institutions are now following a trend in implementing strategies that rely on intrinsic motivations rather than the extrinsic motivations that the traditional _____ s foster.

Exam Probability: **Low**

33. *Answer choices:*

(see index for correct answer)

- a. levels of analysis
- b. interpersonal communication
- c. Incentive
- d. deep-level diversity

Guidance: level 1

A _____ is monetary compensation paid by an employer to an employee in exchange for work done. Payment may be calculated as a fixed amount for each task completed , or at an hourly or daily rate , or based on an easily measured quantity of work done.

Exam Probability: **Medium**

34. *Answer choices:*

(see index for correct answer)

- a. functional perspective
- b. cultural
- c. hierarchical
- d. Wage

Guidance: level 1

:: ::

Competition law is a law that promotes or seeks to maintain market competition by regulating anti-competitive conduct by companies. Competition law is implemented through public and private enforcement. Competition law is known as " _____ law" in the United States for historical reasons, and as "anti-monopoly law" in China and Russia. In previous years it has been known as trade practices law in the United Kingdom and Australia. In the European Union, it is referred to as both _____ and competition law.

Exam Probability: **Medium**

35. *Answer choices:*

(see index for correct answer)

- a. functional perspective
- b. levels of analysis
- c. Antitrust
- d. surface-level diversity

Guidance: level 1

:: Business law ::

The term is used to designate a range of diverse, if often kindred, concepts. These have historically been addressed in a number of discrete disciplines, notably mathematics, physics, chemistry, ethics, aesthetics, ontology, and theology.

Exam Probability: **Medium**

36. *Answer choices:*

(see index for correct answer)

- a. License
- b. Complex structured finance transactions
- c. Unfair business practices
- d. Equity of redemption

:: Business law ::

A _____ is a group of people who jointly supervise the activities of an organization, which can be either a for-profit business, nonprofit organization, or a government agency. Such a board's powers, duties, and responsibilities are determined by government regulations and the organization's own constitution and bylaws. These authorities may specify the number of members of the board, how they are to be chosen, and how often they are to meet.

Exam Probability: **Low**

37. *Answer choices:*

(see index for correct answer)

- a. Consularization
- b. Time-and-a-half
- c. Board of directors
- d. Sole proprietorship

:: ::

_____ is the consumption and saving opportunity gained by an entity within a specified timeframe, which is generally expressed in monetary terms. For households and individuals, "_____ is the sum of all the wages, salaries, profits, interest payments, rents, and other forms of earnings received in a given period of time."

Exam Probability: **Low**

38. *Answer choices:*

(see index for correct answer)

- a. corporate values
- b. open system
- c. deep-level diversity
- d. Income

Guidance: level 1

:: Legal doctrines and principles ::

In the United States, the _____ is a legal rule, based on constitutional law, that prevents evidence collected or analyzed in violation of the defendant's constitutional rights from being used in a court of law. This may be considered an example of a prophylactic rule formulated by the judiciary in order to protect a constitutional right. The _____ may also, in some circumstances at least, be considered to follow directly from the constitutional language, such as the Fifth Amendment's command that no person "shall be compelled in any criminal case to be a witness against himself" and that no person "shall be deprived of life, liberty or property without due process of law".

Exam Probability: **Medium**

39. *Answer choices:*

(see index for correct answer)

- a. Acquiescence
- b. Eminent domain
- c. Parol evidence
- d. Act of state doctrine

Guidance: level 1

:: ::

An _____ , for United States federal income tax, is a closely held corporation that makes a valid election to be taxed under Subchapter S of Chapter 1 of the Internal Revenue Code. In general, _____ s do not pay any income taxes. Instead, the corporation's income or losses are divided among and passed through to its shareholders. The shareholders must then report the income or loss on their own individual income tax returns.

Exam Probability: **High**

40. *Answer choices:*

(see index for correct answer)

- a. hierarchical perspective
- b. Sarbanes-Oxley act of 2002
- c. empathy
- d. co-culture

Guidance: level 1

:: ::

_____ is a legal term which, in its broadest sense, is a synonym for anyone in a position of trust and so can refer to any person who holds property, authority, or a position of trust or responsibility for the benefit of another. A _____ can also refer to a person who is allowed to do certain tasks but not able to gain income. Although in the strictest sense of the term a _____ is the holder of property on behalf of a beneficiary, the more expansive sense encompasses persons who serve, for example, on the board of _____ s of an institution that operates for a charity, for the benefit of the general public, or a person in the local government.

Exam Probability: **Low**

41. *Answer choices:*

(see index for correct answer)

- a. Trustee
- b. process perspective
- c. empathy
- d. Character

Guidance: level 1

:: Data management ::

_____ is a form of intellectual property that grants the creator of an original creative work an exclusive legal right to determine whether and under what conditions this original work may be copied and used by others, usually for a limited term of years. The exclusive rights are not absolute but limited by limitations and exceptions to _____ law, including fair use. A major limitation on _____ on ideas is that _____ protects only the original expression of ideas, and not the underlying ideas themselves.

Exam Probability: **Medium**

42. *Answer choices:*

(see index for correct answer)

- a. Two-phase commit protocol
- b. DMAIC
- c. Copyright
- d. Information integration

Guidance: level 1

:: Mortgage ::

_____ is a legal process in which a lender attempts to recover the balance of a loan from a borrower who has stopped making payments to the lender by forcing the sale of the asset used as the collateral for the loan.

Exam Probability: **Medium**

43. *Answer choices:*

(see index for correct answer)

- a. Repayment mortgage
- b. Mortgage bank
- c. AEPROSER
- d. Lenders mortgage insurance

Guidance: level 1

:: ::

In financial markets, a share is a unit used as mutual funds, limited partnerships, and real estate investment trusts. The owner of _____ in the corporation/company is a shareholder of the corporation. A share is an indivisible unit of capital, expressing the ownership relationship between the company and the shareholder. The denominated value of a share is its face value, and the total of the face value of issued _____ represent the capital of a company, which may not reflect the market value of those _____ .

Exam Probability: **Low**

44. *Answer choices:*

(see index for correct answer)

- a. Shares
- b. hierarchical

- c. levels of analysis
- d. empathy

Guidance: level 1

:: Commerce ::

_____ relates to "the exchange of goods and services, especially on a large scale". It includes legal, economic, political, social, cultural and technological systems that operate in a country or in international trade.

Exam Probability: **Low**

45. *Answer choices:*

(see index for correct answer)

- a. Commerce
- b. Export restriction
- c. Bunker adjustment factor
- d. Card association

Guidance: level 1

:: Labour relations ::

_____ is a field of study that can have different meanings depending on the context in which it is used. In an international context, it is a subfield of labor history that studies the human relations with regard to work – in its broadest sense – and how this connects to questions of social inequality. It explicitly encompasses unregulated, historical, and non-Western forms of labor. Here, _____ define "for or with whom one works and under what rules. These rules determine the type of work, type and amount of remuneration, working hours, degrees of physical and psychological strain, as well as the degree of freedom and autonomy associated with the work."

Exam Probability: **High**

46. *Answer choices:*

(see index for correct answer)

- a. Big labor
- b. Labor relations
- c. Boulwarism
- d. Merit shop

Guidance: level 1

:: Fair use ::

_____ is a doctrine in the law of the United States that permits limited use of copyrighted material without having to first acquire permission from the copyright holder. _____ is one of the limitations to copyright intended to balance the interests of copyright holders with the public interest in the wider distribution and use of creative works by allowing as a defense to copyright infringement claims certain limited uses that might otherwise be considered infringement.

Exam Probability: **Medium**

47. *Answer choices:*

(see index for correct answer)

- a. Transformation
- b. Nominative use
- c. Fair use
- d. Derivative work

Guidance: level 1

:: ::

_____ is property that is movable. In common law systems, _____ may also be called chattels or personalty. In civil law systems, _____ is often called movable property or movables – any property that can be moved from one location to another.

Exam Probability: **Medium**

48. *Answer choices:*

(see index for correct answer)

- a. cultural
- b. imperative
- c. open system
- d. deep-level diversity

Guidance: level 1

:: Contract law ::

_____ is an equitable remedy in the law of contract, whereby a court issues an order requiring a party to perform a specific act, such as to complete performance of the contract. It is typically available in the sale of land, but otherwise is not generally available if damages are an appropriate alternative. _____ is almost never available for contracts of personal service, although performance may also be ensured through the threat of proceedings for contempt of court.

Exam Probability: **Medium**

49. *Answer choices:*

(see index for correct answer)

- a. Offeree
- b. Complete contract
- c. Substantial performance

- d. Pactum de quota litis

Guidance: level 1

:: Business law ::

An _____ is a natural person, business, or corporation that provides goods or services to another entity under terms specified in a contract or within a verbal agreement. Unlike an employee, an _____ does not work regularly for an employer but works as and when required, during which time they may be subject to law of agency. _____ s are usually paid on a freelance basis. Contractors often work through a limited company or franchise, which they themselves own, or may work through an umbrella company.

Exam Probability: **High**

50. *Answer choices:*

(see index for correct answer)

- a. Power harassment
- b. Limited partnership
- c. Family and Medical Leave Act of 1993
- d. Independent contractor

Guidance: level 1

:: ::

An _____ is an area of the production, distribution, or trade, and consumption of goods and services by different agents. Understood in its broadest sense, `The _____ is defined as a social domain that emphasize the practices, discourses, and material expressions associated with the production, use, and management of resources`. Economic agents can be individuals, businesses, organizations, or governments. Economic transactions occur when two parties agree to the value or price of the transacted good or service, commonly expressed in a certain currency. However, monetary transactions only account for a small part of the economic domain.

Exam Probability: **Low**

51. *Answer choices:*

(see index for correct answer)

- a. functional perspective
- b. open system
- c. Economy
- d. Sarbanes-Oxley act of 2002

Guidance: level 1

:: Legal terms ::

_____ , or non-absolute contributory negligence outside the United States, is a partial legal defense that reduces the amount of damages that a plaintiff can recover in a negligence-based claim, based upon the degree to which the plaintiff's own negligence contributed to cause the injury. When the defense is asserted, the factfinder, usually a jury, must decide the degree to which the plaintiff's negligence and the combined negligence of all other relevant actors all contributed to cause the plaintiff's damages. It is a modification of the doctrine of contributory negligence that disallows any recovery by a plaintiff whose negligence contributed even minimally to causing the damages.

Exam Probability: **High**

52. *Answer choices:*

(see index for correct answer)

- a. Chain of title
- b. Comparative negligence
- c. Misfeasance
- d. Family purpose doctrine

Guidance: level 1

:: ::

A _____ , in common law jurisdictions, is a civil wrong that causes a claimant to suffer loss or harm resulting in legal liability for the person who commits the _____ ious act. It can include the intentional infliction of emotional distress, negligence, financial losses, injuries, invasion of privacy, and many other things.

Exam Probability: **High**

53. *Answer choices:*

(see index for correct answer)

- a. process perspective
- b. Tort
- c. functional perspective
- d. empathy

Guidance: level 1

:: ::

_____ is a means of protection from financial loss. It is a form of risk management, primarily used to hedge against the risk of a contingent or uncertain loss

Exam Probability: **High**

54. *Answer choices:*

(see index for correct answer)

- a. functional perspective
- b. personal values
- c. similarity-attraction theory
- d. levels of analysis

Guidance: level 1

:: ::

_____ is a judicial device in common law legal systems whereby a court may prevent, or "estop" a person from making assertions or from going back on his or her word; the person being sanctioned is "estopped". _____ may prevent someone from bringing a particular claim. Legal doctrines of _____ are based in both common law and equity.

Exam Probability: **Medium**

55. *Answer choices:*
(see index for correct answer)

- a. Estoppel
- b. functional perspective
- c. Sarbanes-Oxley act of 2002
- d. hierarchical perspective

:: Arbitration law ::

The United States Arbitration Act , more commonly referred to as the
_____ or FAA, is an act of Congress that provides for judicial
facilitation of private dispute resolution through arbitration. It applies in
both state courts and federal courts, as was held constitutional in Southland
Corp. v. Keating. It applies where the transaction contemplated by the parties
"involves" interstate commerce and is predicated on an exercise of the Commerce
Clause powers granted to Congress in the U.S. Constitution.

Exam Probability: **Medium**

56. *Answer choices:*

(see index for correct answer)

- a. Uniform Arbitration Act
- b. Federal Arbitration Act
- c. Title 9 of the United States Code
- d. UNCITRAL Model Law on International Commercial Arbitration

:: Negotiable instrument law ::

In the United States, The Preservation of Consumers' Claims and Defenses [_____ Rule], formally known as the "Trade Regulation Rule Concerning Preservation of Consumers' Claims and Defenses," protects consumers when merchants sell a consumer's credit contracts to other lenders. Specifically, it preserves consumers' right to assert the same legal claims and defenses against anyone who purchases the credit contract, as they would have against the seller who originally provided the credit. [16 Code of Federal Regulations Part 433]

Exam Probability: **High**

57. *Answer choices:*

(see index for correct answer)

- a. Burton v. United States
- b. Regulation CC
- c. holder in due course doctrine
- d. Holder in due course

Guidance: level 1

:: Chemical industry ::

The _____ for the Protection of Literary and Artistic Works, usually known as the _____ , is an international agreement governing copyright, which was first accepted in Berne, Switzerland, in 1886.

Exam Probability: **Medium**

58. *Answer choices:*

(see index for correct answer)

- a. Berne Convention
- b. Middle German Chemical Triangle
- c. Chemical leasing
- d. ConverDyn

Guidance: level 1

:: Competition regulators ::

The _____ is an independent agency of the United States government, established in 1914 by the _____ Act. Its principal mission is the promotion of consumer protection and the elimination and prevention of anticompetitive business practices, such as coercive monopoly. It is headquartered in the _____ Building in Washington, D.C.

Exam Probability: **Low**

59. *Answer choices:*

(see index for correct answer)

- a. National Board for Prices and Incomes
- b. Industrial Commission
- c. Queensland Competition Authority
- d. Federal Trade Commission

Guidance: level 1

Finance

Finance is a field that is concerned with the allocation (investment) of assets and liabilities over space and time, often under conditions of risk or uncertainty. Finance can also be defined as the science of money management. Participants in the market aim to price assets based on their risk level, fundamental value, and their expected rate of return. Finance can be split into three sub-categories: public finance, corporate finance and personal finance.

:: Business law ::

A _____ is an arrangement where parties, known as partners, agree to cooperate to advance their mutual interests. The partners in a _____ may be individuals, businesses, interest-based organizations, schools, governments or combinations. Organizations may partner to increase the likelihood of each achieving their mission and to amplify their reach. A _____ may result in issuing and holding equity or may be only governed by a contract.

Exam Probability: **Medium**

1. *Answer choices:*

(see index for correct answer)

- a. Enhanced use lease
- b. European Patent Convention
- c. Partnership
- d. Subordination

Guidance: level 1

:: Generally Accepted Accounting Principles ::

Financial statements prepared and presented by a company typically follow an external standard that specifically guides their preparation. These standards vary across the globe and are typically overseen by some combination of the private accounting profession in that specific nation and the various government regulators. Variations across countries may be considerable, making cross-country evaluation of financial data challenging.

2. *Answer choices:*

(see index for correct answer)

- a. Standard Business Reporting
- b. Contributed capital
- c. Operating income
- d. Gross sales

Guidance: level 1

:: Generally Accepted Accounting Principles ::

Expenditure is an outflow of money to another person or group to pay for an item or service, or for a category of costs. For a tenant, rent is an _____ . For students or parents, tuition is an _____ . Buying food, clothing, furniture or an automobile is often referred to as an _____ . An _____ is a cost that is "paid" or "remitted", usually in exchange for something of value. Something that seems to cost a great deal is "expensive". Something that seems to cost little is "inexpensive". " _____ s of the table" are _____ s of dining, refreshments, a feast, etc.

Exam Probability: **High**

3. *Answer choices:*

(see index for correct answer)

- a. Closing entries
- b. Expense
- c. Long-term liabilities
- d. Generally Accepted Accounting Practice

Guidance: level 1

:: Inventory ::

In business and accounting/accountancy, _____ or continuous inventory describes systems of inventory where information on inventory quantity and availability is updated on a continuous basis as a function of doing business. Generally this is accomplished by connecting the inventory system with order entry and in retail the point of sale system. In this case, book inventory would be exactly the same as, or almost the same, as the real inventory.

Exam Probability: **Medium**

4. *Answer choices:*

(see index for correct answer)

- a. just-in-time manufacturing
- b. Safety stock
- c. Stock-taking
- d. Cost of goods sold

Guidance: level 1

:: Debt ::

A _____ is a monetary amount owed to a creditor that is unlikely to be paid and, or which the creditor is not willing to take action to collect for various reasons, often due to the debtor not having the money to pay, for example due to a company going into liquidation or insolvency. There are various technical definitions of what constitutes a _____ , depending on accounting conventions, regulatory treatment and the institution provisioning. In the USA, bank loans with more than ninety days' arrears become "problem loans". Accounting sources advise that the full amount of a _____ be written off to the profit and loss account or a provision for _____ s as soon as it is foreseen.

Exam Probability: **Medium**

5. *Answer choices:*

(see index for correct answer)

- a. Default
- b. Borrowing base
- c. Bad debt
- d. Bailout

Guidance: level 1

:: Management accounting ::

_____ s are costs that change as the quantity of the good or service that a business produces changes. _____ s are the sum of marginal costs over all units produced. They can also be considered normal costs. Fixed costs and _____ s make up the two components of total cost. Direct costs are costs that can easily be associated with a particular cost object. However, not all _____ s are direct costs. For example, variable manufacturing overhead costs are _____ s that are indirect costs, not direct costs. _____ s are sometimes called unit-level costs as they vary with the number of units produced.

Exam Probability: **Medium**

6. *Answer choices:*

(see index for correct answer)

- a. Cost accounting
- b. Management accounting in supply chains
- c. Chartered Institute of Management Accountants
- d. Fixed cost

Guidance: level 1

:: ::

A shareholder is an individual or institution that legally owns one or more shares of stock in a public or private corporation. Shareholders may be referred to as members of a corporation. Legally, a person is not a shareholder in a corporation until their name and other details are entered in the corporation's register of shareholders or members.

7. *Answer choices:*

(see index for correct answer)

- a. hierarchical
- b. Stockholder
- c. surface-level diversity
- d. levels of analysis

Guidance: level 1

:: Money ::

Cash and _____ s are the most liquid current assets found on a business's balance sheet. _____ s are short-term commitments "with temporarily idle cash and easily convertible into a known cash amount". An investment normally counts to be a _____ when it has a short maturity period of 90 days or less, and can be included in the cash and _____ s balance from the date of acquisition when it carries an insignificant risk of changes in the asset value; with more than 90 days maturity, the asset is not considered as cash and _____ s. Equity investments mostly are excluded from _____ s, unless they are essentially _____ s, for instance, if the preferred shares acquired within a short maturity period and with specified recovery date.

8. *Answer choices:*

(see index for correct answer)

- a. Relative theory of money
- b. Limping bimetallism
- c. Cash equivalent
- d. Ideal money

Guidance: level 1

:: Consumer theory ::

A _____ is a technical term in psychology, economics and philosophy usually used in relation to choosing between alternatives. For example, someone prefers A over B if they would rather choose A than B.

Exam Probability: **Low**

9. *Answer choices:*

(see index for correct answer)

- a. Expenditure function
- b. Quality bias
- c. Consumer sovereignty
- d. Preference

Guidance: level 1

:: Management accounting ::

_____ is the process of recording, classifying, analyzing, summarizing, and allocating costs associated with a process, after that developing various courses of action to control the costs. Its goal is to advise the management on how to optimize business practices and processes based on cost efficiency and capability. _____ provides the detailed cost information that management needs to control current operations and plan for the future.

Exam Probability: **Medium**

10. *Answer choices:*

(see index for correct answer)

- a. Management control system
- b. Factory overhead
- c. Inventory valuation
- d. Environmental full-cost accounting

Guidance: level 1

:: ::

Pharmaceutical _____ is the creation of a particular pharmaceutical product to fit the unique need of a patient. To do this, _____ pharmacists combine or process appropriate ingredients using various tools.

11. *Answer choices:*

(see index for correct answer)

- a. functional perspective
- b. Sarbanes-Oxley act of 2002
- c. cultural
- d. Compounding

Guidance: level 1

:: ::

_____ or accountancy is the measurement, processing, and communication of financial information about economic entities such as businesses and corporations. The modern field was established by the Italian mathematician Luca Pacioli in 1494. _____ , which has been called the "language of business", measures the results of an organization's economic activities and conveys this information to a variety of users, including investors, creditors, management, and regulators. Practitioners of _____ are known as accountants. The terms " _____ " and "financial reporting" are often used as synonyms.

12. *Answer choices:*

(see index for correct answer)

- a. corporate values
- b. Accounting
- c. information systems assessment
- d. open system

Guidance: level 1

:: Investment ::

The _____ is a measure of an investment's rate of return. The term internal refers to the fact that the calculation excludes external factors, such as the risk-free rate, inflation, the cost of capital, or various financial risks.

Exam Probability: **Medium**

13. *Answer choices:*

(see index for correct answer)

- a. Portable alpha
- b. Value averaging
- c. Spell Capital Partners
- d. Internal rate of return

Guidance: level 1

:: Generally Accepted Accounting Principles ::

The first published description of the process is found in Luca Pacioli`s 1494 work Summa de arithmetica, in the section titled Particularis de Computis et Scripturis. Although he did not use the term, he essentially prescribed a technique similar to a post-closing _____ .

Exam Probability: **Medium**

14. *Answer choices:*

(see index for correct answer)

- a. Trial balance
- b. Generally Accepted Accounting Practice
- c. Petty cash
- d. Completed-contract method

Guidance: level 1

:: Accounting journals and ledgers ::

A _____ , in accounting, is the logging of a transaction in an accounting journal that shows a company's debit and credit balances. The _____ can consist of several recordings, each of which is either a debit or a credit. The total of the debits must equal the total of the credits or the _____ is considered unbalanced. Journal entries can record unique items or recurring items such as depreciation or bond amortization. In accounting software, journal entries are usually entered using a separate module from accounts payable, which typically has its own subledger, that indirectly affects the general ledger. As a result, journal entries directly change the account balances on the general ledger. A properly documented _____ consists of the correct date, amount that will be debited, amount that will be credited, description of transaction, and unique reference number .

Exam Probability: **Medium**

15. *Answer choices:*

(see index for correct answer)

- a. Subsidiary ledger
- b. Journal entry
- c. Subledger
- d. Check register

Guidance: level 1

:: Accounting terminology ::

_____ of something is, in finance, the adding together of interest or different investments over a period of time. It holds specific meanings in accounting, where it can refer to accounts on a balance sheet that represent liabilities and non-cash-based assets used in _____ -based accounting. These types of accounts include, among others, accounts payable, accounts receivable, goodwill, deferred tax liability and future interest expense.

Exam Probability: **Medium**

16. *Answer choices:*

(see index for correct answer)

- a. Capital surplus
- b. Fund accounting
- c. Capital expenditure
- d. Checkoff

Guidance: level 1

:: Mutualism (movement) ::

A _____ is a professionally managed investment fund that pools money from many investors to purchase securities. These investors may be retail or institutional in nature.

Exam Probability: **Low**

17. *Answer choices:*

(see index for correct answer)

- a. Communal work
- b. Mutual fund
- c. Winslow Carlton
- d. Ayni

Guidance: level 1

:: ::

An _____ is an asset that lacks physical substance. It is defined in opposition to physical assets such as machinery and buildings. An _____ is usually very hard to evaluate. Patents, copyrights, franchises, goodwill, trademarks, and trade names. The general interpretation also includes software and other intangible computer based assets are all examples of _____ s. _____ s generally—though not necessarily—suffer from typical market failures of non-rivalry and non-excludability.

Exam Probability: **Low**

18. *Answer choices:*

(see index for correct answer)

- a. co-culture
- b. Intangible asset
- c. hierarchical perspective

- d. process perspective

Guidance: level 1

:: ::

The U.S. _____ is an independent agency of the United States federal government. The SEC holds primary responsibility for enforcing the federal securities laws, proposing securities rules, and regulating the securities industry, the nation's stock and options exchanges, and other activities and organizations, including the electronic securities markets in the United States.

Exam Probability: **Low**

19. *Answer choices:*

(see index for correct answer)

- a. information systems assessment
- b. levels of analysis
- c. Securities and Exchange Commission
- d. process perspective

Guidance: level 1

:: Stock market ::

A _____ , equity market or share market is the aggregation of buyers and sellers of stocks , which represent ownership claims on businesses; these may include securities listed on a public stock exchange, as well as stock that is only traded privately. Examples of the latter include shares of private companies which are sold to investors through equity crowdfunding platforms. Stock exchanges list shares of common equity as well as other security types, e.g. corporate bonds and convertible bonds.

Exam Probability: **Low**

20. *Answer choices:*

(see index for correct answer)

- a. Alternative display facility
- b. Intellidex
- c. Open outcry
- d. Stock market

Guidance: level 1

:: Fixed income analysis ::

The _____ , book yield or redemption yield of a bond or other fixed-interest security, such as gilts, is the internal rate of return earned by an investor who buys the bond today at the market price, assuming that the bond is held until maturity, and that all coupon and principal payments are made on schedule. _____ is the discount rate at which the sum of all future cash flows from the bond is equal to the current price of the bond. The YTM is often given in terms of Annual Percentage Rate , but more often market convention is followed. In a number of major markets the convention is to quote annualized yields with semi-annual compounding ; thus, for example, an annual effective yield of 10.25% would be quoted as 10.00%, because $1.05 \times 1.05 = 1.1025$ and $2 \times 5 = 10$.

Exam Probability: **High**

21. *Answer choices:*

(see index for correct answer)

- a. LIBOR market model
- b. Embedded option
- c. Yield to maturity
- d. Bond duration closed-form formula

Guidance: level 1

:: Fraud ::

In law, _____ is intentional deception to secure unfair or unlawful gain, or to deprive a victim of a legal right. _____ can violate civil law, a criminal law, or it may cause no loss of money, property or legal right but still be an element of another civil or criminal wrong. The purpose of _____ may be monetary gain or other benefits, for example by obtaining a passport, travel document, or driver's license, or mortgage _____, where the perpetrator may attempt to qualify for a mortgage by way of false statements.

Exam Probability: **Medium**

22. *Answer choices:*

(see index for correct answer)

- a. Parcel mule scam
- b. Swatting
- c. Shell corporation
- d. Customer not present

Guidance: level 1

:: Capital (economics) ::

In Economics and Accounting, the _____ is the cost of a company's funds, or, from an investor's point of view "the required rate of return on a portfolio company's existing securities". It is used to evaluate new projects of a company. It is the minimum return that investors expect for providing capital to the company, thus setting a benchmark that a new project has to meet.

23. *Answer choices:*

(see index for correct answer)

- a. Structural capital
- b. operating capital
- c. Cost of capital
- d. financial capital

Guidance: level 1

:: Investment ::

_____ , and investment appraisal, is the planning process used to determine whether an organization's long term investments such as new machinery, replacement of machinery, new plants, new products, and research development projects are worth the funding of cash through the firm's capitalization structure . It is the process of allocating resources for major capital, or investment, expenditures. One of the primary goals of _____ investments is to increase the value of the firm to the shareholders.

Exam Probability: **Low**

24. *Answer choices:*

(see index for correct answer)

- a. Umbrella fund

- b. Advocis
- c. Lawcard
- d. Capital budgeting

Guidance: level 1

:: ::

An _____ , for United States federal income tax, is a closely held
corporation that makes a valid election to be taxed under Subchapter S of
Chapter 1 of the Internal Revenue Code. In general, _____ s do not pay any
income taxes. Instead, the corporation's income or losses are divided among and
passed through to its shareholders. The shareholders must then report the
income or loss on their own individual income tax returns.

Exam Probability: **Medium**

25. *Answer choices:*

(see index for correct answer)

- a. S corporation
- b. surface-level diversity
- c. hierarchical
- d. functional perspective

Guidance: level 1

:: Generally Accepted Accounting Principles ::

An _____ or profit and loss account is one of the financial statements of a company and shows the company's revenues and expenses during a particular period.

Exam Probability: **Low**

26. *Answer choices:*

(see index for correct answer)

- a. Normal balance
- b. Deferred income
- c. Vendor-specific objective evidence
- d. Income statement

Guidance: level 1

:: Costs ::

In microeconomic theory, the _____ , or alternative cost, of making a particular choice is the value of the most valuable choice out of those that were not taken. In other words, opportunity that will require sacrifices.

Exam Probability: **Medium**

27. *Answer choices:*

(see index for correct answer)

- a. Opportunity cost
- b. Cost reduction
- c. Quality costs
- d. Cost competitiveness of fuel sources

Guidance: level 1

:: Financial accounting ::

_____ in accounting is the process of treating investments in associate companies. Equity accounting is usually applied where an investor entity holds 20–50% of the voting stock of the associate company. The investor records such investments as an asset on its balance sheet. The investor's proportional share of the associate company's net income increases the investment , and proportional payments of dividends decrease it. In the investor's income statement, the proportional share of the investor's net income or net loss is reported as a single-line item.

Exam Probability: **Medium**

28. *Answer choices:*

(see index for correct answer)

- a. Equity method
- b. Accounting identity

- c. Net worth
- d. Authorised capital

Guidance: level 1

:: Planning ::

_____ is a high level plan to achieve one or more goals under conditions of uncertainty. In the sense of the "art of the general," which included several subsets of skills including tactics, siegecraft, logistics etc., the term came into use in the 6th century C.E. in East Roman terminology, and was translated into Western vernacular languages only in the 18th century. From then until the 20th century, the word "_____" came to denote "a comprehensive way to try to pursue political ends, including the threat or actual use of force, in a dialectic of wills" in a military conflict, in which both adversaries interact.

Exam Probability: **High**

29. *Answer choices:*

(see index for correct answer)

- a. Default effect
- b. Counterplan
- c. Strategy
- d. Strategic communication

Guidance: level 1

:: Actuarial science ::

_____ is the possibility of losing something of value. Values can be gained or lost when taking _____ resulting from a given action or inaction, foreseen or unforeseen. _____ can also be defined as the intentional interaction with uncertainty. Uncertainty is a potential, unpredictable, and uncontrollable outcome; _____ is a consequence of action taken in spite of uncertainty.

Exam Probability: **Low**

30. *Answer choices:*

(see index for correct answer)

- a. Computational finance
- b. Time value of money
- c. Risk
- d. Extreme value theory

Guidance: level 1

:: Portfolio theories ::

In finance, the _____ is a model used to determine a theoretically appropriate required rate of return of an asset, to make decisions about adding assets to a well-diversified portfolio.

31. *Answer choices:*

(see index for correct answer)

- a. Returns-based style analysis
- b. Intertemporal portfolio choice
- c. Capital asset pricing model
- d. Efficient frontier

Guidance: level 1

:: Generally Accepted Accounting Principles ::

_____ , or non-current liabilities, are liabilities that are due beyond a year or the normal operation period of the company. The normal operation period is the amount of time it takes for a company to turn inventory into cash. On a classified balance sheet, liabilities are separated between current and _____ to help users assess the company's financial standing in short-term and long-term periods. _____ give users more information about the long-term prosperity of the company, while current liabilities inform the user of debt that the company owes in the current period. On a balance sheet, accounts are listed in order of liquidity, so _____ come after current liabilities. In addition, the specific long-term liability accounts are listed on the balance sheet in order of liquidity. Therefore, an account due within eighteen months would be listed before an account due within twenty-four months. Examples of _____ are bonds payable, long-term loans, capital leases, pension liabilities, post-retirement healthcare liabilities, deferred compensation, deferred revenues, deferred income taxes, and derivative liabilities.

32. *Answer choices:*

(see index for correct answer)

- a. Statement of recommended practice
- b. Net income
- c. Earnings before interest, taxes, depreciation, and amortization
- d. Long-term liabilities

Guidance: level 1

:: Materials ::

A _____ , also known as a feedstock, unprocessed material, or primary commodity, is a basic material that is used to produce goods, finished products, energy, or intermediate materials which are feedstock for future finished products. As feedstock, the term connotes these materials are bottleneck assets and are highly important with regard to producing other products. An example of this is crude oil, which is a _____ and a feedstock used in the production of industrial chemicals, fuels, plastics, and pharmaceutical goods; lumber is a _____ used to produce a variety of products including all types of furniture. The term " _____ " denotes materials in minimally processed or unprocessed in states; e.g., raw latex, crude oil, cotton, coal, raw biomass, iron ore, air, logs, or water i.e. "...any product of agriculture, forestry, fishing and any other mineral that is in its natural form or which has undergone the transformation required to prepare it for internationally marketing in substantial volumes."

33. *Answer choices:*

(see index for correct answer)

- a. Raw material
- b. Biocompatible material
- c. Cross-laminates
- d. Muka

Guidance: level 1

:: Basel II ::

All businesses take risks based on two factors: the probability an adverse circumstance will come about and the cost of such adverse circumstance. Risk management is the study of how to control risks and balance the possibility of gains.

Exam Probability: **Medium**

34. *Answer choices:*

(see index for correct answer)

- a. Advanced measurement approach
- b. Advanced IRB
- c. Market risk
- d. Jaime Caruana

:: Generally Accepted Accounting Principles ::

In accounting, an economic item's _____ is the original nominal monetary value of that item. _____ accounting involves reporting assets and liabilities at their _____ s, which are not updated for changes in the items' values. Consequently, the amounts reported for these balance sheet items often differ from their current economic or market values.

Exam Probability: **Low**

35. *Answer choices:*

(see index for correct answer)

- a. Operating income before depreciation and amortization
- b. Operating profit
- c. Historical cost
- d. Net realizable value

:: Elementary geometry ::

The _____ is the front of an animal's head that features three of the head's sense organs, the eyes, nose, and mouth, and through which animals express many of their emotions. The _____ is crucial for human identity, and damage such as scarring or developmental deformities affects the psyche adversely.

Exam Probability: **Low**

36. *Answer choices:*

(see index for correct answer)

- a. Golden angle
- b. Angular diameter
- c. Central angle
- d. Transversal

Guidance: level 1

:: Financial ratios ::

_____ or asset turns is a financial ratio that measures the efficiency of a company's use of its assets in generating sales revenue or sales income to the company.

Exam Probability: **Low**

37. *Answer choices:*

(see index for correct answer)

- a. Average collection period
- b. Treynor ratio
- c. Asset turnover
- d. Sterling ratio

Guidance: level 1

:: Accounting terminology ::

Total _____ is a method of Accounting cost which entails the full cost of manufacturing or providing a service. TAC includes not just the costs of materials and labour, but also of all manufacturing overheads . The cost of each cost center can be direct or indirect. The direct cost can be easily identified with individual cost centers. Whereas indirect cost cannot be easily identified with the cost center. The distribution of overhead among the departments is called apportionment.

Exam Probability: **Low**

38. *Answer choices:*

(see index for correct answer)

- a. Adjusting entries
- b. Internal auditing
- c. Accounts payable
- d. Absorption costing

:: Costs ::

_____ is the sum of costs of all resources consumed in the process of making a product. The _____ is classified into three categories: direct materials cost, direct labor cost and manufacturing overhead.

Exam Probability: **Medium**

39. *Answer choices:*

(see index for correct answer)

- a. Manufacturing cost
- b. Joint cost
- c. Road Logistics Costing in South Africa
- d. Direct materials cost

:: Financial accounting ::

_____ is the value of all the non-financial and financial assets owned by an institutional unit or sector minus the value of all its outstanding liabilities. Since financial assets minus outstanding liabilities equal net financial assets, _____ can also be conveniently expressed as non-financial assets plus net financial assets. _____ can apply to companies, individuals, governments or economic sectors such as the sector of financial corporations or to entire countries.

Exam Probability: **Medium**

40. *Answer choices:*

(see index for correct answer)

- a. Intangibles
- b. Exit rate
- c. Capital account
- d. Net worth

Guidance: level 1

:: Accounting systems ::

In bookkeeping, a _____ statement is a process that explains the difference on a specified date between the bank balance shown in an organization's bank statement, as supplied by the bank and the corresponding amount shown in the organization's own accounting records.

Exam Probability: **Low**

41. *Answer choices:*

(see index for correct answer)

- a. Confidence accounting
- b. Bank reconciliation
- c. Single-entry bookkeeping
- d. Open-book accounting

Guidance: level 1

:: Funds ::

_____ value is the value of an entity's assets minus the value of its liabilities, often in relation to open-end or mutual funds, since shares of such funds registered with the U.S. Securities and Exchange Commission are redeemed at their _____ value. It is also a key figure with regard to hedge funds and venture capital funds when calculating the value of the underlying investments in these funds by investors. This may also be the same as the book value or the equity value of a business. _____ value may represent the value of the total equity, or it may be divided by the number of shares outstanding held by investors, thereby representing the _____ value per share.

Exam Probability: **High**

42. *Answer choices:*

(see index for correct answer)

- a. Icapital.biz Berhad

- b. Income fund
- c. Montana Management
- d. Net asset

Guidance: level 1

:: Personal finance ::

_____ is income not spent, or deferred consumption. Methods of _____ include putting money aside in, for example, a deposit account, a pension account, an investment fund, or as cash. _____ also involves reducing expenditures, such as recurring costs. In terms of personal finance, _____ generally specifies low-risk preservation of money, as in a deposit account, versus investment, wherein risk is a lot higher; in economics more broadly, it refers to any income not used for immediate consumption.

Exam Probability: **Medium**

43. *Answer choices:*

(see index for correct answer)

- a. Certified Financial Planner Board of Standards
- b. Coverdell Education Savings Account
- c. Repossession
- d. Take a penny, leave a penny

Guidance: level 1

_____ involves decision making. It can include judging the merits of multiple options and selecting one or more of them. One can make a _____ between imagined options or between real options followed by the corresponding action. For example, a traveler might choose a route for a journey based on the preference of arriving at a given destination as soon as possible. The preferred route can then follow from information such as the length of each of the possible routes, traffic conditions, etc. The arrival at a _____ can include more complex motivators such as cognition, instinct, and feeling.

Exam Probability: **Medium**

44. *Answer choices:*

(see index for correct answer)

- a. imperative
- b. interpersonal communication
- c. hierarchical perspective
- d. information systems assessment

Guidance: level 1

:: Occupations ::

An _____ is a practitioner of accounting or accountancy, which is the measurement, disclosure or provision of assurance about financial information that helps managers, investors, tax authorities and others make decisions about allocating resource.

Exam Probability: **Low**

45. *Answer choices:*

(see index for correct answer)

- a. Drafter
- b. Union organizer
- c. Key worker
- d. Accountant

Guidance: level 1

:: Subprime mortgage crisis ::

The _____ Group, Inc., is an American multinational investment bank and financial services company headquartered in New York City. It offers services in investment management, securities, asset management, prime brokerage, and securities underwriting.

Exam Probability: **High**

46. *Answer choices:*

(see index for correct answer)

- a. Money market fund
- b. Goldman Sachs
- c. Secondary Mortgage Market Enhancement Act
- d. Housing and Economic Recovery Act of 2008

Guidance: level 1

:: Financial markets ::

The _____ , also called the aftermarket and follow on public offering is the financial market in which previously issued financial instruments such as stock, bonds, options, and futures are bought and sold. Another frequent usage of " _____ " is to refer to loans which are sold by a mortgage bank to investors such as Fannie Mae and Freddie Mac.

Exam Probability: **Medium**

47. *Answer choices:*

(see index for correct answer)

- a. Latino Community Foundation
- b. Derivatives market
- c. TradersStudio
- d. Secondary market

:: Business economics ::

In finance, _____ is the risk of losses caused by interest rate changes. The prices of most financial instruments, such as stocks and bonds move inversely with interest rates, so investors are subject to capital loss when rates rise.

Exam Probability: **High**

48. *Answer choices:*

(see index for correct answer)

- a. Tradespace
- b. Leontief production function
- c. Gross operating surplus
- d. Residual value

:: Generally Accepted Accounting Principles ::

_____ is the accounting classification of an account. It is part of double-entry book-keeping technique.

49. *Answer choices:*

(see index for correct answer)

- a. Profit
- b. Engagement letter
- c. Income statement
- d. Normal balance

Guidance: level 1

:: ::

_____ is the process of making predictions of the future based on past and present data and most commonly by analysis of trends. A commonplace example might be estimation of some variable of interest at some specified future date. Prediction is a similar, but more general term. Both might refer to formal statistical methods employing time series, cross-sectional or longitudinal data, or alternatively to less formal judgmental methods. Usage can differ between areas of application: for example, in hydrology the terms "forecast" and " _____ " are sometimes reserved for estimates of values at certain specific future times, while the term "prediction" is used for more general estimates, such as the number of times floods will occur over a long period.

Exam Probability: **High**

50. *Answer choices:*

(see index for correct answer)

- a. hierarchical
- b. empathy
- c. cultural
- d. Forecasting

Guidance: level 1

:: Financial risk ::

_____ is any of various types of risk associated with financing, including financial transactions that include company loans in risk of default. Often it is understood to include only downside risk, meaning the potential for financial loss and uncertainty about its extent.

Exam Probability: **High**

51. *Answer choices:*

(see index for correct answer)

- a. Immunization
- b. Foreign exchange hedge
- c. Financial risk
- d. Collar

Guidance: level 1

:: Business economics ::

A _____ is a term used primarily in cost accounting to describe something to which costs are assigned. Common examples of _____ s are: product lines, geographic territories, customers, departments or anything else for which management would like to quantify cost.

Exam Probability: **Medium**

52. *Answer choices:*

(see index for correct answer)

- a. European embedded value
- b. Vendor finance
- c. Rate risk
- d. Cost object

Guidance: level 1

:: Insolvency ::

_____ is the process in accounting by which a company is brought to an end in the United Kingdom, Republic of Ireland and United States. The assets and property of the company are redistributed. _____ is also sometimes referred to as winding-up or dissolution, although dissolution technically refers to the last stage of _____ . The process of _____ also arises when customs, an authority or agency in a country responsible for collecting and safeguarding customs duties, determines the final computation or ascertainment of the duties or drawback accruing on an entry.

Exam Probability: **Medium**

53. *Answer choices:*

(see index for correct answer)

- a. Liquidation
- b. Debt consolidation
- c. Conservatorship
- d. United Kingdom insolvency law

Guidance: level 1

:: ::

A _____ , in the word's original meaning, is a sheet of paper on which one performs work. They come in many forms, most commonly associated with children's school work assignments, tax forms, and accounting or other business environments. Software is increasingly taking over the paper-based _____ .

54. *Answer choices:*

(see index for correct answer)

- a. empathy
- b. Worksheet
- c. personal values
- d. surface-level diversity

Guidance: level 1

:: Accounting terminology ::

Accounts are typically defined by an identifier and a caption or header and are coded by account type. In computerized accounting systems with computable quantity accounting, the accounts can have a quantity measure definition.

Exam Probability: **Medium**

55. *Answer choices:*

(see index for correct answer)

- a. Accounts payable
- b. Accrued liabilities
- c. Chart of accounts
- d. General ledger

:: Financial ratios ::

The _____ is a liquidity ratio that measures whether a firm has enough resources to meet its short-term obligations. It compares a firm's current assets to its current liabilities, and is expressed as follows.

Exam Probability: **Low**

56. *Answer choices:*

(see index for correct answer)

- a. Debt service coverage ratio
- b. Information ratio
- c. Sales density
- d. Current ratio

:: ::

_____ is a marketing communication that employs an openly sponsored, non-personal message to promote or sell a product, service or idea. Sponsors of _____ are typically businesses wishing to promote their products or services. _____ is differentiated from public relations in that an advertiser pays for and has control over the message. It differs from personal selling in that the message is non-personal, i.e., not directed to a particular individual. _____ is communicated through various mass media, including traditional media such as newspapers, magazines, television, radio, outdoor _____ or direct mail; and new media such as search results, blogs, social media, websites or text messages. The actual presentation of the message in a medium is referred to as an advertisement, or "ad" or advert for short.

Exam Probability: **High**

57. *Answer choices:*

(see index for correct answer)

- a. co-culture
- b. Advertising
- c. surface-level diversity
- d. hierarchical

Guidance: level 1

:: Actuarial science ::

_____ is the addition of interest to the principal sum of a loan or deposit, or in other words, interest on interest. It is the result of reinvesting interest, rather than paying it out, so that interest in the next period is then earned on the principal sum plus previously accumulated interest. _____ is standard in finance and economics.

Exam Probability: **Low**

58. *Answer choices:*

(see index for correct answer)

- a. Compound interest
- b. Tail value at risk
- c. Coherent risk measure
- d. SWAG

Guidance: level 1

:: Marketing ::

_____ is a financial mechanism in which a debtor obtains the right to delay payments to a creditor, for a defined period of time, in exchange for a charge or fee. Essentially, the party that owes money in the present purchases the right to delay the payment until some future date. The discount, or charge, is the difference between the original amount owed in the present and the amount that has to be paid in the future to settle the debt.

Exam Probability: **Medium**

59. *Answer choices:*

(see index for correct answer)

- a. Global Center for Health Innovation
- b. Alpha consumer
- c. MARC USA
- d. Discounting

Guidance: level 1

Human resource management

Human resource (HR) management is the strategic approach to the effective management of organization workers so that they help the business gain a competitive advantage. It is designed to maximize employee performance in service of an employer's strategic objectives. HR is primarily concerned with the management of people within organizations, focusing on policies and on systems. HR departments are responsible for overseeing employee-benefits design, employee recruitment, training and development, performance appraisal, and rewarding (e.g., managing pay and benefit systems). HR also concerns itself with organizational change and industrial relations, that is, the balancing of organizational practices with requirements arising from collective bargaining and from governmental laws.

:: Labour relations ::

A _____ , also known as a post-entry closed shop, is a form of a union security clause. Under this, the employer agrees to either only hire labor union members or to require that any new employees who are not already union members become members within a certain amount of time. Use of the _____ varies widely from nation to nation, depending on the level of protection given trade unions in general.

Exam Probability: **High**

1. *Answer choices:*

(see index for correct answer)

- a. Jesse Simons
- b. Union shop
- c. Merit shop
- d. Minnesota Nurses Association

Guidance: level 1

:: ::

A trade union is an association of workers forming a legal unit or legal personhood, usually called a "bargaining unit", which acts as bargaining agent and legal representative for a unit of employees in all matters of law or right arising from or in the administration of a collective agreement. Labour unions typically fund the formal organisation, head office, and legal team functions of the labour union through regular fees or union dues. The delegate staff of the labour union representation in the workforce are made up of workplace volunteers who are appointed by members in democratic elections.

2. *Answer choices:*

(see index for correct answer)

- a. open system
- b. empathy
- c. hierarchical
- d. Labor union

Guidance: level 1

:: Labor ::

_____ refers to the process of grouping activities into departments.
Division of labour creates specialists who need coordination. This coordination
is facilitated by grouping specialists together in departments.

Exam Probability: **Medium**

3. *Answer choices:*

(see index for correct answer)

- a. Eurosclerosis
- b. Paper organization
- c. Economic activism
- d. Lump of labour fallacy

:: Human resource management ::

_____ , also known as organizational socialization, is management jargon first created in 1988 that refers to the mechanism through which new employees acquire the necessary knowledge, skills, and behaviors in order to become effective organizational members and insiders.

Exam Probability: **Low**

4. *Answer choices:*

(see index for correct answer)

- a. Autonomous work group
- b. Chartered Institute of Personnel and Development
- c. Onboarding
- d. CEO succession

:: Human resource management ::

_____ is an institutional process that maximizes performance levels and competency for an organization. The process includes all the activities needed to maintain a productive workforce, such as field service management, human resource management, performance and training management, data collection, recruiting, budgeting, forecasting, scheduling and analytics.

Exam Probability: **High**

5. *Answer choices:*

- a. Workforce management
- b. Co-determination
- c. Employeeship
- d. The war for talent

Guidance: level 1

:: Job interview ::

An _____ is a survey conducted with an individual who is separating from an organization or relationship. Most commonly, this occurs between an employee and an organization, a student and an educational institution, or a member and an association. An organization can use the information gained from an _____ to assess what should be improved, changed, or remain intact. More so, an organization can use the results from _____ s to reduce employee, student, or member turnover and increase productivity and engagement, thus reducing the high costs associated with turnover. Some examples of the value of conducting _____ s include shortening the recruiting and hiring process, reducing absenteeism, improving innovation, sustaining performance, and reducing possible litigation if issues mentioned in the _____ are addressed. It is important for each organization to customize its own _____ in order to maintain the highest levels of survey validity and reliability.

Exam Probability: **Medium**

6. *Answer choices:*

(see index for correct answer)

- a. Informational interview
- b. Microsoft interview
- c. Situation, Task, Action, Result
- d. Programming interview

Guidance: level 1

:: Problem solving ::

A _____ is a unit or formation established to work on a single defined task or activity. Originally introduced by the United States Navy, the term has now caught on for general usage and is a standard part of NATO terminology. Many non-military organizations now create " _____ s" or task groups for temporary activities that might have once been performed by ad hoc committees.

Exam Probability: **High**

7. *Answer choices:*

(see index for correct answer)

- a. Task force
- b. Nursing process
- c. How to Solve It
- d. Lateral computing

Guidance: level 1

:: Behavioral and social facets of systemic risk ::

_____ is the difficulty in understanding an issue and effectively making decisions when one has too much information about that issue. Generally, the term is associated with the excessive quantity of daily information.

_____ most likely originated from information theory, which are studies in the storage, preservation, communication, compression, and extraction of information. The term, _____ , was first used in Bertram Gross' 1964 book, The Managing of Organizations, and it was further popularized by Alvin Toffler in his bestselling 1970 book Future Shock. Speier et al. stated.

8. *Answer choices:*

(see index for correct answer)

- a. Media transparency
- b. Emotional contagion
- c. virtuous cycle
- d. Attentive user interface

Guidance: level 1

:: Employment of foreign-born ::

_____ refers to the international labor pool of workers, including those employed by multinational companies and connected through a global system of networking and production, immigrant workers, transient migrant workers, telecommuting workers, those in export-oriented employment, contingent work or other precarious employment. As of 2012, the global labor pool consisted of approximately 3 billion workers, around 200 million unemployed.

Exam Probability: **High**

9. *Answer choices:*

(see index for correct answer)

- a. Optional Practical Training
- b. Reverse brain drain

- c. H-2B visa
- d. Global workforce

:: Human resource management ::

_____ are the people who make up the workforce of an organization, business sector, or economy. "Human capital" is sometimes used synonymously with " _____ ", although human capital typically refers to a narrower effect . Likewise, other terms sometimes used include manpower, talent, labor, personnel, or simply people.

Exam Probability: **Medium**

10. *Answer choices:*

(see index for correct answer)

- a. E-HRM
- b. Flextime
- c. Behavioral Competencies
- d. Human resources

:: Majority–minority relations ::

_____ , also known as reservation in India and Nepal, positive discrimination / action in the United Kingdom, and employment equity in Canada and South Africa, is the policy of promoting the education and employment of members of groups that are known to have previously suffered from discrimination. Historically and internationally, support for _____ has sought to achieve goals such as bridging inequalities in employment and pay, increasing access to education, promoting diversity, and redressing apparent past wrongs, harms, or hindrances.

Exam Probability: **High**

11. *Answer choices:*

(see index for correct answer)

- a. Affirmative action
- b. cultural dissonance
- c. positive discrimination

Guidance: level 1

:: Management ::

_____ is a set of activities that ensure goals are met in an effective and efficient manner. _____ can focus on the performance of an organization, a department, an employee, or the processes in place to manage particular tasks. _____ standards are generally organized and disseminated by senior leadership at an organization, and by task owners.

12. *Answer choices:*

(see index for correct answer)

- a. Perth leadership outcome model
- b. Event management
- c. Performance management
- d. Management buyout

Guidance: level 1

:: Human resource management ::

A _____ is a group of people with different functional expertise working toward a common goal. It may include people from finance, marketing, operations, and human resources departments. Typically, it includes employees from all levels of an organization. Members may also come from outside an organization .

Exam Probability: **High**

13. *Answer choices:*

(see index for correct answer)

- a. Reward management
- b. Cross-functional team

- c. Job analysis
- d. Functional job analysis

Guidance: level 1

:: Psychometrics ::

In statistics and research, _____ is typically a measure based on the correlations between different items on the same test . It measures whether several items that propose to measure the same general construct produce similar scores. For example, if a respondent expressed agreement with the statements "I like to ride bicycles" and "I've enjoyed riding bicycles in the past", and disagreement with the statement "I hate bicycles", this would be indicative of good _____ of the test.

Exam Probability: **High**

14. *Answer choices:*

(see index for correct answer)

- a. Survey methodology
- b. Bipolar spectrum diagnostic scale
- c. Adaptive comparative judgement
- d. Test

Guidance: level 1

:: Fundamental analysis ::

_____ , also known as letter stock or restricted securities, is stock of a company that is not fully transferable until certain conditions have been met. Upon satisfaction of those conditions, the stock is no longer restricted, and becomes transferable to the person holding the award. _____ is often used as a form of employee compensation, in which case it typically becomes transferrable upon the satisfaction of certain conditions, such as continued employment for a period of time or the achievement of particular product-development milestones, earnings per share goals or other financial targets. _____ is a popular alternative to stock options, particularly for executives, due to favorable accounting rules and income tax treatment.

Exam Probability: **Medium**

15. *Answer choices:*

(see index for correct answer)

- a. Growth stock
- b. Economic Value Added
- c. Earnings per share
- d. Restricted stock

Guidance: level 1

:: Business ethics ::

A _____ is a person who exposes any kind of information or activity that is deemed illegal, unethical, or not correct within an organization that is either private or public. The information of alleged wrongdoing can be classified in many ways: violation of company policy/rules, law, regulation, or threat to public interest/national security, as well as fraud, and corruption. Those who become _____ s can choose to bring information or allegations to surface either internally or externally. Internally, a _____ can bring his/her accusations to the attention of other people within the accused organization such as an immediate supervisor. Externally, a _____ can bring allegations to light by contacting a third party outside of an accused organization such as the media, government, law enforcement, or those who are concerned. _____ s, however, take the risk of facing stiff reprisal and retaliation from those who are accused or alleged of wrongdoing.

Exam Probability: **Medium**

16. *Answer choices:*

(see index for correct answer)

- a. Workplace bullying
- b. Evolution of corporate social responsibility in India
- c. Integrity management
- d. Corporate social entrepreneurship

Guidance: level 1

:: ::

In business strategy, _____ is establishing a competitive advantage by having the lowest cost of operation in the industry. _____ is often driven by company efficiency, size, scale, scope and cumulative experience .A _____ strategy aims to exploit scale of production, well-defined scope and other economies , producing highly standardized products, using advanced technology.In recent years, more and more companies have chosen a strategic mix to achieve market leadership. These patterns consist of simultaneous _____ , superior customer service and product leadership. Walmart has succeeded across the world due to its _____ strategy. The company has cut down on exesses at every point of production and thus are able to provide the consumers with quality products at low prices.

Exam Probability: **Low**

17. *Answer choices:*

(see index for correct answer)

- a. interpersonal communication
- b. personal values
- c. Cost leadership
- d. functional perspective

Guidance: level 1

:: Evaluation methods ::

In social psychology, _____ is the process of looking at oneself in order to assess aspects that are important to one's identity. It is one of the motives that drive self-evaluation, along with self-verification and self-enhancement. Sedikides suggests that the _____ motive will prompt people to seek information to confirm their uncertain self-concept rather than their certain self-concept and at the same time people use _____ to enhance their certainty of their own self-knowledge. However, the _____ motive could be seen as quite different from the other two self-evaluation motives. Unlike the other two motives through _____ people are interested in the accuracy of their current self view, rather than improving their self-view. This makes _____ the only self-evaluative motive that may cause a person's self-esteem to be damaged.

Exam Probability: **Medium**

18. *Answer choices:*

(see index for correct answer)

- a. Gender evaluation methodology
- b. Moral statistics
- c. Position weight matrix
- d. Event correlation

Guidance: level 1

:: Sociological terminology ::

In moral and political philosophy, the _____ is a theory or model that originated during the Age of Enlightenment and usually concerns the legitimacy of the authority of the state over the individual. _____ arguments typically posit that individuals have consented, either explicitly or tacitly, to surrender some of their freedoms and submit to the authority in exchange for protection of their remaining rights or maintenance of the social order. The relation between natural and legal rights is often a topic of _____ theory. The term takes its name from The _____ , a 1762 book by Jean-Jacques Rousseau that discussed this concept. Although the antecedents of _____ theory are found in antiquity, in Greek and Stoic philosophy and Roman and Canon Law, the heyday of the _____ was the mid-17th to early 19th centuries, when it emerged as the leading doctrine of political legitimacy.

Exam Probability: **High**

19. *Answer choices:*

(see index for correct answer)

- a. iron cage
- b. Enculturation
- c. Social contract
- d. Symbolic capital

Guidance: level 1

:: Trade union legislation ::

The _____ is the name for several legislative bills on US labor law which have been proposed and sometimes introduced into one or both chambers of the U.S. Congress.

Exam Probability: **Medium**

20. *Answer choices:*

(see index for correct answer)

- a. Trade Union and Labour Relations Act 1974
- b. Labor Management Relations Act of 1947
- c. National Labor Relations Act
- d. Trade Union Act 1984

Guidance: level 1

:: Recruitment ::

_____ is a specialized recruitment service which organizations pay to seek out and recruit highly qualified candidates for senior-level and executive jobs . Headhunters may also seek out and recruit other highly specialized and/or skilled positions in organizations for which there is strong competition in the job market for the top talent, such as senior data analysts or computer programmers. The method usually involves commissioning a third-party organization, typically an _____ firm, but possibly a standalone consultant or consulting firm, to research the availability of suitable qualified candidates working for competitors or related businesses or organizations. Having identified a shortlist of qualified candidates who match the client's requirements, the _____ firm may act as an intermediary to contact the individual and see if they might be interested in moving to a new employer. The _____ firm may also carry out initial screening of the candidate, negotiations on remuneration and benefits, and preparing the employment contract. In some markets there has been a move towards using _____ for lower positions driven by the fact that there are less candidates for some positions even on lower levels than executive.

Exam Probability: **High**

21. *Answer choices:*

(see index for correct answer)

- a. Acqui-hiring
- b. S.I.R. Method of Recruiting
- c. Candidate submittal
- d. Executive search

Guidance: level 1

:: ::

Domestic violence is violence or other abuse by one person against another in a domestic setting, such as in marriage or cohabitation. It may be termed intimate partner violence when committed by a spouse or partner in an intimate relationship against the other spouse or partner, and can take place in heterosexual or same-sex relationships, or between former spouses or partners. Domestic violence can also involve violence against children, parents, or the elderly. It takes a number of forms, including physical, verbal, emotional, economic, religious, reproductive, and sexual abuse, which can range from subtle, coercive forms to marital rape and to violent physical abuse such as choking, beating, female genital mutilation, and acid throwing that results in disfigurement or death. Domestic murders include stoning, bride burning, honor killings, and dowry deaths.

Exam Probability: **High**

22. *Answer choices:*

(see index for correct answer)

- a. Family violence
- b. co-culture
- c. open system
- d. personal values

Guidance: level 1

:: Asset ::

In financial accounting, an _____ is any resource owned by the business. Anything tangible or intangible that can be owned or controlled to produce value and that is held by a company to produce positive economic value is an _____ . Simply stated, _____ s represent value of ownership that can be converted into cash . The balance sheet of a firm records the monetary value of the _____ s owned by that firm. It covers money and other valuables belonging to an individual or to a business.

Exam Probability: **Low**

23. *Answer choices:*

(see index for correct answer)

- a. Current asset
- b. Asset

Guidance: level 1

:: Power (social and political) ::

In a notable study of power conducted by social psychologists John R. P. French and Bertram Raven in 1959, power is divided into five separate and distinct forms. In 1965 Raven revised this model to include a sixth form by separating the informational power base as distinct from the _____ base.

Exam Probability: **High**

24. *Answer choices:*

(see index for correct answer)

- a. Expert power
- b. Referent power
- c. Hard power

Guidance: level 1

:: ::

_____ is a belief that hard work and diligence have a moral benefit and an inherent ability, virtue or value to strengthen character and individual abilities. It is a set of values centered on importance of work and manifested by determination or desire to work hard. Social ingrainment of this value is considered to enhance character through hard work that is respective to an individual's field of work.

Exam Probability: **Low**

25. *Answer choices:*

(see index for correct answer)

- a. functional perspective
- b. personal values
- c. co-culture
- d. process perspective

Guidance: level 1

:: Cognitive biases ::

The _____ is a type of immediate judgement discrepancy, or cognitive bias, where a person making an initial assessment of another person, place, or thing will assume ambiguous information based upon concrete information. A simplified example of the _____ is when an individual noticing that the person in the photograph is attractive, well groomed, and properly attired, assumes, using a mental heuristic, that the person in the photograph is a good person based upon the rules of that individual's social concept. This constant error in judgment is reflective of the individual's preferences, prejudices, ideology, aspirations, and social perception. The _____ is an evaluation by an individual and can affect the perception of a decision, action, idea, business, person, group, entity, or other whenever concrete data is generalized or influences ambiguous information.

Exam Probability: **Low**

26. *Answer choices:*

(see index for correct answer)

- a. Halo effect
- b. Duration neglect
- c. Psychological projection
- d. Anchoring

Guidance: level 1

:: Options (finance) ::

_____ is a contractual agreement between a corporation and recipients of phantom shares that bestow upon the grantee the right to a cash payment at a designated time or in association with a designated event in the future, which payment is to be in an amount tied to the market value of an equivalent number of shares of the corporation's stock. Thus, the amount of the payout will increase as the stock price rises, and decrease if the stock falls, but without the recipient actually receiving any stock. Like other forms of stock-based compensation plans, _____ broadly serves to align the interests of recipients and shareholders, incent contribution to share value, and encourage the retention or continued participation of contributors. Recipients are typically employees, but may also be directors, third-party vendors, or others.

Exam Probability: **High**

27. *Answer choices:*

(see index for correct answer)

- a. Margrabe's formula
- b. Phantom stock
- c. Naked call
- d. Real options valuation

Guidance: level 1

:: Meetings ::

A _____ is a body of one or more persons that is subordinate to a deliberative assembly. Usually, the assembly sends matters into a _____ as a way to explore them more fully than would be possible if the assembly itself were considering them. _____ s may have different functions and their type of work differ depending on the type of the organization and its needs.

Exam Probability: **Medium**

28. *Answer choices:*

(see index for correct answer)

- a. Program book
- b. Minutes
- c. Speed geeking
- d. Committee

Guidance: level 1

:: United States federal labor legislation ::

The _____ of 1967 is a US labor law that forbids employment discrimination against anyone at least 40 years of age in the United States . In 1967, the bill was signed into law by President Lyndon B. Johnson. The ADEA prevents age discrimination and provides equal employment opportunity under conditions that were not explicitly covered in Title VII of the Civil Rights Act of 1964. It also applies to the standards for pensions and benefits provided by employers, and requires that information concerning the needs of older workers be provided to the general public.

29. *Answer choices:*

(see index for correct answer)

- a. Adamson Act
- b. Water Resources Development Act of 2007
- c. Contract Work Hours and Safety Standards Act
- d. Age Discrimination in Employment Act

Guidance: level 1

:: Trade union legislation ::

The _____ of 1935 is a foundational statute of United States labor law which guarantees the right of private sector employees to organize into trade unions, engage in collective bargaining, and take collective action such as strikes. The act was written by Senator Robert F. Wagner, passed by the 74th United States Congress, and signed into law by President Franklin D. Roosevelt.

Exam Probability: **High**

30. *Answer choices:*

(see index for correct answer)

- a. Employment Act 1980
- b. Trade Union Act 1984

- c. National Labor Relations Act
- d. Padlock Law

Guidance: level 1

:: Human resource management ::

_____ is a flexible hours schedule that allows workers to alter workday start and finish times. In contrast to traditional work arrangements that require employees to work a standard 9 a.m. to 5 p.m. day, _____ typically involves a "core" period of the day during which employees are required to be at work , and a "bandwidth" period within which all required hours must be worked . The working day outside of the "core" period is "flexible time", in which employees can choose when they work, subject to achieving total daily, weekly or monthly hours within the "bandwidth" period set by employers, and subject to the necessary work being done. The total working time required of employees on _____ schedules is the same as that required under traditional work schedules. A _____ policy allows staff to determine when they will work, while a flexplace policy allows staff to determine where they will work. Advantages include allowing employees to coordinate their work hours with public transport schedules, with the schedules of their children, and with daily traffic patterns to avoid high congestion times such as rush hour. Some claim that flexible working will change the nature of the way we work. The idea of _____ was invented by Christel Kammerer.

Exam Probability: **Low**

31. *Answer choices:*

(see index for correct answer)

- a. Senior management
- b. Flextime
- c. Employee silence
- d. Management by observation

Guidance: level 1

:: ::

A _____ is a fund into which a sum of money is added during an employee's employment years, and from which payments are drawn to support the person's retirement from work in the form of periodic payments. A _____ may be a "defined benefit plan" where a fixed sum is paid regularly to a person, or a "defined contribution plan" under which a fixed sum is invested and then becomes available at retirement age. _____ s should not be confused with severance pay; the former is usually paid in regular installments for life after retirement, while the latter is typically paid as a fixed amount after involuntary termination of employment prior to retirement.

Exam Probability: **High**

32. *Answer choices:*
(see index for correct answer)

- a. interpersonal communication
- b. empathy
- c. Pension
- d. functional perspective

:: Occupational safety and health ::

A safety data sheet , _____ , or product safety data sheet is a document that lists information relating to occupational safety and health for the use of various substances and products. SDSs are a widely used system for cataloging information on chemicals, chemical compounds, and chemical mixtures. SDS information may include instructions for the safe use and potential hazards associated with a particular material or product, along with spill-handling procedures. SDS formats can vary from source to source within a country depending on national requirements.

Exam Probability: **Medium**

33. *Answer choices:*

(see index for correct answer)

- a. Material safety data sheet
- b. Robert A. Kehoe
- c. Burn pit
- d. Wildfire

:: Trade unions ::

An _____ is a form of union security agreement where the employer may hire union or non-union workers, and employees need not join the union in order to remain employed. However, the non-union worker must pay a fee to cover collective bargaining costs. The fee paid by non-union members under the _____ is known as the "agency fee".

Exam Probability: **Low**

34. *Answer choices:*

(see index for correct answer)

- a. Union wage premium
- b. Trade union
- c. Anti-union violence
- d. Agency shop

Guidance: level 1

:: Business ethics ::

_____ is a type of harassment technique that relates to a sexual nature and the unwelcome or inappropriate promise of rewards in exchange for sexual favors. _____ includes a range of actions from mild transgressions to sexual abuse or assault. Harassment can occur in many different social settings such as the workplace, the home, school, churches, etc. Harassers or victims may be of any gender.

Exam Probability: **High**

35. *Answer choices:*

(see index for correct answer)

- a. Third-party technique
- b. Corporate social responsibility
- c. Impact investing
- d. Sexual harassment

Guidance: level 1

:: Employment compensation ::

An _____ is an employee benefit program that assists employees with personal problems and/or work-related problems that may impact their job performance, health, mental and emotional well-being. EAPs generally offer free and confidential assessments, short-term counseling, referrals, and follow-up services for employees and their household members. EAP counselors also work in a consultative role with managers and supervisors to address employee and organizational challenges and needs. Many corporations, academic institution and/or government agencies are active in helping organizations prevent and cope with workplace violence, trauma, and other emergency response situations. There is a variety of support programs offered for employees. Even though EAPs are mainly aimed at work-related problems, there are a variety of programs that can assist with problems outside of the workplace. EAPs have grown over the years, and are more desirable economically and socially.

Exam Probability: **Low**

36. *Answer choices:*

(see index for correct answer)

- a. Workers Compensation Act 1987
- b. Health Reimbursement Account
- c. Sliding wage scale
- d. Employee assistance program

Guidance: level 1

:: ::

_____ is the administration of an organization, whether it is a business, a not-for-profit organization, or government body. _____ includes the activities of setting the strategy of an organization and coordinating the efforts of its employees to accomplish its objectives through the application of available resources, such as financial, natural, technological, and human resources. The term " _____ " may also refer to those people who manage an organization.

Exam Probability: **High**

37. *Answer choices:*

(see index for correct answer)

- a. Management
- b. corporate values
- c. Sarbanes-Oxley act of 2002
- d. open system

Guidance: level 1

:: Psychometrics ::

Electronic assessment, also known as e-assessment, _____ , computer assisted/mediated assessment and computer-based assessment, is the use of information technology in various forms of assessment such as educational assessment, health assessment, psychiatric assessment, and psychological assessment. This may utilize an online computer connected to a network. This definition embraces a wide range of student activity ranging from the use of a word processor to on-screen testing. Specific types of e-assessment include multiple choice, online/electronic submission, computerized adaptive testing and computerized classification testing.

Exam Probability: **Low**

38. *Answer choices:*

(see index for correct answer)

- a. Guttman scale
- b. Online assessment
- c. Person-fit analysis
- d. Survey methodology

Guidance: level 1

:: Recruitment ::

_____ is a tool companies and organizations use as a way to communicate the good and the bad characteristics of the job during the hiring process of new employees, or as a tool to reestablish job specificity for existing employees. _____ s should provide the individuals with a well-rounded description that details what obligations the individual can expect to perform while working for that specific company. Descriptions may include, but are not limited to, work environment, expectations, and Company policies .

Exam Probability: **Low**

39. *Answer choices:*

(see index for correct answer)

- a. Riviera Partners
- b. Vacancy led recruitment
- c. Curriculum vitae
- d. Realistic job preview

Guidance: level 1

:: Trade unions ::

A _____ , in North America, or union branch , in the United Kingdom and other countries, is a local branch of a usually national trade union. The terms used for sub-branches of _____ s vary from country to country and include "shop committee", "shop floor committee", "board of control", "chapel", and others.

40. *Answer choices:*

(see index for correct answer)

- a. Union democracy
- b. Local union
- c. Global Labour University
- d. Company union

Guidance: level 1

:: ::

An _____ is a process where candidates are examined to determine their suitability for specific types of employment, especially management or military command. The candidates' personality and aptitudes are determined by techniques including interviews, group exercises, presentations, examinations and psychometric testing.

Exam Probability: **Low**

41. *Answer choices:*

(see index for correct answer)

- a. cultural
- b. deep-level diversity

- c. information systems assessment
- d. Assessment center

Guidance: level 1

:: Unemployment ::

_____ is the support service provided by responsible organizations, keen to support individuals who are exiting the business – to help former employees transition to new jobs and help them re-orient themselves in the job market. A consultancy firm usually provides the _____ services which are paid for by the former employer and are achieved usually through practical advice, training materials and workshops. Some companies may offer psychological support.

Exam Probability: **High**

42. *Answer choices:*

(see index for correct answer)

- a. Outplacement
- b. Labour Force Survey
- c. Short time
- d. Youth unemployment

Guidance: level 1

:: Human resource management ::

_____ refers to the anticipation of required human capital for an organization and the planning to meet those needs. The field increased in popularity after McKinsey's 1997 research and the 2001 book on The War for Talent. _____ in this context does not refer to the management of entertainers.

Exam Probability: **Medium**

43. *Answer choices:*
(see index for correct answer)

- a. Senior management
- b. Mechanical aptitude
- c. Talent management
- d. Cross-cultural capital

Guidance: level 1

:: ::

_____ consists of using generic or ad hoc methods in an orderly manner to find solutions to problems. Some of the problem-solving techniques developed and used in philosophy, artificial intelligence, computer science, engineering, mathematics, or medicine are related to mental problem-solving techniques studied in psychology.

44. *Answer choices:*

(see index for correct answer)

- a. Character
- b. Problem solving
- c. corporate values
- d. information systems assessment

Guidance: level 1

:: Employment compensation ::

A _____ is the minimum income necessary for a worker to meet their basic needs. Needs are defined to include food, housing, and other essential needs such as clothing. The goal of a _____ is to allow a worker to afford a basic but decent standard of living. Due to the flexible nature of the term "needs", there is not one universally accepted measure of what a _____ is and as such it varies by location and household type.

Exam Probability: **High**

45. *Answer choices:*

(see index for correct answer)

- a. Sick leave
- b. Interactive accommodation process

- c. Family meal
- d. Living wage

Guidance: level 1

:: Employment compensation ::

_____ is time off from work that workers can use to stay home to address their health and safety needs without losing pay. Paid _____ is a statutory requirement in many nations. Most European, many Latin American, a few African and a few Asian countries have legal requirements for paid _____ .

Exam Probability: **Medium**

46. *Answer choices:*

(see index for correct answer)

- a. Annual leave
- b. Flexible spending account
- c. Employee assistance program
- d. Sick leave

Guidance: level 1

:: Multiple choice ::

The _____ is a standardized psychometric test of adult personality and psychopathology. Psychologists and other mental health professionals use various versions of the MMPI to help develop treatment plans; assist with differential diagnosis; help answer legal questions ; screen job candidates during the personnel selection process; or as part of a therapeutic assessment procedure.

Exam Probability: **Low**

47. *Answer choices:*

(see index for correct answer)

- a. Minnesota Multiphasic Personality Inventory
- b. Eysenck Personality Questionnaire
- c. Eddy Test
- d. Multiple choice

Guidance: level 1

:: ::

_____ is a form of development in which a person called a coach supports a learner or client in achieving a specific personal or professional goal by providing training and guidance. The learner is sometimes called a coachee. Occasionally, _____ may mean an informal relationship between two people, of whom one has more experience and expertise than the other and offers advice and guidance as the latter learns; but _____ differs from mentoring in focusing on specific tasks or objectives, as opposed to more general goals or overall development.

48. *Answer choices:*

(see index for correct answer)

- a. surface-level diversity
- b. Coaching
- c. process perspective
- d. corporate values

Guidance: level 1

:: Self ::

_____ is a term that has been used in various psychology theories, often in different ways. The term was originally introduced by the organismic theorist Kurt Goldstein for the motive to realize one`s full potential. In Goldstein`s view, it is the organism`s master motive, the only real motive: "the tendency to actualize itself as fully as possible is the basic drive ... the drive of _____ ." Carl Rogers similarly wrote of "the curative force in psychotherapy  man`s tendency to actualize himself, to become his potentialities ... to express and activate all the capacities of the organism." The concept was brought most fully to prominence in Abraham Maslow`s hierarchy of needs theory as the final level of psychological development that can be achieved when all basic and mental needs are essentially fulfilled and the "actualization" of the full personal potential takes place, although he adapted this viewpoint later on in life to be more flexible.

49. *Answer choices:*

- a. Self-presentation
- b. Self-actualization
- c. impression management
- d. a person

Guidance: level 1

:: Workplace ::

_____ is asystematic determination of a subject's merit, worth and significance, using criteria governed by a set of standards. It can assist an organization, program, design, project or any other intervention or initiative to assess any aim, realisable concept/proposal, or any alternative, to help in decision-making; or to ascertain the degree of achievement or value in regard to the aim and objectives and results of any such action that has been completed. The primary purpose of _____, in addition to gaining insight into prior or existing initiatives, is to enable reflection and assist in the identification of future change.

Exam Probability: **High**

50. *Answer choices:*

- a. Control freak
- b. Workplace phobia

- c. 360-degree feedback
- d. Work motivation

Guidance: level 1

:: Recruitment ::

Recruitment refers to the overall process of attracting, shortlisting, selecting and appointing suitable candidates for jobs within an organization. Recruitment can also refer to processes involved in choosing individuals for unpaid roles. Managers, human resource generalists and recruitment specialists may be tasked with carrying out recruitment, but in some cases public-sector employment agencies, commercial recruitment agencies, or specialist search consultancies are used to undertake parts of the process. Internet-based technologies which support all aspects of recruitment have become widespread.

Exam Probability: **Medium**

51. *Answer choices:*

(see index for correct answer)

- a. Employee referral
- b. Silicon Milkroundabout
- c. Employment discrimination against persons with criminal records in the United States
- d. Telephone interview

Guidance: level 1

:: Trade unions in the United States ::

_____ is a labor union in the United States and Canada with roughly 300,000 active members. The union's members work predominantly in the hotel, food service, laundry, warehouse, and casino gaming industries. The union was formed in 2004 by the merger of Union of Needletrades, Industrial, and Textile Employees and Hotel Employees and Restaurant Employees Union .

Exam Probability: **Medium**

52. *Answer choices:*

(see index for correct answer)

- a. Patent Office Professional Association
- b. California Faculty Association
- c. Pennsylvania Association of Staff Nurses and Allied Professionals
- d. Coalition of Labor Union Women

Guidance: level 1

:: Ethically disputed business practices ::

An _____ in US labor law refers to certain actions taken by employers or unions that violate the National Labor Relations Act of 1935 29 U.S.C. § 151–169 and other legislation. Such acts are investigated by the National Labor Relations Board .

53. *Answer choices:*

(see index for correct answer)

- a. Insider trading
- b. Cream skimming
- c. Boiler room
- d. Market saturation

Guidance: level 1

:: Human resource management ::

_____ are transactions in which the ownership of companies, other business organizations, or their operating units are transferred or consolidated with other entities. As an aspect of strategic management, M&A can allow enterprises to grow or downsize, and change the nature of their business or competitive position.

Exam Probability: **Medium**

54. *Answer choices:*

(see index for correct answer)

- a. human resource
- b. Virtual management

- c. Mergers and acquisitions
- d. Labour is not a commodity

Guidance: level 1

:: Employment ::

_____ s are experiential learning opportunities, similar to internships but generally shorter, provided by partnerships between educational institutions and employers to give students short practical experiences in their field of study. In medicine it may refer to a visiting physician who is not part of the regular staff. In law, it usually refers to rigorous legal work opportunities undertaken by law students for law school credit and pay, similar to that of a junior attorney. It is derived from Latin externus and from English -ship.

Exam Probability: **Medium**

55. *Answer choices:*

(see index for correct answer)

- a. Liaison officer
- b. Payroll tax
- c. EuroMayDay
- d. delayering

Guidance: level 1

:: Training ::

A _____ is commonly known as an individual taking part in a _____ program or a graduate program within a company after having graduated from university or college.

Exam Probability: **Medium**

56. *Answer choices:*
(see index for correct answer)

- a. Screencast
- b. International Society for Performance Improvement
- c. ActivePresenter
- d. Trainee

Guidance: level 1

:: Organizational behavior ::

In organizational behavior and industrial and organizational psychology, _____ is an individual's psychological attachment to the organization. The basis behind many of these studies was to find ways to improve how workers feel about their jobs so that these workers would become more committed to their organizations. _____ predicts work variables such as turnover, organizational citizenship behavior, and job performance. Some of the factors such as role stress, empowerment, job insecurity and employability, and distribution of leadership have been shown to be connected to a worker's sense of _____ .

Exam Probability: **High**

57. *Answer choices:*
(see index for correct answer)

- a. Self-policing
- b. Civic virtue
- c. Counterproductive norms
- d. Organizational commitment

Guidance: level 1

:: Business ethics ::

_____ is a pejorative term for a workplace that has very poor, socially unacceptable working conditions. The work may be difficult, dangerous, climatically challenged or underpaid. Workers in _____ s may work long hours with low pay, regardless of laws mandating overtime pay or a minimum wage; child labor laws may also be violated. The Fair Labor Association's "2006 Annual Public Report" inspected factories for FLA compliance in 18 countries including Bangladesh, El Salvador, Colombia, Guatemala, Malaysia, Thailand, Tunisia, Turkey, China, India, Vietnam, Honduras, Indonesia, Brazil, Mexico, and the US. The U.S. Department of Labor's "2015 Findings on the Worst Forms of Child Labor" found that "18 countries did not meet the International Labour Organization's recommendation for an adequate number of inspectors."

Exam Probability: **Medium**

58. *Answer choices:*

(see index for correct answer)

- a. Destructionism
- b. Sweatshop
- c. Equator Principles
- d. Videntifier

Guidance: level 1

:: Socialism ::

In sociology, _____ is the process of internalizing the norms and ideologies of society. _____ encompasses both learning and teaching and is thus "the means by which social and cultural continuity are attained".

59. *Answer choices:*

(see index for correct answer)

- a. Anti-Stalinist left
- b. Socialization
- c. Proletarian internationalism
- d. Socialist realism

Guidance: level 1

Information systems

Information systems (IS) are formal, sociotechnical, organizational systems designed to collect, process, store, and distribute information. In a sociotechnical perspective Information Systems are composed by four components: technology, process, people and organizational structure.

:: Information systems ::

In artificial intelligence, an _____ is a computer system that emulates the decision-making ability of a human expert. _____ s are designed to solve complex problems by reasoning through bodies of knowledge, represented mainly as if–then rules rather than through conventional procedural code. The first _____ s were created in the 1970s and then proliferated in the 1980s. _____ s were among the first truly successful forms of artificial intelligence software. However, some experts point out that _____ s were not part of true artificial intelligence since they lack the ability to learn autonomously from external data. An _____ is divided into two subsystems: the inference engine and the knowledge base. The knowledge base represents facts and rules. The inference engine applies the rules to the known facts to deduce new facts. Inference engines can also include explanation and debugging abilities.

Exam Probability: **Medium**

1. *Answer choices:*

(see index for correct answer)

- a. Automated information system
- b. Shadow IT
- c. Policy appliances
- d. Expert system

Guidance: level 1

:: Domain name system ::

The _____ is a hierarchical and decentralized naming system for computers, services, or other resources connected to the Internet or a private network. It associates various information with domain names assigned to each of the participating entities. Most prominently, it translates more readily memorized domain names to the numerical IP addresses needed for locating and identifying computer services and devices with the underlying network protocols. By providing a worldwide, distributed directory service, the _____ has been an essential component of the functionality of the Internet since 1985.

Exam Probability: **Medium**

2. *Answer choices:*

(see index for correct answer)

- a. Dot Aero Council
- b. Domain registration
- c. Stop Online Piracy Act
- d. Gauss Research Laboratory

Guidance: level 1

:: Online companies ::

_____ is a business directory service and crowd-sourced review forum, and a public company of the same name that is headquartered in San Francisco, California. The company develops, hosts and markets the _____ .com website and the _____ mobile app, which publish crowd-sourced reviews about businesses. It also operates an online reservation service called _____ Reservations.

Exam Probability: **Medium**

3. *Answer choices:*

- a. Yelp
- b. ClickBank
- c. Adzuna
- d. PrivatePhone

Guidance: level 1

:: Advertising techniques ::

The _____ is a story from the Trojan War about the subterfuge that the Greeks used to enter the independent city of Troy and win the war. In the canonical version, after a fruitless 10-year siege, the Greeks constructed a huge wooden horse, and hid a select force of men inside including Odysseus. The Greeks pretended to sail away, and the Trojans pulled the horse into their city as a victory trophy. That night the Greek force crept out of the horse and opened the gates for the rest of the Greek army, which had sailed back under cover of night. The Greeks entered and destroyed the city of Troy, ending the war.

Exam Probability: **High**

4. *Answer choices:*

(see index for correct answer)

- a. Media clip
- b. Trojan horse
- c. Retail Radio
- d. Display window

Guidance: level 1

:: Data analysis ::

_____ , also referred to as text data mining, roughly equivalent to text analytics, is the process of deriving high-quality information from text. High-quality information is typically derived through the devising of patterns and trends through means such as statistical pattern learning. _____ usually involves the process of structuring the input text , deriving patterns within the structured data, and finally evaluation and interpretation of the output. `High quality` in _____ usually refers to some combination of relevance, novelty, and interest. Typical _____ tasks include text categorization, text clustering, concept/entity extraction, production of granular taxonomies, sentiment analysis, document summarization, and entity relation modeling .

Exam Probability: **Low**

5. *Answer choices:*

(see index for correct answer)

- a. Boolean analysis
- b. Grand mean
- c. Multiway data analysis
- d. Exponential smoothing

Guidance: level 1

:: ::

A web _____ or Internet _____ is a software system that is designed to carry out web search , which means to search the World Wide Web in a systematic way for particular information specified in a web search query. The search results are generally presented in a line of results, often referred to as _____ results pages . The information may be a mix of web pages, images, videos, infographics, articles, research papers and other types of files. Some _____ s also mine data available in databases or open directories. Unlike web directories, which are maintained only by human editors, _____ s also maintain real-time information by running an algorithm on a web crawler.Internet content that is not capable of being searched by a web _____ is generally described as the deep web.

Exam Probability: **Low**

6. *Answer choices:*

(see index for correct answer)

- a. similarity-attraction theory
- b. Character
- c. imperative
- d. information systems assessment

Guidance: level 1

:: Enterprise modelling ::

_____ are large-scale application software packages that support business processes, information flows, reporting, and data analytics in complex organizations. While ES are generally packaged enterprise application software systems they can also be bespoke, custom developed systems created to support a specific organization's needs.

Exam Probability: **Low**

7. *Answer choices:*

(see index for correct answer)

- a. Enterprise modelling
- b. Behavior Trees
- c. Enterprise systems
- d. Object-oriented business engineering

Guidance: level 1

:: Fraud ::

In law, _____ is intentional deception to secure unfair or unlawful gain, or to deprive a victim of a legal right. _____ can violate civil law , a criminal law , or it may cause no loss of money, property or legal right but still be an element of another civil or criminal wrong. The purpose of _____ may be monetary gain or other benefits, for example by obtaining a passport, travel document, or driver's license, or mortgage _____ . where the perpetrator may attempt to qualify for a mortgage by way of false statements.

8. *Answer choices:*

(see index for correct answer)

- a. Missing trader fraud
- b. SHERIFF
- c. Fraud
- d. Hijacked journal

Guidance: level 1

:: Information technology management ::

B2B is often contrasted with business-to-consumer . In B2B commerce, it is often the case that the parties to the relationship have comparable negotiating power, and even when they do not, each party typically involves professional staff and legal counsel in the negotiation of terms, whereas B2C is shaped to a far greater degree by economic implications of information asymmetry. However, within a B2B context, large companies may have many commercial, resource and information advantages over smaller businesses. The United Kingdom government, for example, created the post of Small Business Commissioner under the Enterprise Act 2016 to "enable small businesses to resolve disputes" and "consider complaints by small business suppliers about payment issues with larger businesses that they supply."

Exam Probability: **Medium**

9. *Answer choices:*

(see index for correct answer)

- a. Document management system
- b. Business-to-business
- c. IT Project Coordinator
- d. Drill down

Guidance: level 1

:: Information systems ::

A _____ manages the creation and modification of digital content. It typically supports multiple users in a collaborative environment.

Exam Probability: **High**

10. *Answer choices:*
(see index for correct answer)

- a. SAP Information Interchange OnDemand
- b. Content management system
- c. Expert systems for mortgages
- d. Information engineering

Guidance: level 1

:: Confidence tricks ::

_____ is the fraudulent attempt to obtain sensitive information such as usernames, passwords and credit card details by disguising oneself as a trustworthy entity in an electronic communication. Typically carried out by email spoofing or instant messaging, it often directs users to enter personal information at a fake website which matches the look and feel of the legitimate site.

Exam Probability: **Medium**

11. *Answer choices:*

(see index for correct answer)

- a. Phishing
- b. Children of Lieutenant Schmidt
- c. Pigeon drop
- d. First International Bank of Grenada

Guidance: level 1

:: Data management ::

In computing, a _____ , also known as an enterprise _____ , is a system used for reporting and data analysis, and is considered a core component of business intelligence. DWs are central repositories of integrated data from one or more disparate sources. They store current and historical data in one single place that are used for creating analytical reports for workers throughout the enterprise.

Exam Probability: **High**

12. *Answer choices:*

(see index for correct answer)

- a. Copyright
- b. Data warehouse
- c. CERF
- d. Point-in-time recovery

Guidance: level 1

:: Information technology organisations ::

The Internet Corporation for Assigned Names and Numbers is a nonprofit organization responsible for coordinating the maintenance and procedures of several databases related to the namespaces and numerical spaces of the Internet, ensuring the network's stable and secure operation. _____ performs the actual technical maintenance work of the Central Internet Address pools and DNS root zone registries pursuant to the Internet Assigned Numbers Authority function contract. The contract regarding the IANA stewardship functions between _____ and the National Telecommunications and Information Administration of the United States Department of Commerce ended on October 1, 2016, formally transitioning the functions to the global multistakeholder community.

Exam Probability: **High**

13. *Answer choices:*
(see index for correct answer)

- a. Institute of IT Training
- b. BytesForAll
- c. Software Technology Parks of India
- d. InfoPark, Kochi

Guidance: level 1

:: Cloud storage ::

_____ was an online backup service for both Windows and macOS users. Linux support was made available in Q3, 2014. In 2007 _____ was acquired by EMC, and in 2013 _____ was included in the EMC Backup Recovery Systems division's product list.On September 7, 2016, Dell Inc. acquired EMC Corporation to form Dell Technologies, restructuring the original Dell Inc. as a subsidiary of Dell Technologies.. On March 19, 2018 Carbonite acquired _____ from Dell for $148.5 million in cash and in 2019 shut down the service, incorporating _____ 's clients into its own online backup service programs.

Exam Probability: **Low**

14. *Answer choices:*

(see index for correct answer)

- a. GreenButton
- b. Mozy
- c. Rackspace Cloud
- d. Nirvanix

Guidance: level 1

:: ::

A _____ is a control panel usually located directly ahead of a vehicle's driver, displaying instrumentation and controls for the vehicle's operation.

15. *Answer choices:*

(see index for correct answer)

- a. Dashboard
- b. imperative
- c. Sarbanes-Oxley act of 2002
- d. functional perspective

Guidance: level 1

:: ::

A _____ is a telecommunications network that extends over a large geographical distance for the primary purpose of computer networking. _____ s are often established with leased telecommunication circuits.

Exam Probability: **Low**

16. *Answer choices:*

(see index for correct answer)

- a. similarity-attraction theory
- b. Wide Area Network
- c. cultural
- d. deep-level diversity

:: Production economics ::

In microeconomics, _____ are the cost advantages that enterprises obtain due to their scale of operation , with cost per unit of output decreasing with increasing scale.

Exam Probability: **High**

17. *Answer choices:*

(see index for correct answer)

- a. Economic batch quantity
- b. Economies of scale
- c. Productivity world
- d. Capitalist mode of production

:: ::

A _____ is the event in which two or more bodies exert forces on each other in about a relatively short time. Although the most common use of the word _____ refers to incidents in which two or more objects collide with great force, the scientific use of the term implies nothing about the magnitude of the force.

Exam Probability: **High**

18. *Answer choices:*

(see index for correct answer)

- a. hierarchical perspective
- b. cultural
- c. imperative
- d. Collision

Guidance: level 1

:: Telecommunications engineering ::

A _____ is a computer processor that incorporates the functions of a central processing unit on a single integrated circuit , or at most a few integrated circuits. The _____ is a multipurpose, clock driven, register based, digital integrated circuit that accepts binary data as input, processes it according to instructions stored in its memory and provides results as output. _____ s contain both combinational logic and sequential digital logic. _____ s operate on numbers and symbols represented in the binary number system.

19. *Answer choices:*

(see index for correct answer)

- a. Microprocessor
- b. Computer network

Guidance: level 1

:: Supply chain management ::

_____ is the removal of intermediaries in economics from a supply chain, or cutting out the middlemen in connection with a transaction or a series of transactions. Instead of going through traditional distribution channels, which had some type of intermediary , companies may now deal with customers directly, for example via the Internet. Hence, the use of factory direct and direct from the factory to mean the same thing.

Exam Probability: **Low**

20. *Answer choices:*

(see index for correct answer)

- a. XIO Strategies
- b. Wave picking
- c. Disintermediation
- d. Service management

:: World Wide Web Consortium standards ::

_____ is a markup language that defines a set of rules for encoding documents in a format that is both human-readable and machine-readable. The W3C's XML 1.0 Specification and several other related specifications—all of them free open standards—define XML.

Exam Probability: **Medium**

21. *Answer choices:*

(see index for correct answer)

- a. Hypertext markup language
- b. Hyper Text Markup Language

:: ::

_____ is a set of values of subjects with respect to qualitative or quantitative variables.

Exam Probability: **Low**

22. *Answer choices:*

(see index for correct answer)

- a. surface-level diversity
- b. co-culture
- c. functional perspective
- d. deep-level diversity

Guidance: level 1

:: Stochastic processes ::

_____ in its modern meaning is a "new idea, creative thoughts, new imaginations in form of device or method". _____ is often also viewed as the application of better solutions that meet new requirements, unarticulated needs, or existing market needs. Such _____ takes place through the provision of more-effective products, processes, services, technologies, or business models that are made available to markets, governments and society. An _____ is something original and more effective and, as a consequence, new, that "breaks into" the market or society. _____ is related to, but not the same as, invention, as _____ is more apt to involve the practical implementation of an invention to make a meaningful impact in the market or society, and not all _____ s require an invention. _____ often manifests itself via the engineering process, when the problem being solved is of a technical or scientific nature. The opposite of _____ is exnovation.

Exam Probability: **High**

23. *Answer choices:*

(see index for correct answer)

- a. WSSUS model
- b. Killed process
- c. Innovation
- d. Piecewise-deterministic Markov process

Guidance: level 1

:: Game artificial intelligence ::

In computer science, _____ , sometimes called machine intelligence, is intelligence demonstrated by machines, in contrast to the natural intelligence displayed by humans and animals. Colloquially, the term " _____ " is used to describe machines that mimic "cognitive" functions that humans associate with other human minds, such as "learning" and "problem solving".

Exam Probability: **Low**

24. *Answer choices:*

(see index for correct answer)

- a. Jump point search
- b. Zobrist hashing
- c. Logistello
- d. Artificial intelligence

Guidance: level 1

The _____ is the global system of interconnected computer networks that use the _____ protocol suite to link devices worldwide. It is a network of networks that consists of private, public, academic, business, and government networks of local to global scope, linked by a broad array of electronic, wireless, and optical networking technologies. The _____ carries a vast range of information resources and services, such as the inter-linked hypertext documents and applications of the World Wide Web , electronic mail, telephony, and file sharing.

Exam Probability: **Low**

25. *Answer choices:*

(see index for correct answer)

- a. Internet
- b. co-culture
- c. hierarchical
- d. deep-level diversity

Guidance: level 1

Collaborative software or _____ is application software designed to help people involved in a common task to achieve their goals. One of the earliest definitions of collaborative software is "intentional group processes plus software to support them".

Exam Probability: **High**

26. *Answer choices:*

(see index for correct answer)

- a. empathy
- b. co-culture
- c. Groupware
- d. Character

Guidance: level 1

:: Marketing ::

_____ , in marketing, manufacturing, call centres and management, is the use of flexible computer-aided manufacturing systems to produce custom output. Such systems combine the low unit costs of mass production processes with the flexibility of individual customization.

Exam Probability: **Medium**

27. *Answer choices:*

(see index for correct answer)

- a. Mass customization
- b. reverse marketing
- c. elaboration likelihood model
- d. Product requirements document

Guidance: level 1

:: Information technology management ::

_____ within quality management systems and information technology systems is a process—either formal or informal—used to ensure that changes to a product or system are introduced in a controlled and coordinated manner. It reduces the possibility that unnecessary changes will be introduced to a system without forethought, introducing faults into the system or undoing changes made by other users of software. The goals of a _____ procedure usually include minimal disruption to services, reduction in back-out activities, and cost-effective utilization of resources involved in implementing change.

Exam Probability: **High**

28. *Answer choices:*
(see index for correct answer)

- a. Downtime
- b. Revere, Inc.
- c. Service integration and management

- d. Change control

Guidance: level 1

:: Computer access control protocols ::

An _____ is a type of computer communications protocol or cryptographic protocol specifically designed for transfer of authentication data between two entities. It allows the receiving entity to authenticate the connecting entity as well as authenticate itself to the connecting entity by declaring the type of information needed for authentication as well as syntax. It is the most important layer of protection needed for secure communication within computer networks.

Exam Probability: **Low**

29. *Answer choices:*

(see index for correct answer)

- a. NTLMSSP
- b. Authentication protocol
- c. Extensible Authentication Protocol
- d. Reflection attack

Guidance: level 1

:: Network performance ::

_____ is a distributed computing paradigm which brings computer data storage closer to the location where it is needed. Computation is largely or completely performed on distributed device nodes. _____ pushes applications, data and computing power away from centralized points to locations closer to the user. The target of _____ is any application or general functionality needing to be closer to the source of the action where distributed systems technology interacts with the physical world. _____ does not need contact with any centralized cloud, although it may interact with one. In contrast to cloud computing, _____ refers to decentralized data processing at the edge of the network.

Exam Probability: **Low**

30. *Answer choices:*

(see index for correct answer)

- a. Traffic shaping
- b. Iproute2
- c. Spectral efficiency
- d. Edge computing

Guidance: level 1

:: ::

A _____ or data centre is a building, dedicated space within a building, or a group of buildings used to house computer systems and associated components, such as telecommunications and storage systems.

31. *Answer choices:*

(see index for correct answer)

- a. personal values
- b. information systems assessment
- c. imperative
- d. Data center

Guidance: level 1

:: Business planning ::

_____ is an organization's process of defining its strategy, or direction, and making decisions on allocating its resources to pursue this strategy. It may also extend to control mechanisms for guiding the implementation of the strategy. _____ became prominent in corporations during the 1960s and remains an important aspect of strategic management. It is executed by strategic planners or strategists, who involve many parties and research sources in their analysis of the organization and its relationship to the environment in which it competes.

Exam Probability: **Medium**

32. *Answer choices:*

(see index for correct answer)

- a. Stakeholder management
- b. Strategic planning
- c. Business war games
- d. operational planning

Guidance: level 1

:: Commerce websites ::

_____ is an American classified advertisements website with sections devoted to jobs, housing, for sale, items wanted, services, community service, gigs, résumés, and discussion forums.

Exam Probability: **Low**

33. *Answer choices:*

(see index for correct answer)

- a. Sheep Marketplace
- b. CNET
- c. Sallsell
- d. Wigix

Guidance: level 1

:: E-commerce ::

The phrase _____ was originally coined in 1997 by Kevin Duffey at the launch of the Global _____ Forum, to mean "the delivery of electronic commerce capabilities directly into the consumer's hand, anywhere, via wireless technology." Many choose to think of _____ as meaning "a retail outlet in your customer's pocket."

Exam Probability: **Medium**

34. *Answer choices:*

(see index for correct answer)

- a. Government-to-employees
- b. Steam
- c. Mobile commerce
- d. TRANZ 330

Guidance: level 1

:: Product testing ::

_____ is a characteristic of a product or system, whose interfaces are completely understood, to work with other products or systems, at present or in the future, in either implementation or access, without any restrictions.

Exam Probability: **Medium**

35. *Answer choices:*

- a. Testing reliability
- b. Wine tasting
- c. IBM Product Test
- d. Interoperability

Guidance: level 1

:: Survey methodology ::

An _____ is a conversation where questions are asked and answers are given. In common parlance, the word " _____ " refers to a one-on-one conversation between an _____ er and an _____ ee. The _____ er asks questions to which the _____ ee responds, usually so information may be transferred from _____ ee to _____ er . Sometimes, information can be transferred in both directions. It is a communication, unlike a speech, which produces a one-way flow of information.

Exam Probability: **Medium**

36. *Answer choices:*

- a. Survey sampling
- b. Enterprise feedback management
- c. Coverage error
- d. World Association for Public Opinion Research

:: Information technology management ::

_____ is a good-practice framework created by international professional association ISACA for information technology management and IT governance. _____ provides an implementable "set of controls over information technology and organizes them around a logical framework of IT-related processes and enablers."

Exam Probability: **Low**

37. *Answer choices:*

(see index for correct answer)

- a. IT service management
- b. E-Booking
- c. COBIT
- d. Contract management

:: Customer relationship management software ::

_____ Software Corporation is a Global Business Software company based in Austin, TX and was founded in 1972. Its products are aimed at the manufacturing, distribution, retail and services industries.

Exam Probability: **Medium**

38. *Answer choices:*

(see index for correct answer)

- a. LeadMaster CRM
- b. Epicor
- c. Access Commerce
- d. SAP Business One

Guidance: level 1

:: Data management ::

_____ represents the business objects that contain the most valuable, agreed upon information shared across an organization. It can cover relatively static reference data, transactional, unstructured, analytical, hierarchical and metadata. It is the primary focus of the information technology discipline of _____ management .

Exam Probability: **Low**

39. *Answer choices:*

(see index for correct answer)

- a. Master data
- b. Modular concurrency control
- c. Core Data
- d. Australian National Data Service

Guidance: level 1

:: Infographics ::

A _____ is a graphical representation of data, in which "the data is represented by symbols, such as bars in a bar _____ , lines in a line _____ , or slices in a pie _____ ". A _____ can represent tabular numeric data, functions or some kinds of qualitative structure and provides different info.

Exam Probability: **High**

40. *Answer choices:*

(see index for correct answer)

- a. Treemapping
- b. Chartjunk
- c. Chart
- d. VisAD

:: Telecommunication theory ::

In reliability theory and reliability engineering, the term _____ has the following meanings.

Exam Probability: **Medium**

41. *Answer choices:*
(see index for correct answer)

- a. Articulation score
- b. Blind equalization
- c. Multicast-broadcast single-frequency network
- d. Pulse shaping

:: Content management systems ::

_____ is the textual, visual, or aural content that is encountered as part of the user experience on websites. It may include—among other things—text, images, sounds, videos, and animations.

42. *Answer choices:*

(see index for correct answer)

- a. Aiki Framework
- b. TYPO3 Flow
- c. Web content
- d. LiteDiary

Guidance: level 1

:: Human–machine interaction ::

In electrical engineering, a _____ is an electrical component that can "make" or "break" an electrical circuit, interrupting the current or diverting it from one conductor to another. The mechanism of a _____ removes or restores the conducting path in a circuit when it is operated. It may be operated manually, for example, a light _____ or a keyboard button, may be operated by a moving object such as a door, or may be operated by some sensing element for pressure, temperature or flow. A _____ will have one or more sets of contacts, which may operate simultaneously, sequentially, or alternately. _____ es in high-powered circuits must operate rapidly to prevent destructive arcing, and may include special features to assist in rapidly interrupting a heavy current. Multiple forms of actuators are used for operation by hand or to sense position, level, temperature or flow. Special types are used, for example, for control of machinery, to reverse electric motors, or to sense liquid level. Many specialized forms exist. A common use is control of lighting, where multiple _____ es may be wired into one circuit to allow convenient control of light fixtures.

43. *Answer choices:*

(see index for correct answer)

- a. Percussion mallet
- b. Handle
- c. Key
- d. Usability assurance

Guidance: level 1

:: User interfaces ::

The _____ , in the industrial design field of human–computer interaction, is the space where interactions between humans and machines occur. The goal of this interaction is to allow effective operation and control of the machine from the human end, whilst the machine simultaneously feeds back information that aids the operators' decision-making process. Examples of this broad concept of _____ s include the interactive aspects of computer operating systems, hand tools, heavy machinery operator controls, and process controls. The design considerations applicable when creating _____ s are related to or involve such disciplines as ergonomics and psychology.

Exam Probability: **High**

44. *Answer choices:*

(see index for correct answer)

- a. Text-based user interface
- b. User interface
- c. Monome
- d. SDL Passolo

Guidance: level 1

:: Information systems ::

A _____ is an information system used for decision-making, and for the coordination, control, analysis, and visualization of information in an organization; especially in a company.

Exam Probability: **Low**

45. *Answer choices:*

(see index for correct answer)

- a. Document engineering
- b. Management information system
- c. Expert system
- d. Joint Regional Information Exchange System

Guidance: level 1

:: Data transmission ::

In telecommunication a _____ is the means of connecting one location to another for the purpose of transmitting and receiving digital information. It can also refer to a set of electronics assemblies, consisting of a transmitter and a receiver and the interconnecting data telecommunication circuit. These are governed by a link protocol enabling digital data to be transferred from a data source to a data sink.

Exam Probability: **Low**

46. *Answer choices:*

(see index for correct answer)

- a. Standard telegraph level
- b. RVU protocol
- c. Data link
- d. Message format

Guidance: level 1

:: Remote administration software ::

_____ is a protocol used on the Internet or local area network to provide a bidirectional interactive text-oriented communication facility using a virtual terminal connection. User data is interspersed in-band with _____ control information in an 8-bit byte oriented data connection over the Transmission Control Protocol .

Exam Probability: **Low**

47. *Answer choices:*

(see index for correct answer)

- a. LogMeIn
- b. TigerVNC
- c. Back Orifice 2000
- d. Crossloop

Guidance: level 1

:: E-commerce ::

Electronic governance or e-governance is the application of information and communication technology for delivering government services, exchange of information, communication transactions, integration of various stand-alone systems and services between government-to-citizen , _____ , government-to-government , government-to-employees as well as back-office processes and interactions within the entire government framework. Through e-governance, government services are made available to citizens in a convenient, efficient, and transparent manner. The three main target groups that can be distinguished in governance concepts are government, citizens, andbusinesses/interest groups. In e-governance, there are no distinct boundaries.

Exam Probability: **Medium**

48. *Answer choices:*

(see index for correct answer)

- a. AdsML
- b. Government-to-employees
- c. Playism
- d. Government-to-business

Guidance: level 1

:: Data management ::

Data aggregation is the compiling of information from databases with intent to prepare combined datasets for data processing.

Exam Probability: **Medium**

49. *Answer choices:*

(see index for correct answer)

- a. DMAIC
- b. Data set
- c. Automated tiered storage
- d. Distributed concurrency control

Guidance: level 1

:: Google services ::

_____ is a web mapping service developed by Google. It offers satellite imagery, aerial photography, street maps, 360° panoramic views of streets , real-time traffic conditions, and route planning for traveling by foot, car, bicycle and air , or public transportation.

Exam Probability: **High**

50. *Answer choices:*

(see index for correct answer)

- a. Google Map Maker
- b. Google Website Optimizer
- c. Google Calendar
- d. Google Maps

Guidance: level 1

:: Credit cards ::

The _____ Company, also known as Amex, is an American multinational financial services corporation headquartered in Three World Financial Center in New York City. The company was founded in 1850 and is one of the 30 components of the Dow Jones Industrial Average. The company is best known for its charge card, credit card, and traveler's cheque businesses.

Exam Probability: **High**

51. *Answer choices:*

(see index for correct answer)

- a. Credit CARD Act of 2009
- b. Black Card
- c. Wireless identity theft
- d. American Express

Guidance: level 1

:: Information technology management ::

_____ concerns a cycle of organizational activity: the acquisition of information from one or more sources, the custodianship and the distribution of that information to those who need it, and its ultimate disposition through archiving or deletion.

Exam Probability: **High**

52. *Answer choices:*

(see index for correct answer)

- a. Corporate Governance of ICT
- b. Intelligent workload management
- c. Information management
- d. Configuration Management

:: Web analytics ::

A click path or _____ is the sequence of hyperlinks one or more website visitors follows on a given site, presented in the order viewed. A visitor's click path may start within the website or at a separate 3rd party website, often a search engine results page, and it continues as a sequence of successive webpages visited by the user. Click paths take call data and can match it to ad sources, keywords, and/or referring domains, in order to capture data.

Exam Probability: **High**

53. *Answer choices:*

(see index for correct answer)

- a. Piwik
- b. IBM Unica NetInsight
- c. Clickstream
- d. Open Web Analytics

:: ::

_____ are interactive computer-mediated technologies that facilitate the creation and sharing of information, ideas, career interests and other forms of expression via virtual communities and networks. The variety of stand-alone and built-in _____ services currently available introduces challenges of definition; however, there are some common features.

Exam Probability: **Medium**

54. *Answer choices:*

(see index for correct answer)

- a. Social media
- b. Character
- c. hierarchical perspective
- d. information systems assessment

Guidance: level 1

:: Data modeling languages ::

An entity–relationship model describes interrelated things of interest in a specific domain of knowledge. A basic ER model is composed of entity types and specifies relationships that can exist between entities .

Exam Probability: **Low**

55. *Answer choices:*

(see index for correct answer)

- a. TREX
- b. Entity-relationship
- c. Information Object Class
- d. Binary Format Description language

Guidance: level 1

:: Policy ::

A _____ is a statement or a legal document that discloses some or all
of the ways a party gathers, uses, discloses, and manages a customer or
client's data. It fulfills a legal requirement to protect a customer or
client's privacy. Personal information can be anything that can be used to
identify an individual, not limited to the person's name, address, date of
birth, marital status, contact information, ID issue, and expiry date,
financial records, credit information, medical history, where one travels, and
intentions to acquire goods and services. In the case of a business it is often
a statement that declares a party's policy on how it collects, stores, and
releases personal information it collects. It informs the client what specific
information is collected, and whether it is kept confidential, shared with
partners, or sold to other firms or enterprises. Privacy policies typically
represent a broader, more generalized treatment, as opposed to data use
statements, which tend to be more detailed and specific.

Exam Probability: **Low**

56. *Answer choices:*

(see index for correct answer)

- a. Security policy
- b. WS-Policy
- c. Asia-Pacific Network for Global Change Research
- d. Health administration

Guidance: level 1

:: ::

A _____ is an organized collection of data, generally stored and accessed electronically from a computer system. Where _____ s are more complex they are often developed using formal design and modeling techniques.

Exam Probability: **Medium**

57. *Answer choices:*

(see index for correct answer)

- a. interpersonal communication
- b. Database
- c. hierarchical
- d. open system

Guidance: level 1

:: Enterprise architecture ::

Enterprise software, also known as _____ software , is computer software used to satisfy the needs of an organization rather than individual users. Such organizations include businesses, schools, interest-based user groups, clubs, charities, and governments. Enterprise software is an integral part of a information system.

Exam Probability: **Medium**

58. *Answer choices:*

(see index for correct answer)

- a. Reference architecture
- b. Application architecture
- c. Enterprise application
- d. ARID

Guidance: level 1

:: Payment systems ::

_____ is a mobile phone-based money transfer, financing and microfinancing service, launched in 2007 by Vodafone for Safaricom and Vodacom, the largest mobile network operators in Kenya and Tanzania. It has since expanded to Afghanistan, South Africa, India and in 2014 to Romania and in 2015 to Albania. _____ allows users to deposit, withdraw, transfer money and pay for goods and services easily with a mobile device.

Exam Probability: **High**

59. *Answer choices:*

(see index for correct answer)

- a. M-Pesa
- b. Direct corporate access
- c. Yang Cheng Tong
- d. Express Payment System

Guidance: level 1

Marketing

Marketing is the study and management of exchange relationships. Marketing is the business process of creating relationships with and satisfying customers. With its focus on the customer, marketing is one of the premier components of business management.

Marketing is defined by the American Marketing Association as "the activity, set of institutions, and processes for creating, communicating, delivering, and exchanging offerings that have value for customers, clients, partners, and society at large."

:: ::

_____ is the production of products for use or sale using labour and machines, tools, chemical and biological processing, or formulation. The term may refer to a range of human activity, from handicraft to high tech, but is most commonly applied to industrial design, in which raw materials are transformed into finished goods on a large scale. Such finished goods may be sold to other manufacturers for the production of other, more complex products, such as aircraft, household appliances, furniture, sports equipment or automobiles, or sold to wholesalers, who in turn sell them to retailers, who then sell them to end users and consumers.

Exam Probability: **High**

1. *Answer choices:*

(see index for correct answer)

- a. Manufacturing
- b. Character
- c. open system
- d. levels of analysis

Guidance: level 1

:: Financial economics ::

In management, business value is an informal term that includes all forms of value that determine the health and well-being of the firm in the long run. Business value expands concept of value of the firm beyond economic value to include other forms of value such as employee value, _____ , supplier value, channel partner value, alliance partner value, managerial value, and societal value. Many of these forms of value are not directly measured in monetary terms.

Exam Probability: **High**

2. *Answer choices:*

(see index for correct answer)

- a. Capital asset
- b. Indexation
- c. Ask price
- d. Financial innovation

Guidance: level 1

:: Brand management ::

Marketing communications uses different marketing channels and tools in combination: Marketing communication channels focus on any way a business communicates a message to its desired market, or the market in general. A marketing communication tool can be anything from: advertising, personal selling, direct marketing, sponsorship, communication, and promotion to public relations.

3. *Answer choices:*

(see index for correct answer)

- a. Integrated marketing
- b. Brand legacy
- c. Naming rights
- d. Brand relationship

Guidance: level 1

:: Management ::

A _____ is an idea of the future or desired result that a person or a group of people envisions, plans and commits to achieve. People endeavor to reach _____ s within a finite time by setting deadlines.

4. *Answer choices:*

(see index for correct answer)

- a. Organizational space
- b. Business plan
- c. DMSMS
- d. Radical transparency

:: Stochastic processes ::

_____ in its modern meaning is a "new idea, creative thoughts, new imaginations in form of device or method". _____ is often also viewed as the application of better solutions that meet new requirements, unarticulated needs, or existing market needs. Such _____ takes place through the provision of more-effective products, processes, services, technologies, or business models that are made available to markets, governments and society. An _____ is something original and more effective and, as a consequence, new, that "breaks into" the market or society. _____ is related to, but not the same as, invention, as _____ is more apt to involve the practical implementation of an invention to make a meaningful impact in the market or society, and not all _____ s require an invention. _____ often manifests itself via the engineering process, when the problem being solved is of a technical or scientific nature. The opposite of _____ is exnovation.

Exam Probability: **Medium**

5. *Answer choices:*

(see index for correct answer)

- a. Markov kernel
- b. Innovation
- c. Branching random walk
- d. Bernoulli process

A _____ consists of one people who live in the same dwelling and share meals. It may also consist of a single family or another group of people. A dwelling is considered to contain multiple _____ s if meals or living spaces are not shared. The _____ is the basic unit of analysis in many social, microeconomic and government models, and is important to economics and inheritance.

Exam Probability: **Low**

6. *Answer choices:*

(see index for correct answer)

- a. cultural
- b. personal values
- c. information systems assessment
- d. Household

Guidance: level 1

_____ is both a research area and a practical skill encompassing the ability of an individual or organization to "lead" or guide other individuals, teams, or entire organizations. Specialist literature debates various viewpoints, contrasting Eastern and Western approaches to _____ , and also United States versus European approaches. U.S. academic environments define _____ as "a process of social influence in which a person can enlist the aid and support of others in the accomplishment of a common task".

Exam Probability: **Medium**

7. *Answer choices:*

(see index for correct answer)

- a. functional perspective
- b. Leadership
- c. Sarbanes-Oxley act of 2002
- d. process perspective

Guidance: level 1

:: Product management ::

_____ or brand stretching is a marketing strategy in which a firm marketing a product with a well-developed image uses the same brand name in a different product category. The new product is called a spin-off. Organizations use this strategy to increase and leverage brand equity . An example of a _____ is Jello-gelatin creating Jello pudding pops. It increases awareness of the brand name and increases profitability from offerings in more than one product category.

8. *Answer choices:*

(see index for correct answer)

- a. Consumer adoption of technological innovations
- b. Brand extension
- c. Brand equity
- d. Trademark

Guidance: level 1

:: Survey methodology ::

A _____ is the procedure of systematically acquiring and recording information about the members of a given population. The term is used mostly in connection with national population and housing _____ es; other common _____ es include agriculture, business, and traffic _____ es. The United Nations defines the essential features of population and housing _____ es as "individual enumeration, universality within a defined territory, simultaneity and defined periodicity", and recommends that population _____ es be taken at least every 10 years. United Nations recommendations also cover _____ topics to be collected, official definitions, classifications and other useful information to co-ordinate international practice.

9. *Answer choices:*

- a. Political forecasting
- b. National Health Interview Survey
- c. Group concept mapping
- d. Census

Guidance: level 1

:: Direct marketing ::

_____ is a method of direct marketing in which a salesperson solicits prospective customers to buy products or services, either over the phone or through a subsequent face to face or Web conferencing appointment scheduled during the call. _____ can also include recorded sales pitches programmed to be played over the phone via automatic dialing.

Exam Probability: **Low**

10. *Answer choices:*

- a. Junk fax
- b. The Cobra Group
- c. American Family Publishers
- d. Peter Lemongello

:: Logistics ::

_____ is generally the detailed organization and implementation of a complex operation. In a general business sense, _____ is the management of the flow of things between the point of origin and the point of consumption in order to meet requirements of customers or corporations. The resources managed in _____ may include tangible goods such as materials, equipment, and supplies, as well as food and other consumable items. The _____ of physical items usually involves the integration of information flow, materials handling, production, packaging, inventory, transportation, warehousing, and often security.

Exam Probability: **Medium**

11. *Answer choices:*

(see index for correct answer)

- a. Navy lighterage pontoons
- b. Logistics
- c. Phase jitter modulation
- d. Serial shipping container code

:: Marketing ::

_____ is multi-channel online marketing technique focused at reaching a specific audience on their smartphones, tablets, or any other related devices through websites, E-mail, SMS and MMS, social media, or mobile applications. _____ can provide customers with time and location sensitive, personalized information that promotes goods, services and ideas. In a more theoretical manner, academic Andreas Kaplan defines _____ as "any marketing activity conducted through a ubiquitous network to which consumers are constantly connected using a personal mobile device".

Exam Probability: **Low**

12. *Answer choices:*

(see index for correct answer)

- a. Alpha consumer
- b. Discoverability
- c. Buy one, get one free
- d. Discounting

Guidance: level 1

:: Health promotion ::

_____ , as defined by the World _____ Organization , is "a state of complete physical, mental and social well-being and not merely the absence of disease or infirmity." This definition has been subject to controversy, as it may have limited value for implementation. _____ may be defined as the ability to adapt and manage physical, mental and social challenges throughout life.

13. *Answer choices:*

(see index for correct answer)

- a. Health
- b. Choosing Wisely
- c. Maria Gomori
- d. Patient navigators

Guidance: level 1

:: Marketing ::

A _____ is the quantity of payment or compensation given by one party to another in return for one unit of goods or services.. A _____ is influenced by both production costs and demand for the product. A _____ may be determined by a monopolist or may be imposed on the firm by market conditions.

14. *Answer choices:*

(see index for correct answer)

- a. Price
- b. Blind taste test

- c. Corporate identity
- d. Outsourcing relationship management

Guidance: level 1

:: Market research ::

_____ is the action of defining, gathering, analyzing, and distributing intelligence about products, customers, competitors, and any aspect of the environment needed to support executives and managers in strategic decision making for an organization.

Exam Probability: **Low**

15. *Answer choices:*

(see index for correct answer)

- a. Shanghai Metals Market
- b. Monroe Mendelsohn Research
- c. Competitive intelligence
- d. Early adopter

Guidance: level 1

:: Management ::

A _____ describes the rationale of how an organization creates, delivers, and captures value, in economic, social, cultural or other contexts. The process of _____ construction and modification is also called _____ innovation and forms a part of business strategy.

Exam Probability: **High**

16. *Answer choices:*

(see index for correct answer)

- a. Performance management
- b. Business model
- c. Data Item Descriptions
- d. Manager Tools Podcast

Guidance: level 1

:: Brand management ::

_____ refers to the extent to which customers are able to recall or recognise a brand. _____ is a key consideration in consumer behavior, advertising management, brand management and strategy development. The consumer's ability to recognise or recall a brand is central to purchasing decision-making. Purchasing cannot proceed unless a consumer is first aware of a product category and a brand within that category. Awareness does not necessarily mean that the consumer must be able to recall a specific brand name, but he or she must be able to recall sufficient distinguishing features for purchasing to proceed. For instance, if a consumer asks her friend to buy her some gum in a "blue pack", the friend would be expected to know which gum to buy, even though neither friend can recall the precise brand name at the time.

Exam Probability: **Low**

17. *Answer choices:*

(see index for correct answer)

- a. Brand awareness
- b. Brand loyalty
- c. Branded content
- d. Brand-new

Guidance: level 1

:: Legal terms ::

A _____ is a person who is called upon to issue a response to a communication made by another. The term is used in legal contexts, in survey methodology, and in psychological conditioning.

18. *Answer choices:*

(see index for correct answer)

- a. Respondent
- b. Demise
- c. Direct evidence
- d. Curator bonis

Guidance: level 1

:: Social psychology ::

_____ s is a qualitative methodology used to describe consumers on psychological attributes. _____ s have been applied to the study of personality, values, opinions, attitudes, interests, and lifestyles. While _____ s are often equated with lifestyle research, it has been argued that _____ s should apply to the study of cognitive attributes such as attitudes, interests, opinions, and beliefs while lifestyle should apply to the study of overt behavior . Because this area of research focuses on activities, interests, and opinions, _____ factors are sometimes abbreviated to `AIO variables`.

19. *Answer choices:*

(see index for correct answer)

- a. coercive persuasion
- b. fear appeal
- c. Psychographic
- d. objectification

Guidance: level 1

:: ::

_____ is the administration of an organization, whether it is a business, a not-for-profit organization, or government body. _____ includes the activities of setting the strategy of an organization and coordinating the efforts of its employees to accomplish its objectives through the application of available resources, such as financial, natural, technological, and human resources. The term " _____ " may also refer to those people who manage an organization.

Exam Probability: **Low**

20. *Answer choices:*

(see index for correct answer)

- a. Sarbanes-Oxley act of 2002

- b. empathy
- c. Management
- d. deep-level diversity

Guidance: level 1

:: Market research ::

An _____ or lighthouse customer is an early customer of a given company, product, or technology. The term originates from Everett M. Rogers' Diffusion of Innovations .

Exam Probability: **Low**

21. *Answer choices:*

(see index for correct answer)

- a. Nielsen VideoScan
- b. Customer satisfaction research
- c. Early adopter
- d. INDEX

Guidance: level 1

:: Network theory ::

A _____ is a social structure made up of a set of social actors, sets of dyadic ties, and other social interactions between actors. The _____ perspective provides a set of methods for analyzing the structure of whole social entities as well as a variety of theories explaining the patterns observed in these structures. The study of these structures uses _____ analysis to identify local and global patterns, locate influential entities, and examine network dynamics.

Exam Probability: **Medium**

22. *Answer choices:*
(see index for correct answer)

- a. K shortest path routing
- b. Agent network topology
- c. Similarity
- d. Social network

Guidance: level 1

:: ::

_____ or commercialisation is the process of introducing a new product or production method into commerce—making it available on the market. The term often connotes especially entry into the mass market , but it also includes a move from the laboratory into commerce. Many technologies begin in a research and development laboratory or in an inventor's workshop and may not be practical for commercial use in their infancy . The "development" segment of the "research and development" spectrum requires time and money as systems are engineered with a view to making the product or method a paying commercial proposition. The product launch of a new product is the final stage of new product development - at this point advertising, sales promotion, and other marketing efforts encourage commercial adoption of the product or method. Beyond _____ can lie consumerization .

Exam Probability: **Low**

23. *Answer choices:*

(see index for correct answer)

- a. Sarbanes-Oxley act of 2002
- b. open system
- c. corporate values
- d. hierarchical perspective

Guidance: level 1

:: ::

Competition arises whenever at least two parties strive for a goal which cannot be shared: where one's gain is the other's loss .

24. *Answer choices:*

(see index for correct answer)

- a. Competitor
- b. deep-level diversity
- c. Character
- d. cultural

Guidance: level 1

:: Commerce ::

_____ relates to "the exchange of goods and services, especially on a large scale". It includes legal, economic, political, social, cultural and technological systems that operate in a country or in international trade.

Exam Probability: **Medium**

25. *Answer choices:*

(see index for correct answer)

- a. Sell-side analyst
- b. Council of the Americas
- c. International Marketmakers Combination
- d. Coincidence of wants

:: Marketing ::

_____ or stock is the goods and materials that a business holds for the ultimate goal of resale .

Exam Probability: **Low**

26. *Answer choices:*

(see index for correct answer)

- a. Packshot
- b. Presentation folder
- c. Inventory
- d. Intent scale translation

:: Direct marketing ::

_____ is a form of direct marketing using databases of customers or potential customers to generate personalized communications in order to promote a product or service for marketing purposes. The method of communication can be any addressable medium, as in direct marketing.

27. *Answer choices:*

(see index for correct answer)

- a. Database marketing
- b. Guthy-Renker
- c. Inktel
- d. Synapse Group, Inc.

Guidance: level 1

:: Types of marketing ::

_____ was first defined as a form of marketing developed from direct response marketing campaigns which emphasizes customer retention and satisfaction, rather than a focus on sales transactions.

Exam Probability: **Medium**

28. *Answer choices:*

(see index for correct answer)

- a. Secret brand
- b. Shopper marketing
- c. Vertical disintegration
- d. Guerrilla marketing

:: Direct selling ::

_____ consists of two main business models: single-level marketing, in which a direct seller makes money by buying products from a parent organization and selling them directly to customers, and multi-level marketing , in which the direct seller may earn money from both direct sales to customers and by sponsoring new direct sellers and potentially earning a commission from their efforts.

Exam Probability: **Low**

29. *Answer choices:*

(see index for correct answer)

- a. The Longaberger Company
- b. Direct Selling News
- c. CVSL
- d. Direct Selling Association

:: Marketing ::

_____ , sometimes called trigger-based or event-driven marketing, is a marketing strategy that uses two-way communication channels to allow consumers to connect with a company directly. Although this exchange can take place in person, in the last decade it has increasingly taken place almost exclusively online through email, social media, and blogs.

Exam Probability: **Low**

30. *Answer choices:*

(see index for correct answer)

- a. One Town One Product
- b. Online lead generation
- c. Audience development
- d. Buyer decision process

Guidance: level 1

:: Evaluation methods ::

_____ is a scientific method of observation to gather non-numerical data. This type of research "refers to the meanings, concepts definitions, characteristics, metaphors, symbols, and description of things" and not to their "counts or measures." This research answers why and how a certain phenomenon may occur rather than how often. _____ approaches are employed across many academic disciplines, focusing particularly on the human elements of the social and natural sciences; in less academic contexts, areas of application include qualitative market research, business, service demonstrations by non-profits, and journalism.

31. *Answer choices:*

(see index for correct answer)

- a. Random digit dialing
- b. Advanced Concept Technology Demonstration
- c. Naturalistic observation
- d. Qualitative research

Guidance: level 1

:: Management occupations ::

_____ ship is the process of designing, launching and running a new business, which is often initially a small business. The people who create these businesses are called _____ s.

Exam Probability: **Low**

32. *Answer choices:*

(see index for correct answer)

- a. Entrepreneur
- b. Store manager
- c. Chief reputation officer
- d. Sport management

:: ::

_____ Motor Company is an American multinational automaker that has its main headquarter in Dearborn, Michigan, a suburb of Detroit. It was founded by Henry _____ and incorporated on June 16, 1903. The company sells automobiles and commercial vehicles under the _____ brand and most luxury cars under the Lincoln brand. _____ also owns Brazilian SUV manufacturer Troller, an 8% stake in Aston Martin of the United Kingdom and a 32% stake in Jiangling Motors. It also has joint-ventures in China , Taiwan , Thailand , Turkey , and Russia . The company is listed on the New York Stock Exchange and is controlled by the _____ family; they have minority ownership but the majority of the voting power.

Exam Probability: **High**

33. *Answer choices:*

(see index for correct answer)

- a. surface-level diversity
- b. corporate values
- c. functional perspective
- d. co-culture

:: Debt ::

_____ is the trust which allows one party to provide money or resources to another party wherein the second party does not reimburse the first party immediately , but promises either to repay or return those resources at a later date. In other words, _____ is a method of making reciprocity formal, legally enforceable, and extensible to a large group of unrelated people.

Exam Probability: **Medium**

34. *Answer choices:*

(see index for correct answer)

- a. Least developed country
- b. Peak debt
- c. Credit
- d. Financial assistance

Guidance: level 1

:: Basic financial concepts ::

_____ is a sustained increase in the general price level of goods and services in an economy over a period of time. When the general price level rises, each unit of currency buys fewer goods and services; consequently, _____ reflects a reduction in the purchasing power per unit of money a loss of real value in the medium of exchange and unit of account within the economy. The measure of _____ is the _____ rate, the annualized percentage change in a general price index, usually the consumer price index, over time. The opposite of _____ is deflation.

35. *Answer choices:*

(see index for correct answer)

- a. Forward guidance
- b. Maturity
- c. Present value of benefits
- d. Financial transaction

Guidance: level 1

:: Marketing ::

_____ is a marketing practice of individuals or organizations . It allows them to sell products or services to other companies or organizations that resell them, use them in their products or services or use them to support their works.

Exam Probability: **Medium**

36. *Answer choices:*

(see index for correct answer)

- a. Business marketing
- b. Demonstrator model
- c. Private-label

- d. Pink money

Guidance: level 1

:: ::

A _____ is a graphic mark, emblem, or symbol used to aid and promote public identification and recognition. It may be of an abstract or figurative design or include the text of the name it represents as in a wordmark.

Exam Probability: **High**

37. *Answer choices:*
(see index for correct answer)

- a. process perspective
- b. corporate values
- c. functional perspective
- d. Logo

Guidance: level 1

:: Reputation management ::

A _____ is an astronomical object consisting of a luminous spheroid of plasma held together by its own gravity. The nearest _____ to Earth is the Sun. Many other _____ s are visible to the naked eye from Earth during the night, appearing as a multitude of fixed luminous points in the sky due to their immense distance from Earth. Historically, the most prominent _____ s were grouped into constellations and asterisms, the brightest of which gained proper names. Astronomers have assembled _____ catalogues that identify the known _____ s and provide standardized stellar designations. However, most of the estimated 300 sextillion _____ s in the Universe are invisible to the naked eye from Earth, including all _____ s outside our galaxy, the Milky Way.

Exam Probability: **Medium**

38. *Answer choices:*

(see index for correct answer)

- a. Star
- b. Hilltop algorithm
- c. personal brand
- d. Reputation system

Guidance: level 1

:: Television commercials ::

_____ is a characteristic that distinguishes physical entities that have biological processes, such as signaling and self-sustaining processes, from those that do not, either because such functions have ceased , or because they never had such functions and are classified as inanimate. Various forms of _____ exist, such as plants, animals, fungi, protists, archaea, and bacteria. The criteria can at times be ambiguous and may or may not define viruses, viroids, or potential synthetic _____ as "living". Biology is the science concerned with the study of _____ .

Exam Probability: **High**

39. *Answer choices:*

(see index for correct answer)

- a. Godzilla vs. Charles Barkley
- b. TenderCrisp
- c. Space Chair
- d. Life

Guidance: level 1

:: ::

_____ Corporation is an American multinational technology company with headquarters in Redmond, Washington. It develops, manufactures, licenses, supports and sells computer software, consumer electronics, personal computers, and related services. Its best known software products are the _____ Windows line of operating systems, the _____ Office suite, and the Internet Explorer and Edge Web browsers. Its flagship hardware products are the Xbox video game consoles and the _____ Surface lineup of touchscreen personal computers. As of 2016, it is the world's largest software maker by revenue, and one of the world's most valuable companies. The word " _____ " is a portmanteau of "microcomputer" and "software". _____ is ranked No. 30 in the 2018 Fortune 500 rankings of the largest United States corporations by total revenue.

Exam Probability: **Low**

40. *Answer choices:*

(see index for correct answer)

- a. functional perspective
- b. empathy
- c. imperative
- d. corporate values

Guidance: level 1

:: Commodities ::

In economics, a _____ is an economic good or service that has full or substantial fungibility: that is, the market treats instances of the good as equivalent or nearly so with no regard to who produced them. Most commodities are raw materials, basic resources, agricultural, or mining products, such as iron ore, sugar, or grains like rice and wheat. Commodities can also be mass-produced unspecialized products such as chemicals and computer memory.

Exam Probability: **Medium**

41. *Answer choices:*

(see index for correct answer)

- a. Sample grade
- b. Commoditization
- c. Commodity
- d. Commodity pathway diversion

Guidance: level 1

:: ::

_____ , or auditory perception, is the ability to perceive sounds by detecting vibrations, changes in the pressure of the surrounding medium through time, through an organ such as the ear. The academic field concerned with _____ is auditory science.

Exam Probability: **Medium**

42. *Answer choices:*

(see index for correct answer)

- a. Hearing
- b. process perspective
- c. surface-level diversity
- d. imperative

Guidance: level 1

:: Brokered programming ::

An _____ is a form of television commercial, which generally includes a toll-free telephone number or website. Most often used as a form of direct response television , long-form _____ s are typically 28:30 or 58:30 minutes in length. _____ s are also known as paid programming . This phenomenon started in the United States, where _____ s were typically shown overnight , outside peak prime time hours for commercial broadcasters. Some television stations chose to air _____ s as an alternative to the former practice of signing off. Some channels air _____ s 24 hours. Some stations also choose to air _____ s during the daytime hours mostly on weekends to fill in for unscheduled network or syndicated programming. By 2009, most _____ spending in the U.S. occurred during the early morning, daytime and evening hours, or in the afternoon. Stations in most countries around the world have instituted similar media structures. The _____ industry is worth over $200 billion.

Exam Probability: **High**

43. *Answer choices:*

(see index for correct answer)

- a. Toonzai
- b. Infomercial
- c. Brokered programming
- d. Leased access

Guidance: level 1

:: Marketing ::

_____ is "commercial competition characterized by the repeated cutting of prices below those of competitors". One competitor will lower its price, then others will lower their prices to match. If one of them reduces their price again, a new round of reductions starts. In the short term, _____ s are good for buyers, who can take advantage of lower prices. Often they are not good for the companies involved because the lower prices reduce profit margins and can threaten their survival.

Exam Probability: **High**

44. *Answer choices:*

(see index for correct answer)

- a. Electronic money
- b. Price war
- c. Product churning
- d. Business-to-employee

:: ::

_____ is a marketing communication that employs an openly sponsored, non-personal message to promote or sell a product, service or idea. Sponsors of _____ are typically businesses wishing to promote their products or services. _____ is differentiated from public relations in that an advertiser pays for and has control over the message. It differs from personal selling in that the message is non-personal, i.e., not directed to a particular individual. _____ is communicated through various mass media, including traditional media such as newspapers, magazines, television, radio, outdoor _____ or direct mail; and new media such as search results, blogs, social media, websites or text messages. The actual presentation of the message in a medium is referred to as an advertisement, or "ad" or advert for short.

Exam Probability: **High**

45. *Answer choices:*

(see index for correct answer)

- a. interpersonal communication
- b. Advertising
- c. deep-level diversity
- d. process perspective

:: Business ::

In commerce, _____ is the product of an interaction between an organization and a customer over the duration of their relationship. This interaction is made up of three parts: the customer journey, the brand touchpoints the customer interacts with, and the environments the _____ s during their experience. A good _____ means that the individual's experience during all points of contact matches the individual's expectations. Gartner asserts the importance of managing the customer's experience.

Exam Probability: **Low**

46. *Answer choices:*

(see index for correct answer)

- a. Customer experience
- b. Business strategy mapping
- c. E-lancing
- d. Encore fellowships

Guidance: level 1

:: Television commercials ::

_____ is a phenomenon whereby something new and somehow valuable is formed. The created item may be intangible or a physical object.

47. *Answer choices:*

(see index for correct answer)

- a. Frozen Peas
- b. Creativity
- c. Swimblack
- d. Write the Future

Guidance: level 1

:: Marketing ::

_____ is based on a marketing concept which can be adopted by an organization as a strategy for business expansion. Where implemented, a franchisor licenses its know-how, procedures, intellectual property, use of its business model, brand, and rights to sell its branded products and services to a franchisee. In return the franchisee pays certain fees and agrees to comply with certain obligations, typically set out in a Franchise Agreement.

Exam Probability: **High**

48. *Answer choices:*

(see index for correct answer)

- a. Buy one, get one free
- b. Cult brand

- c. Branding national myths and symbols
- d. Franchising

Guidance: level 1

:: Marketing ::

A _____ is an overall experience of a customer that distinguishes an organization or product from its rivals in the eyes of the customer. _____ s are used in business, marketing, and advertising. Name _____ s are sometimes distinguished from generic or store _____ s.

Exam Probability: **Medium**

49. *Answer choices:*

(see index for correct answer)

- a. Brand
- b. Fixed value-added resource
- c. Profit chart
- d. In-game advertising

Guidance: level 1

:: ::

In production, research, retail, and accounting, a _____ is the value of money that has been used up to produce something or deliver a service, and hence is not available for use anymore. In business, the _____ may be one of acquisition, in which case the amount of money expended to acquire it is counted as _____ . In this case, money is the input that is gone in order to acquire the thing. This acquisition _____ may be the sum of the _____ of production as incurred by the original producer, and further _____ s of transaction as incurred by the acquirer over and above the price paid to the producer. Usually, the price also includes a mark-up for profit over the _____ of production.

Exam Probability: **High**

50. *Answer choices:*

(see index for correct answer)

- a. Cost
- b. personal values
- c. co-culture
- d. corporate values

Guidance: level 1

:: Marketing ::

The _____ is a foundation model for businesses. The _____ has been defined as the "set of marketing tools that the firm uses to pursue its marketing objectives in the target market". Thus the _____ refers to four broad levels of marketing decision, namely: product, price, place, and promotion. Marketing practice has been occurring for millennia, but marketing theory emerged in the early twentieth century. The contemporary _____, or the 4 Ps, which has become the dominant framework for marketing management decisions, was first published in 1960. In services marketing, an extended _____ is used, typically comprising 7 Ps, made up of the original 4 Ps extended by process, people, and physical evidence. Occasionally service marketers will refer to 8 Ps, comprising these 7 Ps plus performance.

Exam Probability: **High**

51. *Answer choices:*

(see index for correct answer)

- a. Marketing mix
- b. Factor analysis
- c. Adobe Experience Manager
- d. Kronos Effect

Guidance: level 1

:: ::

According to the philosopher Piyush Mathur , "Tangibility is the property that a phenomenon exhibits if it has and/or transports mass and/or energy and/or momentum".

52. *Answer choices:*

(see index for correct answer)

- a. empathy
- b. imperative
- c. process perspective
- d. surface-level diversity

Guidance: level 1

:: Project management ::

_____ is the right to exercise power, which can be formalized by a state and exercised by way of judges, appointed executives of government, or the ecclesiastical or priestly appointed representatives of a God or other deities.

Exam Probability: **Low**

53. *Answer choices:*

(see index for correct answer)

- a. IPMA
- b. Phased implementation
- c. Authority

- d. Graphical path method

Guidance: level 1

:: Business terms ::

A _____ is a short statement of why an organization exists, what its overall goal is, identifying the goal of its operations: what kind of product or service it provides, its primary customers or market, and its geographical region of operation. It may include a short statement of such fundamental matters as the organization's values or philosophies, a business's main competitive advantages, or a desired future state—the "vision".

Exam Probability: **Medium**

54. *Answer choices:*
(see index for correct answer)

- a. churn rate
- b. front office
- c. customer base
- d. Mission statement

Guidance: level 1

:: ::

In logic and philosophy, an _____ is a series of statements , called the premises or premisses , intended to determine the degree of truth of another statement, the conclusion. The logical form of an _____ in a natural language can be represented in a symbolic formal language, and independently of natural language formally defined " _____ s" can be made in math and computer science.

Exam Probability: **High**

55. *Answer choices:*

(see index for correct answer)

- a. Argument
- b. co-culture
- c. imperative
- d. deep-level diversity

Guidance: level 1

:: ::

Distribution is one of the four elements of the marketing mix. Distribution is the process of making a product or service available for the consumer or business user who needs it. This can be done directly by the producer or service provider, or using indirect channels with distributors or intermediaries. The other three elements of the marketing mix are product, pricing, and promotion.

56. *Answer choices:*

(see index for correct answer)

- a. hierarchical
- b. co-culture
- c. imperative
- d. Distribution channel

Guidance: level 1

:: Marketing ::

_____ s are structured marketing strategies designed by merchants to encourage customers to continue to shop at or use the services of businesses associated with each program. These programs exist covering most types of commerce, each one having varying features and rewards-schemes.

Exam Probability: **High**

57. *Answer choices:*

(see index for correct answer)

- a. Customer newsletter service
- b. Private-label
- c. Generic trademark

- d. Processing fluency

:: Business models ::

_____ es are privately owned corporations, partnerships, or sole proprietorships that have fewer employees and/or less annual revenue than a regular-sized business or corporation. Businesses are defined as "small" in terms of being able to apply for government support and qualify for preferential tax policy varies depending on the country and industry.
_____ es range from fifteen employees under the Australian Fair Work Act 2009, fifty employees according to the definition used by the European Union, and fewer than five hundred employees to qualify for many U.S. _____ Administration programs. While _____ es can also be classified according to other methods, such as annual revenues, shipments, sales, assets, or by annual gross or net revenue or net profits, the number of employees is one of the most widely used measures.

Exam Probability: **Medium**

58. *Answer choices:*

(see index for correct answer)

- a. Product-service system
- b. Small business
- c. Professional open source
- d. Microfranchising

:: Marketing ::

_____ is the percentage of a market accounted for by a specific entity. In a survey of nearly 200 senior marketing managers, 67% responded that they found the revenue- "dollar _____" metric very useful, while 61% found "unit _____" very useful.

Exam Probability: **Medium**

59. *Answer choices:*

(see index for correct answer)

- a. Corporate anniversary
- b. Content marketing
- c. Market share
- d. Factor analysis

Guidance: level 1

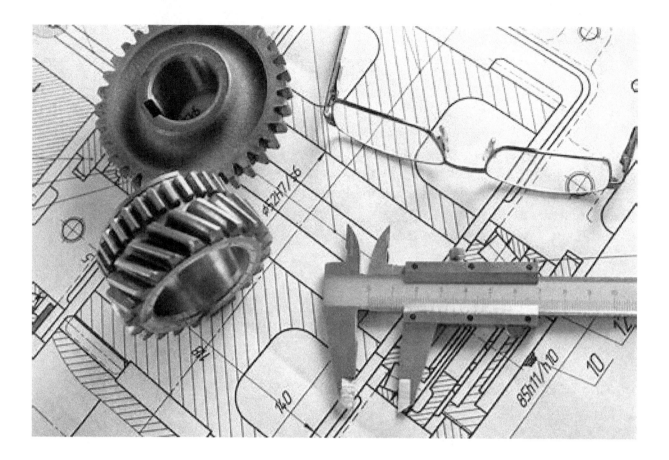

Manufacturing

Manufacturing is the production of merchandise for use or sale using labor and machines, tools, chemical and biological processing, or formulation. The term may refer to a range of human activity, from handicraft to high tech, but is most commonly applied to industrial design , in which raw materials are transformed into finished goods on a large scale. Such finished goods may be sold to other manufacturers for the production of other, more complex products, such as aircraft, household appliances, furniture, sports equipment or automobiles, or sold to wholesalers, who in turn sell them to retailers, who then sell them to end users and consumers.

:: Costs ::

In microeconomic theory, the _____ , or alternative cost, of making a particular choice is the value of the most valuable choice out of those that were not taken. In other words, opportunity that will require sacrifices.

Exam Probability: **Low**

1. *Answer choices:*

(see index for correct answer)

- a. Social cost
- b. Incremental cost-effectiveness ratio
- c. Cost curve
- d. Opportunity cost

Guidance: level 1

:: Management ::

An _____ is a loosely coupled, self-organizing network of firms that combine their economic output to provide products and services offerings to the market. Firms in the _____ may operate independently, for example, through market mechanisms, or cooperatively through agreements and contracts. They provide value added service or product to the OEM .

Exam Probability: **Low**

2. *Answer choices:*

(see index for correct answer)

- a. Crisis management
- b. Coworking
- c. Product breakdown structure
- d. Extended enterprise

Guidance: level 1

:: Business ::

The seller, or the provider of the goods or services, completes a sale in response to an acquisition, appropriation, requisition or a direct interaction with the buyer at the point of sale. There is a passing of title of the item, and the settlement of a price, in which agreement is reached on a price for which transfer of ownership of the item will occur. The seller, not the purchaser typically executes the sale and it may be completed prior to the obligation of payment. In the case of indirect interaction, a person who sells goods or service on behalf of the owner is known as a _____ man or _____ woman or _____ person, but this often refers to someone selling goods in a store/shop, in which case other terms are also common, including _____ clerk, shop assistant, and retail clerk.

Exam Probability: **Medium**

3. *Answer choices:*

(see index for correct answer)

- a. Mavis Amankwah

- b. Business analysis
- c. Co-creation
- d. Sales

Guidance: level 1

:: ::

In sales, commerce and economics, a _____ is the recipient of a good, service, product or an idea - obtained from a seller, vendor, or supplier via a financial transaction or exchange for money or some other valuable consideration.

Exam Probability: **Medium**

4. *Answer choices:*

(see index for correct answer)

- a. cultural
- b. open system
- c. Customer
- d. co-culture

Guidance: level 1

:: Production economics ::

_____ is the creation of a whole that is greater than the simple sum of its parts. The term _____ comes from the Attic Greek word sea synergia from synergos, , meaning "working together".

Exam Probability: **Medium**

5. *Answer choices:*

(see index for correct answer)

- a. Economic batch quantity
- b. Average fixed cost
- c. Isoquant
- d. Foundations of Economic Analysis

Guidance: level 1

:: Building materials ::

_____ is an alloy of iron and carbon, and sometimes other elements. Because of its high tensile strength and low cost, it is a major component used in buildings, infrastructure, tools, ships, automobiles, machines, appliances, and weapons.

Exam Probability: **High**

6. *Answer choices:*

(see index for correct answer)

- a. Reed mat
- b. Formwork
- c. Steel
- d. Structural building components

Guidance: level 1

:: Costs ::

_____ is the process used by companies to reduce their costs and increase their profits. Depending on a company's services or product, the strategies can vary. Every decision in the product development process affects cost.

Exam Probability: **Medium**

7. *Answer choices:*

(see index for correct answer)

- a. Average cost
- b. Customer Cost
- c. Cost reduction
- d. Cost of poor quality

Guidance: level 1

:: Help desk ::

Data center management is the collection of tasks performed by those responsible for managing ongoing operation of a data center This includes Business service management and planning for the future.

Exam Probability: **High**

8. *Answer choices:*

(see index for correct answer)

- a. OTRS
- b. Virtual help desk
- c. HEAT
- d. Computer-aided maintenance

Guidance: level 1

:: Project management ::

_____ is a work methodology emphasizing the parallelisation of tasks , which is sometimes called simultaneous engineering or integrated product development using an integrated product team approach. It refers to an approach used in product development in which functions of design engineering, manufacturing engineering, and other functions are integrated to reduce the time required to bring a new product to market.

9. *Answer choices:*

(see index for correct answer)

- a. Structured data analysis
- b. Hammock activity
- c. Concurrent engineering
- d. Operational bill

Guidance: level 1

:: Project management ::

_____ is a marketing activity that does an aggregate plan for the production process, in advance of 6 to 18 months, to give an idea to management as to what quantity of materials and other resources are to be procured and when, so that the total cost of operations of the organization is kept to the minimum over that period.

Exam Probability: **Medium**

10. *Answer choices:*

(see index for correct answer)

- a. Product-based planning
- b. ISO 31000

- c. Project accounting
- d. Technology roadmap

Guidance: level 1

:: Waste ::

_____ are unwanted or unusable materials. _____ is any substance which is discarded after primary use, or is worthless, defective and of no use. A by-product by contrast is a joint product of relatively minor economic value. A _____ product may become a by-product, joint product or resource through an invention that raises a _____ product's value above zero.

Exam Probability: **Low**

11. *Answer choices:*

(see index for correct answer)

- a. Ship graveyard
- b. Waste
- c. Business waste
- d. Chaff

Guidance: level 1

:: Distribution, retailing, and wholesaling ::

_____ measures the performance of a system. Certain goals are defined and the _____ gives the percentage to which those goals should be achieved. Fill rate is different from _____ .

Exam Probability: **Low**

12. *Answer choices:*

(see index for correct answer)

- a. Manor
- b. Service level
- c. Free box
- d. Sacrificial leg

Guidance: level 1

:: Production and manufacturing ::

_____ is a production planning, scheduling, and inventory control system used to manage manufacturing processes. Most MRP systems are software-based, but it is possible to conduct MRP by hand as well.

Exam Probability: **Low**

13. *Answer choices:*

(see index for correct answer)

- a. Original design manufacturer
- b. Material requirements planning
- c. First pass yield
- d. Critical to quality

Guidance: level 1

:: Production and manufacturing ::

_____ is a theory of management that analyzes and synthesizes workflows. Its main objective is improving economic efficiency, especially labor productivity. It was one of the earliest attempts to apply science to the engineering of processes and to management. _____ is sometimes known as Taylorism after its founder, Frederick Winslow Taylor.

Exam Probability: **High**

14. *Answer choices:*
(see index for correct answer)

- a. Program evaluation and review technique
- b. Product layout
- c. Nesting
- d. Rolled throughput yield

Guidance: level 1

:: Procurement ::

Purchasing is the formal process of buying goods and services. The _____ can vary from one organization to another, but there are some common key elements.

Exam Probability: **High**

15. *Answer choices:*

(see index for correct answer)

- a. System Design Review
- b. FAPPO
- c. Purchasing process
- d. Second-tier sourcing

Guidance: level 1

:: Project management ::

Rolling-wave planning is the process of project planning in waves as the project proceeds and later details become clearer; similar to the techniques used in agile software development approaches like Scrum..

Exam Probability: **Medium**

16. *Answer choices:*

(see index for correct answer)

- a. Gregory T. Haugan
- b. Graphical path method
- c. Financial plan
- d. Budgeted cost of work performed

Guidance: level 1

:: Decision theory ::

_____ is a method developed in Japan beginning in 1966 to help transform the voice of the customer into engineering characteristics for a product. Yoji Akao, the original developer, described QFD as a "method to transform qualitative user demands into quantitative parameters, to deploy the functions forming quality, and to deploy methods for achieving the design quality into subsystems and component parts, and ultimately to specific elements of the manufacturing process." The author combined his work in quality assurance and quality control points with function deployment used in value engineering.

Exam Probability: **High**

17. *Answer choices:*

(see index for correct answer)

- a. Analysis paralysis
- b. Quality function deployment

- c. Aggregated indices randomization method
- d. Decision field theory

Guidance: level 1

:: E-commerce ::

_____ is the business-to-business or business-to-consumer or business-to-government purchase and sale of supplies, work, and services through the Internet as well as other information and networking systems, such as electronic data interchange and enterprise resource planning.

Exam Probability: **High**

18. *Answer choices:*

(see index for correct answer)

- a. Electronic commerce
- b. GeBIZ
- c. E-procurement
- d. WePay

Guidance: level 1

:: ::

The _____ is a project plan of how the production budget will be spent over a given timescale, for every phase of a business project.

19. *Answer choices:*

(see index for correct answer)

- a. surface-level diversity
- b. information systems assessment
- c. corporate values
- d. Production schedule

Guidance: level 1

:: Costs ::

In economics, _____ is the total economic cost of production and is made up of variable cost, which varies according to the quantity of a good produced and includes inputs such as labour and raw materials, plus fixed cost, which is independent of the quantity of a good produced and includes inputs that cannot be varied in the short term: fixed costs such as buildings and machinery, including sunk costs if any. Since cost is measured per unit of time, it is a flow variable.

20. *Answer choices:*

(see index for correct answer)

- a. Cost curve
- b. Flyaway cost
- c. Total cost
- d. Cost reduction

Guidance: level 1

:: Project management ::

_____ s can take many forms depending on the type of project being implemented and the nature of the organization. The _____ details the project deliverables and describes the major objectives. The objectives should include measurable success criteria for the project.

Exam Probability: **Medium**

21. *Answer choices:*

(see index for correct answer)

- a. Scope statement
- b. Kickoff meeting
- c. Organizational project management
- d. Level of Effort

:: Casting (manufacturing) ::

A _____ is a regularity in the world, man-made design, or abstract ideas. As such, the elements of a _____ repeat in a predictable manner. A geometric _____ is a kind of _____ formed of geometric shapes and typically repeated like a wallpaper design.

Exam Probability: **Medium**

22. *Answer choices:*

(see index for correct answer)

- a. Lost-foam casting
- b. Porosity sealing
- c. Steel casting
- d. Pattern

:: Water ::

_____ is a transparent, tasteless, odorless, and nearly colorless chemical substance, which is the main constituent of Earth's streams, lakes, and oceans, and the fluids of most living organisms. It is vital for all known forms of life, even though it provides no calories or organic nutrients. Its chemical formula is H2O, meaning that each of its molecules contains one oxygen and two hydrogen atoms, connected by covalent bonds. _____ is the name of the liquid state of H2O at standard ambient temperature and pressure. It forms precipitation in the form of rain and aerosols in the form of fog. Clouds are formed from suspended droplets of _____ and ice, its solid state. When finely divided, crystalline ice may precipitate in the form of snow. The gaseous state of _____ is steam or _____ vapor. _____ moves continually through the _____ cycle of evaporation, transpiration , condensation, precipitation, and runoff, usually reaching the sea.

Exam Probability: **High**

23. *Answer choices:*

(see index for correct answer)

- a. Hydraulic head
- b. Metabolic water
- c. Water
- d. Marine ecosystem

Guidance: level 1

:: Project management ::

_____ is a process of setting goals, planning and/or controlling the organizing and leading the execution of any type of activity, such as.

24. *Answer choices:*

(see index for correct answer)

- a. A Guide to the Project Management Body of Knowledge
- b. Design structure matrix
- c. Management process
- d. Resource leveling

Guidance: level 1

:: Process management ::

_____ is a statistics package developed at the Pennsylvania State University by researchers Barbara F. Ryan, Thomas A. Ryan, Jr., and Brian L. Joiner in 1972. It began as a light version of OMNITAB 80, a statistical analysis program by NIST. Statistical analysis software such as _____ automates calculations and the creation of graphs, allowing the user to focus more on the analysis of data and the interpretation of results. It is compatible with other _____ , Inc. software.

25. *Answer choices:*

(see index for correct answer)

- a. Business process discovery
- b. Tampering
- c. Turnaround
- d. Chemical plant cost indexes

Guidance: level 1

:: Business process ::

A _____ or business method is a collection of related, structured activities or tasks by people or equipment which in a specific sequence produce a service or product for a particular customer or customers. _____ es occur at all organizational levels and may or may not be visible to the customers. A _____ may often be visualized as a flowchart of a sequence of activities with interleaving decision points or as a process matrix of a sequence of activities with relevance rules based on data in the process. The benefits of using _____ es include improved customer satisfaction and improved agility for reacting to rapid market change. Process-oriented organizations break down the barriers of structural departments and try to avoid functional silos.

Exam Probability: **High**

26. *Answer choices:*

(see index for correct answer)

- a. Business process management
- b. Steering committee
- c. Business logic
- d. Business process

Guidance: level 1

:: Procurement ::

A _____ is a standard business process whose purpose is to invite suppliers into a bidding process to bid on specific products or services. RfQ generally means the same thing as Call for bids and Invitation for bid .

Exam Probability: **High**

27. *Answer choices:*

(see index for correct answer)

- a. Procurement outsourcing
- b. Full operational capability
- c. Collateral Billing number
- d. Request for quotation

Guidance: level 1

:: Finance ::

_____ is a financial estimate intended to help buyers and owners determine the direct and indirect costs of a product or system. It is a management accounting concept that can be used in full cost accounting or even ecological economics where it includes social costs.

Exam Probability: **Low**

28. *Answer choices:*

(see index for correct answer)

- a. Trading the news
- b. Swisspartners Group
- c. Receivership
- d. Total cost of ownership

Guidance: level 1

:: Quality ::

_____ is a concept first outlined by quality expert Joseph M. Juran in publications, most notably Juran on _____ . Designing for quality and innovation is one of the three universal processes of the Juran Trilogy, in which Juran describes what is required to achieve breakthroughs in new products, services, and processes. Juran believed that quality could be planned, and that most quality crises and problems relate to the way in which quality was planned.

Exam Probability: **Medium**

29. *Answer choices:*

(see index for correct answer)

- a. European Organization for Quality
- b. Quality by Design
- c. Independent test organization
- d. Process architecture

Guidance: level 1

:: Management ::

In inventory management, _____ is the order quantity that minimizes the total holding costs and ordering costs. It is one of the oldest classical production scheduling models. The model was developed by Ford W. Harris in 1913, but R. H. Wilson, a consultant who applied it extensively, and K. Andler are given credit for their in-depth analysis.

Exam Probability: **High**

30. *Answer choices:*

(see index for correct answer)

- a. Crisis management
- b. Economic order quantity
- c. Total Worker Health
- d. Purchasing management

:: Quality ::

The _____ , formerly the _____ Control , is a knowledge-based global community of quality professionals, with nearly 80,000 members dedicated to promoting and advancing quality tools, principles, and practices in their workplaces and communities.

Exam Probability: **High**

31. *Answer choices:*

(see index for correct answer)

- a. Process architecture
- b. Cleaning validation
- c. American Society for Quality
- d. Software Engineering Process Group

:: Information technology management ::

_____ is a collective term for all approaches to prepare , support and help individuals, teams, and organizations in making organizational change. The most common change drivers include: technological evolution, process reviews, crisis, and consumer habit changes; pressure from new business entrants, acquisitions, mergers, and organizational restructuring. It includes methods that redirect or redefine the use of resources, business process, budget allocations, or other modes of operation that significantly change a company or organization. Organizational _____ considers the full organization and what needs to change, while _____ may be used solely to refer to how people and teams are affected by such organizational transition. It deals with many different disciplines, from behavioral and social sciences to information technology and business solutions.

Exam Probability: **Low**

32. *Answer choices:*

(see index for correct answer)

- a. Business-to-business
- b. EDIFACT
- c. Information repository
- d. Information model

Guidance: level 1

:: Marketing ::

_____ or stock control can be broadly defined as "the activity of checking a shop's stock." However, a more focused definition takes into account the more science-based, methodical practice of not only verifying a business' inventory but also focusing on the many related facets of inventory management "within an organisation to meet the demand placed upon that business economically." Other facets of _____ include supply chain management, production control, financial flexibility, and customer satisfaction. At the root of _____ , however, is the _____ problem, which involves determining when to order, how much to order, and the logistics of those decisions.

Exam Probability: **Medium**

33. *Answer choices:*

(see index for correct answer)

- a. Content partnership
- b. Customer interaction tracker
- c. Inventory control
- d. Demand signal repository

Guidance: level 1

:: Computer memory companies ::

_____ Corporation is a Japanese multinational conglomerate headquartered in Tokyo, Japan. Its diversified products and services include information technology and communications equipment and systems, electronic components and materials, power systems, industrial and social infrastructure systems, consumer electronics, household appliances, medical equipment, office equipment, as well as lighting and logistics.

Exam Probability: **High**

34. *Answer choices:*

(see index for correct answer)

- a. Strontium Technology
- b. Winbond
- c. SanDisk
- d. Toshiba

Guidance: level 1

:: Project management ::

_____ is the right to exercise power, which can be formalized by a state and exercised by way of judges, appointed executives of government, or the ecclesiastical or priestly appointed representatives of a God or other deities.

Exam Probability: **Medium**

35. *Answer choices:*

(see index for correct answer)

- a. Defense Acquisition Workforce Improvement Act
- b. Project workforce management
- c. Virtual design and construction
- d. Gantt chart

Guidance: level 1

:: Inventory ::

The _____ is the level of inventory which triggers an action to replenish that particular inventory stock. It is a minimum amount of an item which a firm holds in stock, such that, when stock falls to this amount, the item must be reordered. It is normally calculated as the forecast usage during the replenishment lead time plus safety stock. In the EOQ model, it was assumed that there is no time lag between ordering and procuring of materials. Therefore the _____ for replenishing the stocks occurs at that level when the inventory level drops to zero and because instant delivery by suppliers, the stock level bounce back.

Exam Probability: **High**

36. *Answer choices:*

(see index for correct answer)

- a. Stock mix
- b. Cost of goods available for sale

- c. GMROII
- d. Reorder point

:: Risk analysis ::

Supply-chain risk management is "the implementation of strategies to manage both everyday and exceptional risks along the supply chain based on continuous risk assessment with the objective of reducing vulnerability and ensuring continuity".

Exam Probability: **High**

37. *Answer choices:*

(see index for correct answer)

- a. Extreme risk
- b. Arrow-Lind principle
- c. MOSAIC Threat Assessment Systems
- d. Society for Risk Analysis

:: ::

In production, research, retail, and accounting, a _____ is the value of money that has been used up to produce something or deliver a service, and hence is not available for use anymore. In business, the _____ may be one of acquisition, in which case the amount of money expended to acquire it is counted as _____ . In this case, money is the input that is gone in order to acquire the thing. This acquisition _____ may be the sum of the _____ of production as incurred by the original producer, and further _____ s of transaction as incurred by the acquirer over and above the price paid to the producer. Usually, the price also includes a mark-up for profit over the _____ of production.

Exam Probability: **Medium**

38. *Answer choices:*

(see index for correct answer)

- a. interpersonal communication
- b. personal values
- c. cultural
- d. levels of analysis

Guidance: level 1

:: Alchemical processes ::

In chemistry, a _____ is a special type of homogeneous mixture composed of two or more substances. In such a mixture, a solute is a substance dissolved in another substance, known as a solvent. The mixing process of a _____ happens at a scale where the effects of chemical polarity are involved, resulting in interactions that are specific to solvation. The _____ assumes the phase of the solvent when the solvent is the larger fraction of the mixture, as is commonly the case. The concentration of a solute in a _____ is the mass of that solute expressed as a percentage of the mass of the whole _____ . The term aqueous _____ is when one of the solvents is water.

Exam Probability: **Medium**

39. *Answer choices:*

(see index for correct answer)

- a. Sublimation apparatus
- b. Corporification
- c. Digestion
- d. Congelation

Guidance: level 1

:: Semiconductor companies ::

_____ Corporation is a Japanese multinational conglomerate corporation headquartered in Konan, Minato, Tokyo. Its diversified business includes consumer and professional electronics, gaming, entertainment and financial services. The company owns the largest music entertainment business in the world, the largest video game console business and one of the largest video game publishing businesses, and is one of the leading manufacturers of electronic products for the consumer and professional markets, and a leading player in the film and television entertainment industry. _____ was ranked 97th on the 2018 Fortune Global 500 list.

Exam Probability: **Medium**

40. *Answer choices:*

(see index for correct answer)

- a. Sony
- b. ON Semiconductor
- c. Dynex Semiconductor
- d. EM Microelectronic-Marin

Guidance: level 1

:: Management ::

In economics and marketing, _____ is the process of distinguishing a product or service from others, to make it more attractive to a particular target market. This involves differentiating it from competitors' products as well as a firm's own products. The concept was proposed by Edward Chamberlin in his 1933 The Theory of Monopolistic Competition.

41. *Answer choices:*

(see index for correct answer)

- a. Continuous monitoring
- b. Commercial management
- c. Process management
- d. Iterative and incremental development

Guidance: level 1

:: Industrial equipment ::

_____ s are heat exchangers typically used to provide heat to the bottom of industrial distillation columns. They boil the liquid from the bottom of a distillation column to generate vapors which are returned to the column to drive the distillation separation. The heat supplied to the column by the _____ at the bottom of the column is removed by the condenser at the top of the column.

Exam Probability: **High**

42. *Answer choices:*

(see index for correct answer)

- a. Glass crusher
- b. Cargo net

- c. Reboiler
- d. Multiple-effect evaporator

Guidance: level 1

:: ::

In a supply chain, a _____ , or a seller, is an enterprise that contributes goods or services. Generally, a supply chain _____ manufactures inventory/stock items and sells them to the next link in the chain. Today, these terms refer to a supplier of any good or service.

Exam Probability: **Medium**

43. *Answer choices:*

(see index for correct answer)

- a. functional perspective
- b. Sarbanes-Oxley act of 2002
- c. Vendor
- d. co-culture

Guidance: level 1

:: Project management ::

A _____ is a professional in the field of project management. _____ s have the responsibility of the planning, procurement and execution of a project, in any undertaking that has a defined scope, defined start and a defined finish; regardless of industry. _____ s are first point of contact for any issues or discrepancies arising from within the heads of various departments in an organization before the problem escalates to higher authorities. Project management is the responsibility of a _____ . This individual seldom participates directly in the activities that produce the end result, but rather strives to maintain the progress, mutual interaction and tasks of various parties in such a way that reduces the risk of overall failure, maximizes benefits, and minimizes costs.

Exam Probability: **High**

44. *Answer choices:*

(see index for correct answer)

- a. SQEP
- b. Project accounting
- c. Aggregate planning
- d. Project manager

Guidance: level 1

:: Project management ::

Contemporary business and science treat as a _____ any undertaking, carried out individually or collaboratively and possibly involving research or design, that is carefully planned to achieve a particular aim.

45. *Answer choices:*

(see index for correct answer)

- a. Project sponsorship
- b. Duration
- c. Doctor of Project Management
- d. Risk register

Guidance: level 1

:: Metrics ::

_____ is a computer model developed by the University of Idaho, that uses Landsat satellite data to compute and map evapotranspiration . _____ calculates ET as a residual of the surface energy balance, where ET is estimated by keeping account of total net short wave and long wave radiation at the vegetation or soil surface, the amount of heat conducted into soil, and the amount of heat convected into the air above the surface. The difference in these three terms represents the amount of energy absorbed during the conversion of liquid water to vapor, which is ET. _____ expresses near-surface temperature gradients used in heat convection as indexed functions of radio _____ surface temperature, thereby eliminating the need for absolutely accurate surface temperature and the need for air-temperature measurements.

46. *Answer choices:*

(see index for correct answer)

- a. Guide number
- b. Cleanroom suitability
- c. String metric
- d. Parts-per notation

Guidance: level 1

:: E-commerce ::

_____ is the activity of buying or selling of products on online services or over the Internet. Electronic commerce draws on technologies such as mobile commerce, electronic funds transfer, supply chain management, Internet marketing, online transaction processing, electronic data interchange , inventory management systems, and automated data collection systems.

Exam Probability: **Low**

47. *Answer choices:*

(see index for correct answer)

- a. ISO 8583
- b. Urban Ladder
- c. Types of E-commerce
- d. Gazaro

:: Production and manufacturing ::

An _____ is a manufacturing process in which parts are added as the semi-finished assembly moves from workstation to workstation where the parts are added in sequence until the final assembly is produced. By mechanically moving the parts to the assembly work and moving the semi-finished assembly from work station to work station, a finished product can be assembled faster and with less labor than by having workers carry parts to a stationary piece for assembly.

Exam Probability: **Medium**

48. *Answer choices:*

(see index for correct answer)

- a. Master production schedule
- b. Wireless DNC
- c. Copacker
- d. Assembly line

:: Project management ::

A _____ is one of a series of numbered markers placed along a road or boundary at intervals of one mile or occasionally, parts of a mile. They are typically located at the side of the road or in a median or central reservation. They are alternatively known as mile markers, mileposts or mile posts . Mileage is the distance along the road from a fixed commencement point. Commonly the term " _____ " may also refer to markers placed at other distances, such as every kilometre.

Exam Probability: **Medium**

49. *Answer choices:*

(see index for correct answer)

- a. Product description
- b. Site survey
- c. Milestone
- d. Cost estimate

Guidance: level 1

:: Industrial processes ::

A _____ is a device used for high-temperature heating. The name derives from Latin word fornax, which means oven. The heat energy to fuel a _____ may be supplied directly by fuel combustion, by electricity such as the electric arc _____ , or through induction heating in induction _____ s.

50. *Answer choices:*

(see index for correct answer)

- a. Dry-ice blasting
- b. Furnace
- c. Hydrogenation
- d. Trommel screen

Guidance: level 1

:: Business planning ::

_____ is a critical component to the successful delivery of any project, programme or activity. A stakeholder is any individual, group or organization that can affect, be affected by, or perceive itself to be affected by a programme.

Exam Probability: **High**

51. *Answer choices:*

(see index for correct answer)

- a. Joint decision trap
- b. Strategic planning
- c. Open Options Corporation

- d. Stakeholder management

Guidance: level 1

:: Monopoly (economics) ::

_____ are "efficiencies formed by variety, not volume". For example, a gas station that sells gasoline can sell soda, milk, baked goods, etc through their customer service representatives and thus achieve gasoline companies _____ .

Exam Probability: **Medium**

52. *Answer choices:*
(see index for correct answer)

- a. Network effect
- b. Complementary monopoly
- c. De facto monopoly
- d. Economies of scope

Guidance: level 1

:: Time management ::

_____ is the process of planning and exercising conscious control of time spent on specific activities, especially to increase effectiveness, efficiency, and productivity. It involves a juggling act of various demands upon a person relating to work, social life, family, hobbies, personal interests and commitments with the finiteness of time. Using time effectively gives the person "choice" on spending/managing activities at their own time and expediency.

Exam Probability: **Low**

53. *Answer choices:*

(see index for correct answer)

- a. waiting room
- b. Time management
- c. Getting Things Done
- d. Sufficient unto the day is the evil thereof

Guidance: level 1

:: Production and manufacturing ::

In industry, _____ is a system of maintaining and improving the integrity of production and quality systems through the machines, equipment, processes, and employees that add business value to an organization.

Exam Probability: **High**

54. *Answer choices:*

(see index for correct answer)

- a. ERPNEXT
- b. Technological theory of social production
- c. Engineering validation test
- d. Total productive maintenance

Guidance: level 1

:: Project management ::

In economics, _____ is the assignment of available resources to various uses. In the context of an entire economy, resources can be allocated by various means, such as markets or central planning.

Exam Probability: **Low**

55. *Answer choices:*

(see index for correct answer)

- a. Punch list
- b. Resource allocation
- c. Vertical slice
- d. Scope creep

Guidance: level 1

:: Unit operations ::

_____ is a discipline of thermal engineering that concerns the generation, use, conversion, and exchange of thermal energy between physical systems. _____ is classified into various mechanisms, such as thermal conduction, thermal convection, thermal radiation, and transfer of energy by phase changes. Engineers also consider the transfer of mass of differing chemical species, either cold or hot, to achieve _____ . While these mechanisms have distinct characteristics, they often occur simultaneously in the same system.

Exam Probability: **High**

56. *Answer choices:*

(see index for correct answer)

- a. Sedimentation coefficient
- b. Settling
- c. Unit Operations of Chemical Engineering
- d. Heat transfer

Guidance: level 1

:: Distribution, retailing, and wholesaling ::

The _____ is a distribution channel phenomenon in which forecasts yield supply chain inefficiencies. It refers to increasing swings in inventory in response to shifts in customer demand as one moves further up the supply chain. The concept first appeared in Jay Forrester's Industrial Dynamics and thus it is also known as the Forrester effect. The _____ was named for the way the amplitude of a whip increases down its length. The further from the originating signal, the greater the distortion of the wave pattern. In a similar manner, forecast accuracy decreases as one moves upstream along the supply chain. For example, many consumer goods have fairly consistent consumption at retail but this signal becomes more chaotic and unpredictable as the focus moves away from consumer purchasing behavior.

Exam Probability: **Low**

57. *Answer choices:*

(see index for correct answer)

- a. Bullwhip effect
- b. Sacrificial leg
- c. 350 West Mart Center
- d. Pallet racking

Guidance: level 1

:: Elementary mathematics ::

In mathematics, a _____ is an enumerated collection of objects in which repetitions are allowed. Like a set, it contains members . The number of elements is called the length of the _____ . Unlike a set, the same elements can appear multiple times at different positions in a _____ , and order matters. Formally, a _____ can be defined as a function whose domain is either the set of the natural numbers or the set of the first n natural numbers . The position of an element in a _____ is its rank or index; it is the natural number from which the element is the image. It depends on the context or a specific convention, if the first element has index 0 or 1. When a symbol has been chosen for denoting a _____ , the nth element of the _____ is denoted by this symbol with n as subscript; for example, the nth element of the Fibonacci _____ is generally denoted Fn.

Exam Probability: **Medium**

58. *Answer choices:*

(see index for correct answer)

- a. Square root
- b. Sequence
- c. Like terms
- d. Elementary proof

Guidance: level 1

:: Asset ::

In financial accounting, an _____ is any resource owned by the business. Anything tangible or intangible that can be owned or controlled to produce value and that is held by a company to produce positive economic value is an _____ . Simply stated, _____ s represent value of ownership that can be converted into cash . The balance sheet of a firm records the monetary value of the _____ s owned by that firm. It covers money and other valuables belonging to an individual or to a business.

Exam Probability: **High**

59. *Answer choices:*

(see index for correct answer)

- a. Asset
- b. Current asset

Guidance: level 1

Commerce

Commerce relates to "the exchange of goods and services, especially on a large scale." It includes legal, economic, political, social, cultural and technological systems that operate in any country or internationally.

:: E-commerce ::

_____ is the activity of buying or selling of products on online services or over the Internet. Electronic commerce draws on technologies such as mobile commerce, electronic funds transfer, supply chain management, Internet marketing, online transaction processing, electronic data interchange , inventory management systems, and automated data collection systems.

1. *Answer choices:*

(see index for correct answer)

- a. Spamvertising
- b. Supply chain attack
- c. DigiCash
- d. SAF-T

Guidance: level 1

:: Project management ::

_____ is the right to exercise power, which can be formalized by a state and exercised by way of judges, appointed executives of government, or the ecclesiastical or priestly appointed representatives of a God or other deities.

2. *Answer choices:*

(see index for correct answer)

- a. Project engineering
- b. Risk register
- c. Lean project management

- d. Sequence step algorithm

Guidance: level 1

:: Auctioneering ::

A _____ is one of several similar kinds of auctions. Most commonly, it means an auction in which the auctioneer begins with a high asking price, and lowers it until some participant accepts the price, or it reaches a predetermined reserve price. This has also been called a clock auction or open-outcry descending-price auction. This type of auction is good for auctioning goods quickly, since a sale never requires more than one bid. Strategically, it's similar to a first-price sealed-bid auction.

Exam Probability: **High**

3. *Answer choices:*

(see index for correct answer)

- a. Estate sale
- b. Auction catalog
- c. Dutch auction
- d. Online travel auction

Guidance: level 1

:: International trade ::

An _____ is a good brought into a jurisdiction, especially across a national border, from an external source. The party bringing in the good is called an _____ er. An _____ in the receiving country is an export from the sending country. _____ ation and exportation are the defining financial transactions of international trade.

Exam Probability: **High**

4. *Answer choices:*

(see index for correct answer)

- a. National Foreign Trade Council
- b. Mutual recognition agreement
- c. Vent for surplus
- d. Import

Guidance: level 1

:: ::

A _____ manages, commands, directs, or regulates the behavior of other devices or systems using control loops. It can range from a single home heating controller using a thermostat controlling a domestic boiler to large Industrial _____ s which are used for controlling processes or machines.

Exam Probability: **High**

5. *Answer choices:*

(see index for correct answer)

- a. personal values
- b. co-culture
- c. cultural
- d. Control system

Guidance: level 1

:: Minimum wage ::

A _____ is the lowest remuneration that employers can legally pay their workers—the price floor below which workers may not sell their labor. Most countries had introduced _____ legislation by the end of the 20th century.

Exam Probability: **High**

6. *Answer choices:*

(see index for correct answer)

- a. Working poor
- b. Minimum wage
- c. Guaranteed minimum income
- d. Minimum wage in Taiwan

:: ::

_____ refers to a business or organization attempting to acquire goods or services to accomplish its goals. Although there are several organizations that attempt to set standards in the _____ process, processes can vary greatly between organizations. Typically the word " _____ " is not used interchangeably with the word "procurement", since procurement typically includes expediting, supplier quality, and transportation and logistics in addition to _____ .

Exam Probability: **Medium**

7. *Answer choices:*

(see index for correct answer)

- a. co-culture
- b. interpersonal communication
- c. Purchasing
- d. functional perspective

:: Commerce ::

_____ , Inc. is an American media-services provider headquartered in Los Gatos, California, founded in 1997 by Reed Hastings and Marc Randolph in Scotts Valley, California. The company's primary business is its subscription-based streaming OTT service which offers online streaming of a library of films and television programs, including those produced in-house. As of April 2019, _____ had over 148 million paid subscriptions worldwide, including 60 million in the United States, and over 154 million subscriptions total including free trials. It is available almost worldwide except in mainland China as well as Syria, North Korea, and Crimea . The company also has offices in the Netherlands, Brazil, India, Japan, and South Korea. _____ is a member of the Motion Picture Association of America .

Exam Probability: **Low**

8. *Answer choices:*

(see index for correct answer)

- a. Acquiring bank
- b. Oniomania
- c. Netflix
- d. PIN pad

Guidance: level 1

:: Confidence tricks ::

_____ is the fraudulent attempt to obtain sensitive information such as usernames, passwords and credit card details by disguising oneself as a trustworthy entity in an electronic communication. Typically carried out by email spoofing or instant messaging, it often directs users to enter personal information at a fake website which matches the look and feel of the legitimate site.

Exam Probability: **High**

9. *Answer choices:*

(see index for correct answer)

- a. Phishing
- b. Fortune telling fraud
- c. Blessing scam
- d. The switch

Guidance: level 1

:: ::

A _____ is a fund into which a sum of money is added during an employee's employment years, and from which payments are drawn to support the person's retirement from work in the form of periodic payments. A _____ may be a "defined benefit plan" where a fixed sum is paid regularly to a person, or a "defined contribution plan" under which a fixed sum is invested and then becomes available at retirement age. _____s should not be confused with severance pay; the former is usually paid in regular installments for life after retirement, while the latter is typically paid as a fixed amount after involuntary termination of employment prior to retirement.

Exam Probability: **Low**

10. *Answer choices:*

(see index for correct answer)

- a. Pension
- b. empathy
- c. Character
- d. process perspective

Guidance: level 1

:: ::

A _____ or _____ s is a type of footwear and not a specific type of shoe. Most _____ s mainly cover the foot and the ankle, while some also cover some part of the lower calf. Some _____ s extend up the leg, sometimes as far as the knee or even the hip. Most _____ s have a heel that is clearly distinguishable from the rest of the sole, even if the two are made of one piece. Traditionally made of leather or rubber, modern _____ s are made from a variety of materials. _____ s are worn both for their functionality protecting the foot and leg from water, extreme cold, mud or hazards or providing additional ankle support for strenuous activities with added traction requirements , or may have hobnails on their undersides to protect against wear and to get better grip; and for reasons of style and fashion.

Exam Probability: **Medium**

11. *Answer choices:*

(see index for correct answer)

- a. Boot
- b. deep-level diversity
- c. hierarchical perspective
- d. co-culture

Guidance: level 1

:: ::

The _____ or just chief executive , is the most senior corporate, executive, or administrative officer in charge of managing an organization especially an independent legal entity such as a company or nonprofit institution. CEOs lead a range of organizations, including public and private corporations, non-profit organizations and even some government organizations . The CEO of a corporation or company typically reports to the board of directors and is charged with maximizing the value of the entity, which may include maximizing the share price, market share, revenues or another element. In the non-profit and government sector, CEOs typically aim at achieving outcomes related to the organization's mission, such as reducing poverty, increasing literacy, etc.

Exam Probability: **High**

12. *Answer choices:*

(see index for correct answer)

- a. Chief executive officer
- b. Sarbanes-Oxley act of 2002
- c. process perspective
- d. open system

Guidance: level 1

:: ::

_____ or accountancy is the measurement, processing, and communication of financial information about economic entities such as businesses and corporations. The modern field was established by the Italian mathematician Luca Pacioli in 1494. _____ , which has been called the "language of business", measures the results of an organization's economic activities and conveys this information to a variety of users, including investors, creditors, management, and regulators. Practitioners of _____ are known as accountants. The terms "_____" and "financial reporting" are often used as synonyms.

Exam Probability: **Low**

13. *Answer choices:*

(see index for correct answer)

- a. functional perspective
- b. Accounting
- c. similarity-attraction theory
- d. imperative

Guidance: level 1

:: Project management ::

In political science, an _____ is a means by which a petition signed by a certain minimum number of registered voters can force a government to choose to either enact a law or hold a public vote in parliament in what is called indirect _____, or under direct _____, the proposition is immediately put to a plebiscite or referendum, in what is called a Popular initiated Referendum or citizen-initiated referendum).

Exam Probability: **High**

14. *Answer choices:*

(see index for correct answer)

- a. Dependency
- b. Australian Institute of Project Management
- c. Organizational project management
- d. Critical path drag

Guidance: level 1

:: Accounting source documents ::

An _____, bill or tab is a commercial document issued by a seller to a buyer, relating to a sale transaction and indicating the products, quantities, and agreed prices for products or services the seller had provided the buyer.

Exam Probability: **Low**

15. *Answer choices:*

(see index for correct answer)

- a. Credit memorandum
- b. Superbill
- c. Bank statement
- d. Invoice

Guidance: level 1

:: Insolvency ::

_____ is a legal process through which people or other entities who cannot repay debts to creditors may seek relief from some or all of their debts. In most jurisdictions, _____ is imposed by a court order, often initiated by the debtor.

Exam Probability: **High**

16. *Answer choices:*

(see index for correct answer)

- a. Bankruptcy
- b. Preferential creditor
- c. Insolvency
- d. Liquidator

:: Business law ::

A _____ is a contractual arrangement calling for the lessee to pay the lessor for use of an asset. Property, buildings and vehicles are common assets that are _____ d. Industrial or business equipment is also _____ d.

Exam Probability: **High**

17. *Answer choices:*

(see index for correct answer)

- a. Hundi
- b. Lease
- c. Firm offer
- d. WIPO Copyright Treaty

:: Auctioneering ::

A _____ is a type of sealed-bid auction. Bidders submit written bids without knowing the bid of the other people in the auction. The highest bidder wins but the price paid is the second-highest bid. This type of auction is strategically similar to an English auction and gives bidders an incentive to bid their true value. The auction was first described academically by Columbia University professor William Vickrey in 1961 though it had been used by stamp collectors since 1893. In 1797 Johann Wolfgang von Goethe sold a manuscript using a sealed-bid, second-price auction.

Exam Probability: **Low**

18. *Answer choices:*

(see index for correct answer)

- a. Online auction
- b. Vickrey auction
- c. Reppert School of Auctioneering
- d. National Auctioneers Association

Guidance: level 1

:: Generally Accepted Accounting Principles ::

Expenditure is an outflow of money to another person or group to pay for an item or service, or for a category of costs. For a tenant, rent is an _____ . For students or parents, tuition is an _____ . Buying food, clothing, furniture or an automobile is often referred to as an _____ . An _____ is a cost that is "paid" or "remitted", usually in exchange for something of value. Something that seems to cost a great deal is "expensive". Something that seems to cost little is "inexpensive". " _____ s of the table" are _____ s of dining, refreshments, a feast, etc.

Exam Probability: **High**

19. *Answer choices:*

(see index for correct answer)

- a. Matching principle
- b. Long-term liabilities
- c. Expense
- d. Standard Business Reporting

Guidance: level 1

:: Free market ::

In economics, a _____ is a system in which the prices for goods and services are determined by the open market and by consumers. In a _____, the laws and forces of supply and demand are free from any intervention by a government or other authority and from all forms of economic privilege, monopolies and artificial scarcities. Proponents of the concept of _____ contrast it with a regulated market in which a government intervenes in supply and demand through various methods, such as tariffs, used to restrict trade and to protect the local economy. In an idealized free-market economy, prices for goods and services are set freely by the forces of supply and demand and are allowed to reach their point of equilibrium without intervention by government policy.

Exam Probability: **Low**

20. *Answer choices:*

(see index for correct answer)

- a. Free market
- b. Piece rate

Guidance: level 1

:: Management ::

_____ is the process of thinking about the activities required to achieve a desired goal. It is the first and foremost activity to achieve desired results. It involves the creation and maintenance of a plan, such as psychological aspects that require conceptual skills. There are even a couple of tests to measure someone's capability of _____ well. As such, _____ is a fundamental property of intelligent behavior. An important further meaning, often just called " _____ " is the legal context of permitted building developments.

Exam Probability: **Low**

21. *Answer choices:*

(see index for correct answer)

- a. Authoritarian leadership style
- b. Product breakdown structure
- c. Planning
- d. Hierarchical organization

Guidance: level 1

:: Income ::

_____ is the application of disciplined analytics that predict consumer behaviour at the micro-market levels and optimize product availability and price to maximize revenue growth. The primary aim of _____ is selling the right product to the right customer at the right time for the right price and with the right pack. The essence of this discipline is in understanding customers' perception of product value and accurately aligning product prices, placement and availability with each customer segment.

Exam Probability: **Medium**

22. *Answer choices:*

(see index for correct answer)

- a. Implied level of government service
- b. Gratuity
- c. Revenue management
- d. Trinity study

Guidance: level 1

:: Income ::

In business and accounting, net income is an entity's income minus cost of goods sold, expenses and taxes for an accounting period. It is computed as the residual of all revenues and gains over all expenses and losses for the period, and has also been defined as the net increase in shareholders' equity that results from a company's operations. In the context of the presentation of financial statements, the IFRS Foundation defines net income as synonymous with profit and loss. The difference between revenue and the cost of making a product or providing a service, before deducting overheads, payroll, taxation, and interest payments. This is different from operating income .

Exam Probability: **Low**

23. *Answer choices:*

(see index for correct answer)

- a. Giganomics
- b. National average salary
- c. Return of investment
- d. Real income

Guidance: level 1

:: ::

_____ is the production of products for use or sale using labour and machines, tools, chemical and biological processing, or formulation. The term may refer to a range of human activity, from handicraft to high tech, but is most commonly applied to industrial design, in which raw materials are transformed into finished goods on a large scale. Such finished goods may be sold to other manufacturers for the production of other, more complex products, such as aircraft, household appliances, furniture, sports equipment or automobiles, or sold to wholesalers, who in turn sell them to retailers, who then sell them to end users and consumers.

Exam Probability: **Low**

24. *Answer choices:*

(see index for correct answer)

- a. co-culture
- b. corporate values
- c. levels of analysis
- d. open system

Guidance: level 1

:: International trade ::

_____ involves the transfer of goods or services from one person or entity to another, often in exchange for money. A system or network that allows _____ is called a market.

25. *Answer choices:*

(see index for correct answer)

- a. ATR.1 certificate
- b. Import sensitive product
- c. Autarky
- d. Quota share

Guidance: level 1

:: Marketing ::

_____ or stock control can be broadly defined as "the activity of checking a shop's stock." However, a more focused definition takes into account the more science-based, methodical practice of not only verifying a business' inventory but also focusing on the many related facets of inventory management "within an organisation to meet the demand placed upon that business economically." Other facets of _____ include supply chain management, production control, financial flexibility, and customer satisfaction. At the root of _____ , however, is the _____ problem, which involves determining when to order, how much to order, and the logistics of those decisions.

Exam Probability: **Low**

26. *Answer choices:*

(see index for correct answer)

- a. Processing fluency
- b. Inventory control
- c. Lead management
- d. The customer is always right

Guidance: level 1

:: ::

The _____ is a political and economic union of 28 member states that
are located primarily in Europe. It has an area of 4,475,757 km2 and an
estimated population of about 513 million. The EU has developed an internal
single market through a standardised system of laws that apply in all member
states in those matters, and only those matters, where members have agreed to
act as one. EU policies aim to ensure the free movement of people, goods,
services and capital within the internal market, enact legislation in justice
and home affairs and maintain common policies on trade, agriculture, fisheries
and regional development. For travel within the Schengen Area, passport
controls have been abolished. A monetary union was established in 1999 and came
into full force in 2002 and is composed of 19 EU member states which use the
euro currency.

Exam Probability: **Medium**

27. *Answer choices:*

(see index for correct answer)

- a. Character
- b. empathy

- c. cultural
- d. Sarbanes-Oxley act of 2002

Guidance: level 1

:: Retailing ::

A _____ or trolley , also known by a variety of other names, is a cart supplied by a shop, especially supermarkets, for use by customers inside the shop for transport of merchandise to the checkout counter during shopping. In many cases customers can then also use the cart to transport their purchased goods to their vehicles, but some carts are designed to prevent them from leaving the shop.

Exam Probability: **High**

28. *Answer choices:*

(see index for correct answer)

- a. Shopping cart
- b. Showrooming
- c. Gondola
- d. Shopping channel

Guidance: level 1

:: E-commerce ::

_____ Inc. was an electronic money corporation founded by David Chaum in 1989. _____ transactions were unique in that they were anonymous due to a number of cryptographic protocols developed by its founder. _____ declared bankruptcy in 1998, and subsequently sold its assets to eCash Technologies, another digital currency company, which was acquired by InfoSpace on Feb. 19, 2002.

Exam Probability: **Medium**

29. *Answer choices:*

(see index for correct answer)

- a. Self-certifying key
- b. Coinye
- c. Online Shopping in Bangladesh
- d. DigiCash

Guidance: level 1

:: ::

A _____ is an organization, usually a group of people or a company, authorized to act as a single entity and recognized as such in law. Early incorporated entities were established by charter . Most jurisdictions now allow the creation of new _____ s through registration.

Exam Probability: **Medium**

30. *Answer choices:*

(see index for correct answer)

- a. surface-level diversity
- b. empathy
- c. process perspective
- d. Corporation

Guidance: level 1

:: Marketing techniques ::

_____ is the activity of dividing a broad consumer or business market, normally consisting of existing and potential customers, into sub-groups of consumers based on some type of shared characteristics. In dividing or segmenting markets, researchers typically look for common characteristics such as shared needs, common interests, similar lifestyles or even similar demographic profiles. The overall aim of segmentation is to identify high yield segments – that is, those segments that are likely to be the most profitable or that have growth potential – so that these can be selected for special attention .

Exam Probability: **Medium**

31. *Answer choices:*

(see index for correct answer)

- a. Market segmentation
- b. Trailer

- c. Self-referential marketing
- d. trade loading

Guidance: level 1

:: ::

An _____ is an area of the production, distribution, or trade, and consumption of goods and services by different agents. Understood in its broadest sense, `The _____ is defined as a social domain that emphasize the practices, discourses, and material expressions associated with the production, use, and management of resources`. Economic agents can be individuals, businesses, organizations, or governments. Economic transactions occur when two parties agree to the value or price of the transacted good or service, commonly expressed in a certain currency. However, monetary transactions only account for a small part of the economic domain.

Exam Probability: **Medium**

32. *Answer choices:*

(see index for correct answer)

- a. interpersonal communication
- b. hierarchical
- c. Economy
- d. open system

Guidance: level 1

:: Service industries ::

_____ is travel for pleasure or business; also the theory and practice of touring, the business of attracting, accommodating, and entertaining tourists, and the business of operating tours. _____ may be international, or within the traveller's country. The World _____ Organization defines _____ more generally, in terms which go "beyond the common perception of _____ as being limited to holiday activity only", as people "traveling to and staying in places outside their usual environment for not more than one consecutive year for leisure and not less than 24 hours, business and other purposes".

Exam Probability: **High**

33. *Answer choices:*

(see index for correct answer)

- a. Maid service
- b. Financial services in South Korea
- c. Tourism
- d. Association of Special Fares Agents

Guidance: level 1

:: Marketing ::

_____ or stock is the goods and materials that a business holds for the ultimate goal of resale .

Exam Probability: **Medium**

34. *Answer choices:*

(see index for correct answer)

- a. Davie-Brown Index
- b. Inventory
- c. Hype cycle
- d. Macromarketing

Guidance: level 1

:: Marketing ::

_____ —an information- and communication-based electronic exchange environment—is a relatively new concept in marketing. Since physical boundaries no longer interfere with buy/sell decisions, the world has grown into several industry specific _____ s which are integration of marketplaces through sophisticated computer and telecommunication technologies. The term _____ was introduced by Jeffrey Rayport and John Sviokla in 1994 in their article "Managing in the _____ " that appeared in Harvard Business Review. In the article the authors distinguished between electronic and conventional markets. In a _____ , information and/or physical goods are exchanged, and transactions take place through computers and networks. These networks consist of blogs, forum threads, and micro-blogging services like Twitter. Businesses and their customers are enabled to create conversations and two-way communications about products and services. These conversations may also happen outside the sphere of control of a given business, when a marketing campaign or customer-service issue captures the attention of web-savvy consumers.

Exam Probability: **Medium**

35. *Answer choices:*

(see index for correct answer)

- a. Interruption marketing
- b. Marketspace
- c. Hype cycle
- d. Geographical pricing

Guidance: level 1

:: E-commerce ::

E-commerce is the activity of buying or selling of products on online services or over the Internet. _____ draws on technologies such as mobile commerce, electronic funds transfer, supply chain management, Internet marketing, online transaction processing, electronic data interchange , inventory management systems, and automated data collection systems.

Exam Probability: **High**

36. *Answer choices:*

(see index for correct answer)

- a. Electronic commerce
- b. Camgirl
- c. BuildDirect
- d. AS 2805

Guidance: level 1

:: Commerce ::

An _____ is a bank that offers card association branded payment cards directly to consumers. The name is derived from the practice of issuing payment to the acquiring bank on behalf of its customer .

Exam Probability: **Medium**

37. *Answer choices:*

(see index for correct answer)

- a. White Elephant Sale
- b. Quickbrowse
- c. Netflix
- d. Issuing bank

Guidance: level 1

:: ::

In a supply chain, a _____ , or a seller, is an enterprise that contributes goods or services. Generally, a supply chain _____ manufactures inventory/stock items and sells them to the next link in the chain. Today, these terms refer to a supplier of any good or service.

Exam Probability: **High**

38. *Answer choices:*

(see index for correct answer)

- a. Vendor
- b. Sarbanes-Oxley act of 2002
- c. interpersonal communication
- d. empathy

Guidance: level 1

:: Management ::

A _____ is an idea of the future or desired result that a person or a group of people envisions, plans and commits to achieve. People endeavor to reach _____ s within a finite time by setting deadlines.

Exam Probability: **High**

39. *Answer choices:*

(see index for correct answer)

- a. Nonconformity
- b. Peer pressure
- c. Goal
- d. Product life-cycle management

Guidance: level 1

:: Marketing analytics ::

_____ is a long-term, forward-looking approach to planning with the fundamental goal of achieving a sustainable competitive advantage. Strategic planning involves an analysis of the company's strategic initial situation prior to the formulation, evaluation and selection of market-oriented competitive position that contributes to the company's goals and marketing objectives.

40. *Answer choices:*

(see index for correct answer)

- • a. Marketing resource management
- • b. Sumall
- • c. Mission-driven marketing
- • d. Marketing accountability

Guidance: level 1

:: Debt ::

_____ , in finance and economics, is payment from a borrower or deposit-taking financial institution to a lender or depositor of an amount above repayment of the principal sum , at a particular rate. It is distinct from a fee which the borrower may pay the lender or some third party. It is also distinct from dividend which is paid by a company to its shareholders from its profit or reserve, but not at a particular rate decided beforehand, rather on a pro rata basis as a share in the reward gained by risk taking entrepreneurs when the revenue earned exceeds the total costs.

Exam Probability: **High**

41. *Answer choices:*

(see index for correct answer)

- a. Vulture fund
- b. Household debt
- c. Interest
- d. Debt compliance

Guidance: level 1

:: Contract law ::

A _____ is a legally-binding agreement which recognises and governs the rights and duties of the parties to the agreement. A _____ is legally enforceable because it meets the requirements and approval of the law. An agreement typically involves the exchange of goods, services, money, or promises of any of those. In the event of breach of _____ , the law awards the injured party access to legal remedies such as damages and cancellation.

Exam Probability: **High**

42. *Answer choices:*

(see index for correct answer)

- a. Morals clause
- b. Contract
- c. Voidable contract
- d. Executory contract

Guidance: level 1

:: Management accounting ::

_____ s are costs that change as the quantity of the good or service that a business produces changes. _____ s are the sum of marginal costs over all units produced. They can also be considered normal costs. Fixed costs and _____ s make up the two components of total cost. Direct costs are costs that can easily be associated with a particular cost object. However, not all _____ s are direct costs. For example, variable manufacturing overhead costs are _____ s that are indirect costs, not direct costs. _____ s are sometimes called unit-level costs as they vary with the number of units produced.

Exam Probability: **Medium**

43. *Answer choices:*

(see index for correct answer)

- a. Direct material price variance
- b. Direct material usage variance
- c. Variable cost
- d. Cash and cash equivalents

Guidance: level 1

:: Management occupations ::

_____ ship is the process of designing, launching and running a new business, which is often initially a small business. The people who create these businesses are called _____ s.

Exam Probability: **Low**

44. *Answer choices:*

(see index for correct answer)

- a. Chief design officer
- b. Chief business development officer
- c. General counsel
- d. Financial secretary

Guidance: level 1

:: Consumer theory ::

A _____ is a technical term in psychology, economics and philosophy usually used in relation to choosing between alternatives. For example, someone prefers A over B if they would rather choose A than B.

Exam Probability: **Low**

45. *Answer choices:*

(see index for correct answer)

- a. Quality bias
- b. Elasticity of intertemporal substitution
- c. Compensated demand
- d. Autonomous consumption

Guidance: level 1

:: Marketing ::

_____ is a concept introduced in a book of the same name in 1999 by marketing expert Seth Godin. _____ is a non-traditional marketing technique that advertises goods and services when advance consent is given.

Exam Probability: **High**

46. *Answer choices:*

(see index for correct answer)

- a. Neuromarketing
- b. Promo
- c. Permission marketing
- d. elaboration likelihood model

Guidance: level 1

:: ::

_____ , also referred to as orthostasis, is a human position in which the body is held in an upright position and supported only by the feet.

47. *Answer choices:*

(see index for correct answer)

- a. corporate values
- b. empathy
- c. Sarbanes-Oxley act of 2002
- d. interpersonal communication

Guidance: level 1

:: ::

_____ are electronic transfer of money from one bank account to another, either within a single financial institution or across multiple institutions, via computer-based systems, without the direct intervention of bank staff.

48. *Answer choices:*

(see index for correct answer)

- a. cultural
- b. Electronic funds transfer
- c. corporate values
- d. functional perspective

Guidance: level 1

:: Real property law ::

A _____ is the grant of authority or rights, stating that the granter formally recognizes the prerogative of the recipient to exercise the rights specified. It is implicit that the granter retains superiority , and that the recipient admits a limited status within the relationship, and it is within that sense that _____ s were historically granted, and that sense is retained in modern usage of the term.

Exam Probability: **High**

49. *Answer choices:*

(see index for correct answer)

- a. Charter
- b. Contract for deed
- c. Lateral and subjacent support
- d. Disseisor

Guidance: level 1

:: Business terms ::

The _____ or reception is an area where visitors arrive and first encounter a staff at a place of business. _____ staff will deal with whatever question the visitor has and put them in contact with a relevant person at the company. Broadly speaking, the _____ includes roles that affect the revenues of the business. The term _____ is in contrast to the term back office which refers to a company's operations, personnel, accounting, payroll and financial departments which do not interact directly with customers.

Exam Probability: **Medium**

50. *Answer choices:*

(see index for correct answer)

- a. Owner Controlled Insurance Program
- b. Front office
- c. Mission statement
- d. organizational capital

Guidance: level 1

:: Supply chain management ::

_____ is a variable pricing strategy, based on understanding, anticipating and influencing consumer behavior in order to maximize revenue or profits from a fixed, time-limited resource . As a specific, inventory-focused branch of revenue management, _____ involves strategic control of inventory to sell the right product to the right customer at the right time for the right price. This process can result in price discrimination, in which customers consuming identical goods or services are charged different prices.

_____ is a large revenue generator for several major industries; Robert Crandall, former Chairman and CEO of American Airlines, gave _____ its name and has called it "the single most important technical development in transportation management since we entered deregulation."

Exam Probability: **Low**

51. *Answer choices:*

(see index for correct answer)

- a. Design for logistics
- b. Supply chain cyber security
- c. Yield management
- d. Security risk

Guidance: level 1

:: Industry ::

_____ describes various measures of the efficiency of production. Often , a _____ measure is expressed as the ratio of an aggregate output to a single input or an aggregate input used in a production process, i.e. output per unit of input. Most common example is the labour _____ measure, e.g., such as GDP per worker. There are many different definitions of _____ and the choice among them depends on the purpose of the _____ measurement and/or data availability. The key source of difference between various _____ measures is also usually related to how the outputs and the inputs are aggregated into scalars to obtain such a ratio-type measure of _____ .

Exam Probability: **Medium**

52. *Answer choices:*

(see index for correct answer)

- a. Recommended exposure limit
- b. Fordism
- c. Productivity
- d. Economic importance of bacteria

Guidance: level 1

:: ::

In international relations, _____ is – from the perspective of governments – a voluntary transfer of resources from one country to another.

53. *Answer choices:*

(see index for correct answer)

- a. Aid
- b. personal values
- c. co-culture
- d. empathy

Guidance: level 1

:: E-commerce ::

The phrase _____ was originally coined in 1997 by Kevin Duffey at the launch of the Global _____ Forum, to mean "the delivery of electronic commerce capabilities directly into the consumer's hand, anywhere, via wireless technology." Many choose to think of _____ as meaning "a retail outlet in your customer's pocket."

Exam Probability: **Medium**

54. *Answer choices:*

(see index for correct answer)

- a. Mobile ticketing
- b. Online food ordering

- c. Mobile commerce
- d. ITransact

Guidance: level 1

:: Management ::

Logistics is generally the detailed organization and implementation of a complex operation. In a general business sense, logistics is the management of the flow of things between the point of origin and the point of consumption in order to meet requirements of customers or corporations. The resources managed in logistics may include tangible goods such as materials, equipment, and supplies, as well as food and other consumable items. The logistics of physical items usually involves the integration of information flow, materials handling, production, packaging, inventory, transportation, warehousing, and often security.

Exam Probability: **High**

55. *Answer choices:*

(see index for correct answer)

- a. Productive efficiency
- b. Crisis management
- c. Logistics Management
- d. Lead scoring

Guidance: level 1

:: Auctioneering ::

An _____ is a process of buying and selling goods or services by offering them up for bid, taking bids, and then selling the item to the highest bidder. The open ascending price _____ is arguably the most common form of _____ in use today. Participants bid openly against one another, with each subsequent bid required to be higher than the previous bid. An _____ eer may announce prices, bidders may call out their bids themselves , or bids may be submitted electronically with the highest current bid publicly displayed. In a Dutch _____ , the _____ eer begins with a high asking price for some quantity of like items; the price is lowered until a participant is willing to accept the _____ eer`s price for some quantity of the goods in the lot or until the seller`s reserve price is met. While _____ s are most associated in the public imagination with the sale of antiques, paintings, rare collectibles and expensive wines, _____ s are also used for commodities, livestock, radio spectrum and used cars. In economic theory, an _____ may refer to any mechanism or set of trading rules for exchange.

Exam Probability: **High**

56. *Answer choices:*

(see index for correct answer)

- a. Proxy bid
- b. Estate sale
- c. Unique bid auction
- d. Auction

Guidance: level 1

_____ s are formal, sociotechnical, organizational systems designed to collect, process, store, and distribute information. In a sociotechnical perspective, _____ s are composed by four components: task, people, structure , and technology.

Exam Probability: **Low**

57. *Answer choices:*

(see index for correct answer)

- a. levels of analysis
- b. personal values
- c. Information system
- d. interpersonal communication

Guidance: level 1

:: Supply chain management ::

_____ is the removal of intermediaries in economics from a supply chain, or cutting out the middlemen in connection with a transaction or a series of transactions. Instead of going through traditional distribution channels, which had some type of intermediary , companies may now deal with customers directly, for example via the Internet. Hence, the use of factory direct and direct from the factory to mean the same thing.

58. *Answer choices:*

(see index for correct answer)

- a. Disintermediation
- b. Spend analysis
- c. ISO/PAS 28000
- d. Capconn

Guidance: level 1

:: Information technology management ::

_____ s or pop-ups are forms of online advertising on the World Wide Web. A pop-up is a graphical user interface display area, usually a small window, that suddenly appears in the foreground of the visual interface. The pop-up window containing an advertisement is usually generated by JavaScript that uses cross-site scripting, sometimes with a secondary payload that uses Adobe Flash. They can also be generated by other vulnerabilities/security holes in browser security.

Exam Probability: **Low**

59. *Answer choices:*

(see index for correct answer)

- a. Pop-up ad

- b. Digital Fuel
- c. DocSTAR
- d. Aarohan

Guidance: level 1

Business ethics

Business ethics (also known as corporate ethics) is a form of applied ethics or professional ethics, that examines ethical principles and moral or ethical problems that can arise in a business environment. It applies to all aspects of business conduct and is relevant to the conduct of individuals and entire organizations. These ethics originate from individuals, organizational statements or from the legal system. These norms, values, ethical, and unethical practices are what is used to guide business. They help those businesses maintain a better connection with their stakeholders.

:: Corporate governance ::

_____ refers to the practice of members of a corporate board of directors serving on the boards of multiple corporations. A person that sits on multiple boards is known as a multiple director. Two firms have a direct interlock if a director or executive of one firm is also a director of the other, and an indirect interlock if a director of each sits on the board of a third firm. This practice, although widespread and lawful, raises questions about the quality and independence of board decisions.

Exam Probability: **High**

1. *Answer choices:*

(see index for correct answer)

- a. Gender representation on corporate boards of directors
- b. Chief innovation officer
- c. Australian Institute of Company Directors
- d. Interlocking directorate

Guidance: level 1

:: Utilitarianism ::

_____ is a family of consequentialist ethical theories that promotes actions that maximize happiness and well-being for the majority of a population. Although different varieties of _____ admit different characterizations, the basic idea behind all of them is to in some sense maximize utility, which is often defined in terms of well-being or related concepts. For instance, Jeremy Bentham, the founder of _____, described utility as

2. *Answer choices:*

(see index for correct answer)

- a. Global Happiness Organization
- b. Hedonism
- c. Utilitarianism
- d. Paradox of hedonism

Guidance: level 1

:: Electronic waste ::

_____ or e-waste describes discarded electrical or electronic devices. Used electronics which are destined for refurbishment, reuse, resale, salvage, recycling through material recovery, or disposal are also considered e-waste. Informal processing of e-waste in developing countries can lead to adverse human health effects and environmental pollution.

Exam Probability: **Low**

3. *Answer choices:*

(see index for correct answer)

- a. Digger gold
- b. Electronic waste

- c. Solving the E-waste Problem
- d. ReGlobe

Guidance: level 1

:: ::

The _____ of 1973 serves as the enacting legislation to carry out the provisions outlined in The Convention on International Trade in Endangered Species of Wild Fauna and Flora . Designed to protect critically imperiled species from extinction as a "consequence of economic growth and development untempered by adequate concern and conservation", the ESA was signed into law by President Richard Nixon on December 28, 1973. The law requires federal agencies to consult with the Fish and Wildlife Service &/or the NOAA Fisheries Service to ensure their actions are not likely to jeopardize the continued existence of any listed species or result in the destruction or adverse modification of designated critical habitat of such species. The U.S. Supreme Court found that "the plain intent of Congress in enacting" the ESA "was to halt and reverse the trend toward species extinction, whatever the cost." The Act is administered by two federal agencies, the United States Fish and Wildlife Service and the National Marine Fisheries Service .

Exam Probability: **Low**

4. *Answer choices:*

(see index for correct answer)

- a. personal values
- b. Endangered Species Act
- c. surface-level diversity

- d. deep-level diversity

Guidance: level 1

:: Globalization-related theories ::

_____ is an economic system based on the private ownership of the means of production and their operation for profit. Characteristics central to _____ include private property, capital accumulation, wage labor, voluntary exchange, a price system, and competitive markets. In a capitalist market economy, decision-making and investment are determined by every owner of wealth, property or production ability in financial and capital markets, whereas prices and the distribution of goods and services are mainly determined by competition in goods and services markets.

Exam Probability: **Low**

5. *Answer choices:*

(see index for correct answer)

- a. postmodernism
- b. post-industrial
- c. Capitalism

Guidance: level 1

:: ::

A _____ is an organization, usually a group of people or a company, authorized to act as a single entity and recognized as such in law. Early incorporated entities were established by charter . Most jurisdictions now allow the creation of new _____ s through registration.

Exam Probability: **Medium**

6. *Answer choices:*

(see index for correct answer)

- a. Corporation
- b. co-culture
- c. deep-level diversity
- d. personal values

Guidance: level 1

:: ::

_____ is a naturally occurring, yellowish-black liquid found in geological formations beneath the Earth's surface. It is commonly refined into various types of fuels. Components of _____ are separated using a technique called fractional distillation, i.e. separation of a liquid mixture into fractions differing in boiling point by means of distillation, typically using a fractionating column.

Exam Probability: **Medium**

7. *Answer choices:*

(see index for correct answer)

- a. Petroleum
- b. open system
- c. Sarbanes-Oxley act of 2002
- d. process perspective

Guidance: level 1

:: United States federal defense and national security legislation ::

The USA _____ is an Act of the U.S. Congress that was signed into law by President George W. Bush on October 26, 2001. The title of the Act is a contrived three letter initialism preceding a seven letter acronym , which in combination stand for Uniting and Strengthening America by Providing Appropriate Tools Required to Intercept and Obstruct Terrorism Act of 2001. The acronym was created by a 23 year old Congressional staffer, Chris Kyle.

Exam Probability: **High**

8. *Answer choices:*

(see index for correct answer)

- a. Patriot Act
- b. Export Administration Act

Guidance: level 1

In ecology, a _____ is the type of natural environment in which a particular species of organism lives. It is characterized by both physical and biological features. A species` _____ is those places where it can find food, shelter, protection and mates for reproduction.

Exam Probability: **High**

9. *Answer choices:*

(see index for correct answer)

- a. Habitat
- b. process perspective
- c. levels of analysis
- d. open system

Guidance: level 1

:: Corporate scandals ::

The _____ was a privately held international group of financial services companies controlled by Allen Stanford, until it was seized by United States authorities in early 2009. Headquartered in the Galleria Tower II in Uptown Houston, Texas, it had 50 offices in several countries, mainly in the Americas, included the Stanford International Bank, and said it managed US$8.5 billion of assets for more than 30,000 clients in 136 countries on six continents. On February 17, 2009, U.S. Federal agents placed the company into receivership due to charges of fraud. Ten days later, the U.S. Securities and Exchange Commission amended its complaint to accuse Stanford of turning the company into a "massive Ponzi scheme".

Exam Probability: **High**

10. *Answer choices:*

(see index for correct answer)

- a. Madoff investment scandal
- b. Lynn Brewer
- c. Stanford Financial Group
- d. Guinness share-trading fraud

Guidance: level 1

:: Advertising techniques ::

The _____ is a story from the Trojan War about the subterfuge that the Greeks used to enter the independent city of Troy and win the war. In the canonical version, after a fruitless 10-year siege, the Greeks constructed a huge wooden horse, and hid a select force of men inside including Odysseus. The Greeks pretended to sail away, and the Trojans pulled the horse into their city as a victory trophy. That night the Greek force crept out of the horse and opened the gates for the rest of the Greek army, which had sailed back under cover of night. The Greeks entered and destroyed the city of Troy, ending the war.

Exam Probability: **Low**

11. *Answer choices:*

(see index for correct answer)

- a. Inconsistent comparison
- b. Media clip
- c. Below the line
- d. Transpromotional

Guidance: level 1

:: Fraud ::

In law, _____ is intentional deception to secure unfair or unlawful gain, or to deprive a victim of a legal right. _____ can violate civil law, a criminal law, or it may cause no loss of money, property or legal right but still be an element of another civil or criminal wrong. The purpose of _____ may be monetary gain or other benefits, for example by obtaining a passport, travel document, or driver's license, or mortgage _____, where the perpetrator may attempt to qualify for a mortgage by way of false statements.

Exam Probability: **Medium**

12. *Answer choices:*

(see index for correct answer)

- a. Adoption fraud
- b. Swatting
- c. Fraud
- d. Health care fraud

Guidance: level 1

:: ::

The Federal National Mortgage Association , commonly known as _____ , is a United States government-sponsored enterprise and, since 1968, a publicly traded company. Founded in 1938 during the Great Depression as part of the New Deal, the corporation's purpose is to expand the secondary mortgage market by securitizing mortgage loans in the form of mortgage-backed securities , allowing lenders to reinvest their assets into more lending and in effect increasing the number of lenders in the mortgage market by reducing the reliance on locally based savings and loan associations . Its brother organization is the Federal Home Loan Mortgage Corporation , better known as Freddie Mac. As of 2018, _____ is ranked #21 on the Fortune 500 rankings of the largest United States corporations by total revenue.

Exam Probability: **High**

13. *Answer choices:*

(see index for correct answer)

- a. cultural
- b. co-culture
- c. Fannie Mae
- d. functional perspective

Guidance: level 1

:: Utilitarianism ::

_____ is a school of thought that argues that the pursuit of pleasure and intrinsic goods are the primary or most important goals of human life. A hedonist strives to maximize net pleasure . However upon finally gaining said pleasure, happiness may remain stationary.

Exam Probability: **High**

14. *Answer choices:*

(see index for correct answer)

- a. The Theory of Good and Evil
- b. Mere addition paradox
- c. Informed judge
- d. Hedonism

Guidance: level 1

:: ::

The _____ , founded in 1912, is a private, nonprofit organization whose self-described mission is to focus on advancing marketplace trust, consisting of 106 independently incorporated local BBB organizations in the United States and Canada, coordinated under the Council of _____ s in Arlington, Virginia.

Exam Probability: **Low**

15. *Answer choices:*

(see index for correct answer)

- a. levels of analysis
- b. Better Business Bureau
- c. interpersonal communication
- d. similarity-attraction theory

Guidance: level 1

:: Trade unions ::

A _____ was a group formed of private citizens to administer law and order where they considered governmental structures to be inadequate. The term is commonly associated with the frontier areas of the American West in the mid-19th century, where groups attacked cattle rustlers and gangs, and people at gold mining claims. As non-state organizations no functioning checks existed to protect against excessive force or safeguard due process from the committees. In the years prior to the Civil War, some committees worked to free slaves and transport them to freedom.

Exam Probability: **Medium**

16. *Answer choices:*

(see index for correct answer)

- a. Craft unionism
- b. National trade union center

- c. Global Labour University
- d. Opposition to trade unions

Guidance: level 1

:: ::

The American Recovery and Reinvestment Act of 2009 , nicknamed the
_____ , was a stimulus package enacted by the 111th U.S. Congress and
signed into law by President Barack Obama in February 2009. Developed in
response to the Great Recession, the ARRA's primary objective was to save
existing jobs and create new ones as soon as possible. Other objectives were to
provide temporary relief programs for those most affected by the recession and
invest in infrastructure, education, health, and renewable energy.

Exam Probability: **High**

17. *Answer choices:*

(see index for correct answer)

- a. personal values
- b. Recovery Act
- c. cultural
- d. hierarchical perspective

Guidance: level 1

:: Waste ::

_____ is any unwanted material in all forms that can cause harm . Many of today`s household products such as televisions, computers and phones contain toxic chemicals that can pollute the air and contaminate soil and water. Disposing of such waste is a major public health issue.

Exam Probability: **Low**

18. *Answer choices:*

(see index for correct answer)

- a. Waste heat
- b. Controlled waste
- c. Spent caustic
- d. Toxic waste

Guidance: level 1

:: Management ::

A _____ describes the rationale of how an organization creates, delivers, and captures value, in economic, social, cultural or other contexts. The process of _____ construction and modification is also called _____ innovation and forms a part of business strategy.

Exam Probability: **Low**

19. *Answer choices:*

(see index for correct answer)

- a. Management entrenchment
- b. Business model
- c. Work breakdown structure
- d. Radical transparency

Guidance: level 1

:: Mortgage ::

In finance, _____ means making loans to people who may have difficulty maintaining the repayment schedule, sometimes reflecting setbacks, such as unemployment, divorce, medical emergencies, etc. Historically, subprime borrowers were defined as having FICO scores below 600, although "this has varied over time and circumstances."

Exam Probability: **Low**

20. *Answer choices:*

(see index for correct answer)

- a. Negative amortization
- b. Reverse mortgage
- c. Fixed-rate mortgage
- d. Subprime lending

:: Social philosophy ::

The _____ describes the unintended social benefits of an individual's self-interested actions. Adam Smith first introduced the concept in The Theory of Moral Sentiments, written in 1759, invoking it in reference to income distribution. In this work, however, the idea of the market is not discussed, and the word "capitalism" is never used.

Exam Probability: **Low**

21. *Answer choices:*

(see index for correct answer)

- a. Invisible hand
- b. Veil of Ignorance
- c. Societal attitudes towards abortion
- d. Freedom to contract

:: United States federal trade legislation ::

The _____ of 1914 established the Federal Trade Commission. The Act, signed into law by Woodrow Wilson in 1914, outlaws unfair methods of competition and outlaws unfair acts or practices that affect commerce.

Exam Probability: **High**

22. *Answer choices:*

(see index for correct answer)

- a. Federal Trade Commission Act
- b. Cargo Preference Act
- c. Tariff of 1792
- d. McKinley Tariff

Guidance: level 1

:: ::

_____ is an eight-block-long street running roughly northwest to southeast from Broadway to South Street, at the East River, in the Financial District of Lower Manhattan in New York City. Over time, the term has become a metonym for the financial markets of the United States as a whole, the American financial services industry , or New York–based financial interests.

Exam Probability: **High**

23. *Answer choices:*

(see index for correct answer)

- a. cultural
- b. Wall Street
- c. hierarchical perspective
- d. surface-level diversity

Guidance: level 1

:: ::

_____ is a bundle of characteristics, including ways of thinking, feeling, and acting, which humans are said to have naturally. The term is often regarded as capturing what it is to be human, or the essence of humanity. The term is controversial because it is disputed whether or not such an essence exists. Arguments about _____ have been a mainstay of philosophy for centuries and the concept continues to provoke lively philosophical debate. The concept also continues to play a role in science, with neuroscientists, psychologists and social scientists sometimes claiming that their results have yielded insight into _____ . _____ is traditionally contrasted with characteristics that vary among humans, such as characteristics associated with specific cultures. Debates about _____ are related to, although not the same as, debates about the comparative importance of genes and environment in development .

Exam Probability: **Low**

24. *Answer choices:*

(see index for correct answer)

- a. Sarbanes-Oxley act of 2002
- b. Human nature
- c. corporate values
- d. co-culture

Guidance: level 1

:: Private equity ::

In finance, a high-yield bond is a bond that is rated below investment grade. These bonds have a higher risk of default or other adverse credit events, but typically pay higher yields than better quality bonds in order to make them attractive to investors.

Exam Probability: **High**

25. *Answer choices:*

(see index for correct answer)

- a. Private money investing
- b. Junk bond
- c. World Business Angels Association
- d. Fund derivative

Guidance: level 1

:: Labour law ::

An _____ is special or specified circumstances that partially or fully exempt a person or organization from performance of a legal obligation so as to avoid an unreasonable or disproportionate burden or obstacle.

Exam Probability: **High**

26. *Answer choices:*

(see index for correct answer)

- a. Undue hardship
- b. Vesting
- c. Emanation of the state
- d. Occupational disease

Guidance: level 1

:: Auditing ::

_____ refers to the independence of the internal auditor or of the external auditor from parties that may have a financial interest in the business being audited. Independence requires integrity and an objective approach to the audit process. The concept requires the auditor to carry out his or her work freely and in an objective manner.

Exam Probability: **High**

27. *Answer choices:*

(see index for correct answer)

- a. Risk based internal audit
- b. Lease audit
- c. Audit storm
- d. Internal control

Guidance: level 1

:: Human resource management ::

_____ encompasses values and behaviors that contribute to the unique social and psychological environment of a business. The _____ influences the way people interact, the context within which knowledge is created, the resistance they will have towards certain changes, and ultimately the way they share knowledge. _____ represents the collective values, beliefs and principles of organizational members and is a product of factors such as history, product, market, technology, strategy, type of employees, management style, and national culture; culture includes the organization's vision, values, norms, systems, symbols, language, assumptions, environment, location, beliefs and habits.

Exam Probability: **Medium**

28. *Answer choices:*

(see index for correct answer)

- a. Human resource management in public administration

- b. Open-book management
- c. Simultaneous recruiting of new graduates
- d. Organizational culture

Guidance: level 1

:: Marketing ::

_____ is the marketing of products that are presumed to be environmentally safe. It incorporates a broad range of activities, including product modification, changes to the production process, sustainable packaging, as well as modifying advertising. Yet defining _____ is not a simple task where several meanings intersect and contradict each other; an example of this will be the existence of varying social, environmental and retail definitions attached to this term. Other similar terms used are environmental marketing and ecological marketing.

Exam Probability: **Low**

29. *Answer choices:*

(see index for correct answer)

- a. Niche market
- b. Green marketing
- c. Kidification
- d. Generic brand

Guidance: level 1

:: ::

_____ Ltd. is the world's 2nd largest offshore drilling contractor and is based in Vernier, Switzerland. The company has offices in 20 countries, including Switzerland, Canada, United States, Norway, Scotland, India, Brazil, Singapore, Indonesia and Malaysia.

Exam Probability: **Low**

30. *Answer choices:*

(see index for correct answer)

- a. surface-level diversity
- b. Transocean
- c. hierarchical
- d. Sarbanes-Oxley act of 2002

Guidance: level 1

:: ::

_____ is the means to see, hear, or become aware of something or someone through our fundamental senses. The term _____ derives from the Latin word perceptio, and is the organization, identification, and interpretation of sensory information in order to represent and understand the presented information, or the environment.

31. *Answer choices:*

(see index for correct answer)

- a. Character
- b. functional perspective
- c. cultural
- d. Perception

Guidance: level 1

:: ::

The Ethics & Compliance Initiative was formed in 2015 and consists of three nonprofit organizations: the Ethics Research Center, the Ethics & Compliance Association, and the Ethics & Compliance Certification Institute. Based in Arlington, Virginia, United States, ECI is devoted to the advancement of high ethical standards and practices in public and private institutions, and provides research about ethical standards, workplace integrity, and compliance practices and processes.

32. *Answer choices:*

(see index for correct answer)

- a. Ethics Resource Center

- b. levels of analysis
- c. interpersonal communication
- d. open system

Guidance: level 1

:: Carbon finance ::

The _____ is an international treaty which extends the 1992 United Nations Framework Convention on Climate Change that commits state parties to reduce greenhouse gas emissions, based on the scientific consensus that global warming is occurring and it is extremely likely that human-made CO2 emissions have predominantly caused it. The _____ was adopted in Kyoto, Japan on 11 December 1997 and entered into force on 16 February 2005. There are currently 192 parties to the Protocol.

Exam Probability: **Medium**

33. *Answer choices:*
(see index for correct answer)

- a. CEB VER
- b. Reducing emissions from deforestation and forest degradation
- c. Plant A Tree Today Foundation
- d. Carbon Clear

Guidance: level 1

:: Anti-capitalism ::

_____ is a range of economic and social systems characterised by social ownership of the means of production and workers' self-management, as well as the political theories and movements associated with them. Social ownership can be public, collective or cooperative ownership, or citizen ownership of equity. There are many varieties of _____ and there is no single definition encapsulating all of them, with social ownership being the common element shared by its various forms.

Exam Probability: **High**

34. *Answer choices:*

(see index for correct answer)

- a. Deep Green Resistance
- b. Libcom.org
- c. Socialism
- d. Roots of Resistance

Guidance: level 1

:: Confidence tricks ::

A _____ is a form of fraud that lures investors and pays profits to earlier investors with funds from more recent investors. The scheme leads victims to believe that profits are coming from product sales or other means, and they remain unaware that other investors are the source of funds. A _____ can maintain the illusion of a sustainable business as long as new investors contribute new funds, and as long as most of the investors do not demand full repayment and still believe in the non-existent assets they are purported to own.

Exam Probability: **Low**

35. *Answer choices:*

(see index for correct answer)

- a. Blessing scam
- b. Ponzi scheme
- c. Confidence trick
- d. Patent safe

Guidance: level 1

:: United States federal labor legislation ::

The _____ of 1988 is a United States federal law that generally prevents employers from using polygraph tests, either for pre-employment screening or during the course of employment, with certain exemptions.

Exam Probability: **Medium**

36. *Answer choices:*

- a. Employee Polygraph Protection Act
- b. Railway Labor Act
- c. Pension Protection Act of 2006
- d. Uniformed Services Employment and Reemployment Rights Act

Guidance: level 1

:: ::

A _____ is the ability to carry out a task with determined results often within a given amount of time, energy, or both. _____ s can often be divided into domain-general and domain-specific _____ s. For example, in the domain of work, some general _____ s would include time management, teamwork and leadership, self-motivation and others, whereas domain-specific _____ s would be used only for a certain job. _____ usually requires certain environmental stimuli and situations to assess the level of _____ being shown and used.

Exam Probability: **Low**

37. *Answer choices:*

- a. process perspective
- b. hierarchical perspective

- c. cultural
- d. interpersonal communication

Guidance: level 1

:: ::

In regulatory jurisdictions that provide for it , _____ is a group of laws and organizations designed to ensure the rights of consumers as well as fair trade, competition and accurate information in the marketplace. The laws are designed to prevent the businesses that engage in fraud or specified unfair practices from gaining an advantage over competitors. They may also provides additional protection for those most vulnerable in society. _____ laws are a form of government regulation that aim to protect the rights of consumers. For example, a government may require businesses to disclose detailed information about products—particularly in areas where safety or public health is an issue, such as food.

Exam Probability: **Low**

38. *Answer choices:*

(see index for correct answer)

- a. personal values
- b. similarity-attraction theory
- c. co-culture
- d. Consumer Protection

Guidance: level 1

:: Agricultural labor ::

The _____ of America, or more commonly just _____ , is a labor union for farmworkers in the United States. It originated from the merger of two workers' rights organizations, the Agricultural Workers Organizing Committee led by organizer Larry Itliong, and the National Farm Workers Association led by César Chávez and Dolores Huerta. They became allied and transformed from workers' rights organizations into a union as a result of a series of strikes in 1965, when the mostly Filipino farmworkers of the AWOC in Delano, California initiated a grape strike, and the NFWA went on strike in support. As a result of the commonality in goals and methods, the NFWA and the AWOC formed the _____ Organizing Committee on August 22, 1966. This organization was accepted into the AFL-CIO in 1972 and changed its name to the _____ Union.

Exam Probability: **Low**

39. *Answer choices:*

(see index for correct answer)

- a. Texas Farm Workers Union
- b. Farmworker
- c. United Farm Workers
- d. Picking Cotton

Guidance: level 1

:: ::

_____ is the study and management of exchange relationships. _____ is the business process of creating relationships with and satisfying customers. With its focus on the customer, _____ is one of the premier components of business management.

Exam Probability: **Medium**

40. *Answer choices:*

(see index for correct answer)

- a. hierarchical perspective
- b. Character
- c. corporate values
- d. Marketing

Guidance: level 1

:: Toxicology ::

_____ or lead-based paint is paint containing lead. As pigment, lead chromate , Lead oxide, , and lead carbonate are the most common forms. Lead is added to paint to accelerate drying, increase durability, maintain a fresh appearance, and resist moisture that causes corrosion. It is one of the main health and environmental hazards associated with paint. In some countries, lead continues to be added to paint intended for domestic use, whereas countries such as the U.S. and the UK have regulations prohibiting this, although _____ may still be found in older properties painted prior to the introduction of such regulations. Although lead has been banned from household paints in the United States since 1978, paint used in road markings may still contain it. Alternatives such as water-based, lead-free traffic paint are readily available, and many states and federal agencies have changed their purchasing contracts to buy these instead.

Exam Probability: **Low**

41. *Answer choices:*

(see index for correct answer)

- a. Medical toxicology
- b. Toxicofera
- c. Effects range low and effects range median
- d. Lead paint

Guidance: level 1

:: Ethically disputed business practices ::

_____ is the trading of a public company's stock or other securities by individuals with access to nonpublic information about the company. In various countries, some kinds of trading based on insider information is illegal. This is because it is seen as unfair to other investors who do not have access to the information, as the investor with insider information could potentially make larger profits than a typical investor could make. The rules governing _____ are complex and vary significantly from country to country. The extent of enforcement also varies from one country to another. The definition of insider in one jurisdiction can be broad, and may cover not only insiders themselves but also any persons related to them, such as brokers, associates and even family members. A person who becomes aware of non-public information and trades on that basis may be guilty of a crime.

Exam Probability: **Medium**

42. *Answer choices:*

(see index for correct answer)

- a. Trademark troll
- b. Insider trading
- c. Off-label use
- d. Persuasive technology

Guidance: level 1

:: ::

_____ generally refers to a focus on the needs or desires of one's self. A number of philosophical, psychological, and economic theories examine the role of _____ in motivating human action.

Exam Probability: **Medium**

43. *Answer choices:*

(see index for correct answer)

- a. co-culture
- b. information systems assessment
- c. empathy
- d. Self-interest

Guidance: level 1

:: Product certification ::

_____ is food produced by methods that comply with the standards of organic farming. Standards vary worldwide, but organic farming features practices that cycle resources, promote ecological balance, and conserve biodiversity. Organizations regulating organic products may restrict the use of certain pesticides and fertilizers in the farming methods used to produce such products. _____ s typically are not processed using irradiation, industrial solvents, or synthetic food additives.

Exam Probability: **Low**

44. *Answer choices:*

(see index for correct answer)

- a. Organic food
- b. UTZ Certified
- c. Clerk of works
- d. Notified Body

Guidance: level 1

:: Progressive Era in the United States ::

The Clayton Antitrust Act of 1914 , was a part of United States antitrust law with the goal of adding further substance to the U.S. antitrust law regime; the _____ sought to prevent anticompetitive practices in their incipiency. That regime started with the Sherman Antitrust Act of 1890, the first Federal law outlawing practices considered harmful to consumers . The _____ specified particular prohibited conduct, the three-level enforcement scheme, the exemptions, and the remedial measures.

Exam Probability: **Medium**

45. *Answer choices:*

(see index for correct answer)

- a. Clayton Antitrust Act
- b. pragmatism
- c. Clayton Act

:: Power (social and political) ::

_____ is a form of reverence gained by a leader who has strong interpersonal relationship skills. _____ , as an aspect of personal power, becomes particularly important as organizational leadership becomes increasingly about collaboration and influence, rather than command and control.

Exam Probability: **Medium**

46. *Answer choices:*

(see index for correct answer)

- a. Expert power
- b. Referent power
- c. need for power

:: Statutory law ::

_____ or statute law is written law set down by a body of legislature or by a singular legislator . This is as opposed to oral or customary law; or regulatory law promulgated by the executive or common law of the judiciary. Statutes may originate with national, state legislatures or local municipalities.

Exam Probability: **Medium**

47. *Answer choices:*

(see index for correct answer)

- a. incorporation by reference
- b. statute law
- c. ratification
- d. Statutory law

Guidance: level 1

:: Business ethics ::

_____ is a type of international private business self-regulation. While once it was possible to describe CSR as an internal organisational policy or a corporate ethic strategy, that time has passed as various international laws have been developed and various organisations have used their authority to push it beyond individual or even industry-wide initiatives. While it has been considered a form of corporate self-regulation for some time, over the last decade or so it has moved considerably from voluntary decisions at the level of individual organisations, to mandatory schemes at regional, national and even transnational levels.

48. *Answer choices:*

(see index for correct answer)

- a. Jewish business ethics
- b. Corporate social responsibility
- c. Workplace bullying
- d. Anatomy of Greed

Guidance: level 1

:: Social enterprise ::

Corporate social responsibility   is a type of international private business self-regulation. While once it was possible to describe CSR as an internal organisational policy or a corporate ethic strategy, that time has passed as various international laws have been developed and various organisations have used their authority to push it beyond individual or even industry-wide initiatives. While it has been considered a form of corporate self-regulation for some time, over the last decade or so it has moved considerably from voluntary decisions at the level of individual organisations, to mandatory schemes at regional, national and even transnational levels.

Exam Probability: **Low**

49. *Answer choices:*

(see index for correct answer)

- a. Social venture
- b. Corporate citizenship

Guidance: level 1

:: Cultural appropriation ::

_____ is a social and economic order that encourages the acquisition of goods and services in ever-increasing amounts. With the industrial revolution, but particularly in the 20th century, mass production led to an economic crisis: there was overproduction—the supply of goods would grow beyond consumer demand, and so manufacturers turned to planned obsolescence and advertising to manipulate consumer spending. In 1899, a book on _____ published by Thorstein Veblen, called The Theory of the Leisure Class, examined the widespread values and economic institutions emerging along with the widespread "leisure time" in the beginning of the 20th century. In it Veblen "views the activities and spending habits of this leisure class in terms of conspicuous and vicarious consumption and waste. Both are related to the display of status and not to functionality or usefulness."

Exam Probability: **Medium**

50. *Answer choices:*

(see index for correct answer)

- a. Hollywood Indian
- b. Washington Redskins name controversy
- c. Wigger
- d. Consumerism

:: ::

Bernard Lawrence _____ is an American former market maker, investment advisor, financier, fraudster, and convicted felon, who is currently serving a federal prison sentence for offenses related to a massive Ponzi scheme. He is the former non-executive chairman of the NASDAQ stock market, the confessed operator of the largest Ponzi scheme in world history, and the largest financial fraud in U.S. history. Prosecutors estimated the fraud to be worth $64.8 billion based on the amounts in the accounts of _____ 's 4,800 clients as of November 30, 2008.

Exam Probability: **Medium**

51. *Answer choices:*

(see index for correct answer)

- a. hierarchical
- b. imperative
- c. Sarbanes-Oxley act of 2002
- d. Madoff

:: ::

_____ Corporation was an American energy, commodities, and services company based in Houston, Texas. It was founded in 1985 as a merger between Houston Natural Gas and InterNorth, both relatively small regional companies. Before its bankruptcy on December 3, 2001, _____ employed approximately 29,000 staff and was a major electricity, natural gas, communications and pulp and paper company, with claimed revenues of nearly $101 billion during 2000. Fortune named _____ "America's Most Innovative Company" for six consecutive years.

Exam Probability: **Medium**

52. *Answer choices:*

(see index for correct answer)

- a. imperative
- b. functional perspective
- c. Enron
- d. information systems assessment

Guidance: level 1

:: Ethical banking ::

A _____ or community development finance institution - abbreviated in both cases to CDFI - is a financial institution that provides credit and financial services to underserved markets and populations, primarily in the USA but also in the UK. A CDFI may be a community development bank, a community development credit union , a community development loan fund , a community development venture capital fund , a microenterprise development loan fund, or a community development corporation.

Exam Probability: **Medium**

53. *Answer choices:*

(see index for correct answer)

- a. Wilhelm Ernst Barkhoff
- b. The Co-operative Bank
- c. Community development financial institution
- d. Reliance Bank

Guidance: level 1

:: ::

_____ is a product prepared from the leaves of the _____ plant by curing them. The plant is part of the genus Nicotiana and of the Solanaceae family. While more than 70 species of _____ are known, the chief commercial crop is N. tabacum. The more potent variant N. rustica is also used around the world.

54. *Answer choices:*

(see index for correct answer)

- a. Tobacco
- b. corporate values
- c. imperative
- d. levels of analysis

Guidance: level 1

:: Financial markets ::

The _____ is a United States federal government organization, established by Title I of the Dodd–Frank Wall Street Reform and Consumer Protection Act, which was signed into law by President Barack Obama on July 21, 2010. The Office of Financial Research is intended to provide support to the council.

Exam Probability: **High**

55. *Answer choices:*

(see index for correct answer)

- a. Subscription
- b. Convenience yield

- c. Internal financing
- d. Financial Stability Oversight Council

Guidance: level 1

:: Separation of investment and commercial banking ::

The _____ refers to § 619 of the Dodd–Frank Wall Street Reform and Consumer Protection Act . The rule was originally proposed by American economist and former United States Federal Reserve Chairman Paul Volcker to restrict United States banks from making certain kinds of speculative investments that do not benefit their customers. Volcker argued that such speculative activity played a key role in the financial crisis of 2007–2008. The rule is often referred to as a ban on proprietary trading by commercial banks, whereby deposits are used to trade on the bank's own accounts, although a number of exceptions to this ban were included in the Dodd-Frank law.

Exam Probability: **Low**

56. *Answer choices:*

(see index for correct answer)

- a. Bank holding company
- b. GLBA
- c. Independent Commission on Banking
- d. Volcker Rule

Guidance: level 1

A _____ is an astronomical body orbiting a star or stellar remnant that is massive enough to be rounded by its own gravity, is not massive enough to cause thermonuclear fusion, and has cleared its neighbouring region of _____ esimals.

Exam Probability: **High**

57. *Answer choices:*

(see index for correct answer)

- a. co-culture
- b. Planet
- c. deep-level diversity
- d. open system

Guidance: level 1

:: Renewable energy ::

_____ is the conversion of energy from sunlight into electricity, either directly using photovoltaics , indirectly using concentrated _____ , or a combination. Concentrated _____ systems use lenses or mirrors and tracking systems to focus a large area of sunlight into a small beam. Photovoltaic cells convert light into an electric current using the photovoltaic effect.

Exam Probability: **High**

58. *Answer choices:*

(see index for correct answer)

- a. Micro combined heat and power
- b. Solar power
- c. Grid balancing
- d. Small hydro

Guidance: level 1

:: Decentralization ::

_____ or sub _____ mainly refers to the unrestricted growth in many urban areas of housing, commercial development, and roads over large expanses of land, with little concern for urban planning. In addition to describing a particular form of urbanization, the term also relates to the social and environmental consequences associated with this development. In Continental Europe the term "peri-urbanisation" is often used to denote similar dynamics and phenomena, although the term _____ is currently being used by the European Environment Agency. There is widespread disagreement about what constitutes sprawl and how to quantify it. For example, some commentators measure sprawl only with the average number of residential units per acre in a given area. But others associate it with decentralization, discontinuity, segregation of uses, and so forth.

Exam Probability: **High**

59. *Answer choices:*

(see index for correct answer)

- a. egalitarian
- b. Urban sprawl
- c. Ralph Borsodi
- d. Water supply and sanitation in Benin

Guidance: level 1

Accounting

Accounting or accountancy is the measurement, processing, and communication of financial information about economic entities such as businesses and corporations. The modern field was established by the Italian mathematician Luca Pacioli in 1494. Accounting, which has been called the "language of business", measures the results of an organization's economic activities and conveys this information to a variety of users, including investors, creditors, management, and regulators.

:: Business ethics ::

In accounting and in most Schools of economic thought, _____ is a rational and unbiased estimate of the potential market price of a good, service, or asset. It takes into account such objectivity factors as.

Exam Probability: **Medium**

1. *Answer choices:*

(see index for correct answer)

- a. Fair value
- b. Anti-sweatshop movement
- c. Corporate behaviour
- d. Moral hazard

Guidance: level 1

:: United States federal income tax ::

Under United States tax law, the _____ is a dollar amount that non-itemizers may subtract from their income before income tax is applied. Taxpayers may choose either itemized deductions or the _____ , but usually choose whichever results in the lesser amount of tax payable. The _____ is available to US citizens and aliens who are resident for tax purposes and who are individuals, married persons, and heads of household. The _____ is based on filing status and typically increases each year. It is not available to nonresident aliens residing in the United States . Additional amounts are available for persons who are blind and/or are at least 65 years of age.

2. *Answer choices:*

(see index for correct answer)

- a. Standard deduction
- b. Stepped-up basis
- c. Unicap
- d. Physical presence test

Guidance: level 1

:: Generally Accepted Accounting Principles ::

Paid-in capital is capital that is contributed to a corporation by investors
by purchase of stock from the corporation, the primary market, not by purchase
of stock in the open market from other stockholders . It includes share capital
as well as additional paid-in capital.

Exam Probability: **Low**

3. *Answer choices:*

(see index for correct answer)

- a. Operating income
- b. Contributed capital
- c. Cost pool

- d. Expense

Guidance: level 1

:: ::

A _____ is an entity that owes a debt to another entity. The entity may be an individual, a firm, a government, a company or other legal person. The counterparty is called a creditor. When the counterpart of this debt arrangement is a bank, the _____ is more often referred to as a borrower.

Exam Probability: **Medium**

4. *Answer choices:*
(see index for correct answer)

- a. Character
- b. corporate values
- c. empathy
- d. Debtor

Guidance: level 1

:: Marketing ::

_____ or stock is the goods and materials that a business holds for the ultimate goal of resale .

Exam Probability: **Medium**

5. *Answer choices:*

(see index for correct answer)

- a. Aspirational brand
- b. Primary research
- c. Inventory
- d. Paddock girl

Guidance: level 1

:: Real property law ::

_____ is the judicial process whereby a will is "proved" in a court of law and accepted as a valid public document that is the true last testament of the deceased, or whereby the estate is settled according to the laws of intestacy in the state of residence [or real property] of the deceased at time of death in the absence of a legal will.

Exam Probability: **Medium**

6. *Answer choices:*

(see index for correct answer)

- a. M.P.M. Builders, LLC v. Dwyer
- b. Atrisco Land Grant
- c. Massachusetts Land Court
- d. Fee tail

Guidance: level 1

:: International accounting organizations ::

The _____ is the global organization for the accountancy profession. Founded in 1977, IFAC has more than 175 members and associates in more than 130 countries and jurisdictions, representing nearly 3 million accountants employed in public practice, industry and commerce, government, and academe. The organization supports the development, adoption and implementation of international standards for accounting education, ethics, and the public sector as well as audit and assurance. It supports four independent standard-setting boards, which establish international standards on ethics, auditing and assurance, accounting education, and public sector accounting. It also issues guidance to encourage high quality performance by professional accountants in business and small and medium accounting practices.

Exam Probability: **Medium**

7. *Answer choices:*

(see index for correct answer)

- a. International Federation of Accountants
- b. ASEAN Federation of Accountants

- c. Asia-Pacific Management Accounting Association
- d. Pan African Federation of Accountants

:: Accounting terminology ::

In accounting/accountancy, _____ are journal entries usually made at the end of an accounting period to allocate income and expenditure to the period in which they actually occurred. The revenue recognition principle is the basis of making _____ that pertain to unearned and accrued revenues under accrual-basis accounting. They are sometimes called Balance Day adjustments because they are made on balance day.

Exam Probability: **Low**

8. *Answer choices:*

(see index for correct answer)

- a. Accounts payable
- b. Capital appreciation
- c. Accrual
- d. Adjusting entries

:: Legal terms ::

_____ or _____ interest, in law, is anything that functions contrary to a party's interest. This word should not be confused with averse.

Exam Probability: **High**

9. *Answer choices:*

(see index for correct answer)

- a. Principal case
- b. Imperfect self-defense
- c. Divesting abandonment
- d. Adverse

Guidance: level 1

:: Real estate valuation ::

_____ or OMV is the price at which an asset would trade in a competitive auction setting. _____ is often used interchangeably with open _____, fair value or fair _____, although these terms have distinct definitions in different standards, and may or may not differ in some circumstances.

Exam Probability: **Low**

10. *Answer choices:*

(see index for correct answer)

- a. Sales comparison approach
- b. Extraordinary assumptions and hypothetical conditions
- c. Real estate appraisal
- d. E.surv

Guidance: level 1

:: Accounting in the United States ::

_____ is the title of qualified accountants in numerous countries in the English-speaking world. In the United States, the CPA is a license to provide accounting services to the public. It is awarded by each of the 50 states for practice in that state. Additionally, almost every state has passed mobility laws to allow CPAs from other states to practice in their state. State licensing requirements vary, but the minimum standard requirements include passing the Uniform _____ Examination, 150 semester units of college education, and one year of accounting related experience.

Exam Probability: **High**

11. *Answer choices:*

(see index for correct answer)

- a. Other postemployment benefits
- b. Comprehensive Performance Assessment
- c. Governmental Accounting Standards Board
- d. Certified Public Accountant

:: Stock market ::

_____ is a form of stock which may have any combination of features not possessed by common stock including properties of both an equity and a debt instrument, and is generally considered a hybrid instrument. _____ s are senior to common stock, but subordinate to bonds in terms of claim and may have priority over common stock in the payment of dividends and upon liquidation. Terms of the _____ are described in the issuing company's articles of association or articles of incorporation.

Exam Probability: **Low**

12. *Answer choices:*

(see index for correct answer)

- a. Preferred stock
- b. Green sheet
- c. Underwriting contract
- d. Green chip

:: Income ::

_____ is a ratio between the net profit and cost of investment resulting from an investment of some resources. A high ROI means the investment's gains favorably to its cost. As a performance measure, ROI is used to evaluate the efficiency of an investment or to compare the efficiencies of several different investments. In purely economic terms, it is one way of relating profits to capital invested. _____ is a performance measure used by businesses to identify the efficiency of an investment or number of different investments.

Exam Probability: **High**

13. *Answer choices:*

(see index for correct answer)

- a. Return of investment
- b. Family income
- c. Signing bonus
- d. IRD asset

Guidance: level 1

:: Retail financial services ::

A _____ is a prepaid stored-value money card, usually issued by a retailer or bank, to be used as an alternative to cash for purchases within a particular store or related businesses. _____ s are also given out by employers or organizations as rewards or gifts. They may also be distributed by retailers and marketers as part of a promotion strategy, to entice the recipient to come in or return to the store, and at times such cards are called cash cards. _____ s are generally redeemable only for purchases at the relevant retail premises and cannot be cashed out, and in some situations may be subject to an expiry date or fees. American Express, MasterCard, and Visa offer generic _____ s which need not be redeemed at particular stores, and which are widely used for cashback marketing strategies. A feature of these cards is that they are generally anonymous and are disposed of when the stored value on a card is exhausted.

Exam Probability: **High**

14. *Answer choices:*

(see index for correct answer)

- a. Payments Council
- b. Financial management advisor
- c. Merchant services
- d. Financial planner

Guidance: level 1

:: Fraud ::

In law, _____ is intentional deception to secure unfair or unlawful gain, or to deprive a victim of a legal right. _____ can violate civil law , a criminal law , or it may cause no loss of money, property or legal right but still be an element of another civil or criminal wrong. The purpose of _____ may be monetary gain or other benefits, for example by obtaining a passport, travel document, or driver's license, or mortgage _____ , where the perpetrator may attempt to qualify for a mortgage by way of false statements.

Exam Probability: **Medium**

15. *Answer choices:*

(see index for correct answer)

- a. Fraud Alert
- b. Identity theft
- c. Faked death
- d. Unconscious fraud

Guidance: level 1

:: Accounting journals and ledgers ::

The subledger, or _____ , provides details behind entries in the general ledger used in accounting. The subledger shows detail for part of the accounting records such as property and equipment, prepaid expenses, etc. The detail would include such items as date the item was purchased or expense incurred, a description of the item, the original balance, and the net book value. The total of the subledger would match the line item amount on the general ledger. This corresponding line item in the general ledger is referred to as the controlling account. The _____ balance is compared with its controlling account balance as part of the process of preparing a trial balance.

Exam Probability: **Low**

16. *Answer choices:*

(see index for correct answer)

- a. Cash receipts journal
- b. Subsidiary ledger
- c. Sales journal
- d. General journal

Guidance: level 1

:: Generally Accepted Accounting Principles ::

In accounting, _____ , gross margin, sales profit, or credit sales is the difference between revenue and the cost of making a product or providing a service, before deducting overheads, payroll, taxation, and interest payments. This is different from operating profit . Gross margin is the term normally used in the U.S., while _____ is the more common usage in the UK and Australia.

Exam Probability: **Medium**

17. *Answer choices:*

(see index for correct answer)

- a. Gross profit
- b. Net realizable value
- c. Deprival value
- d. Gross sales

Guidance: level 1

:: Stock market ::

_____ is a form of corporate equity ownership, a type of security. The terms voting share and ordinary share are also used frequently in other parts of the world; " _____ " being primarily used in the United States. They are known as Equity shares or Ordinary shares in the UK and other Commonwealth realms. This type of share gives the stockholder the right to share in the profits of the company, and to vote on matters of corporate policy and the composition of the members of the board of directors.

18. *Answer choices:*

(see index for correct answer)

- a. Common stock
- b. Ticker tape
- c. Underwriting contract
- d. Avanza

Guidance: level 1

:: Accounting ::

_____ is the recording of financial transactions, and is part of the process of accounting in business. Transactions include purchases, sales, receipts, and payments by an individual person or an organization/corporation. There are several standard methods of _____ , including the single-entry and double-entry _____ systems. While these may be viewed as "real" _____ , any process for recording financial transactions is a _____ process.

Exam Probability: **High**

19. *Answer choices:*

(see index for correct answer)

- a. Cost allocation

- b. The Progressive Accountant
- c. Profit model
- d. Accountant General

Guidance: level 1

:: Loans ::

In finance, a _____ is the lending of money by one or more individuals, organizations, or other entities to other individuals, organizations etc. The recipient incurs a debt, and is usually liable to pay interest on that debt until it is repaid, and also to repay the principal amount borrowed.

Exam Probability: **Medium**

20. *Answer choices:*

(see index for correct answer)

- a. Forgivable loan
- b. Collateralized loan obligation
- c. Loan-deposit ratio
- d. Private student loan

Guidance: level 1

:: ::

An _____ is a contingent motivator. Traditional _____ s are extrinsic motivators which reward actions to yield a desired outcome. The effectiveness of traditional _____ s has changed as the needs of Western society have evolved. While the traditional _____ model is effective when there is a defined procedure and goal for a task, Western society started to require a higher volume of critical thinkers, so the traditional model became less effective. Institutions are now following a trend in implementing strategies that rely on intrinsic motivations rather than the extrinsic motivations that the traditional _____ s foster.

Exam Probability: **High**

21. *Answer choices:*

(see index for correct answer)

- a. co-culture
- b. Incentive
- c. Character
- d. cultural

Guidance: level 1

:: Financial ratios ::

In finance, the _____ , also known as the acid-test ratio is a type of liquidity ratio which measures the ability of a company to use its near cash or quick assets to extinguish or retire its current liabilities immediately. Quick assets include those current assets that presumably can be quickly converted to cash at close to their book values. It is the ratio between quickly available or liquid assets and current liabilities.

22. *Answer choices:*

(see index for correct answer)

- a. Sortino ratio
- b. Quick ratio
- c. Capitalization rate
- d. Implied multiple

Guidance: level 1

:: Real property law ::

A _____ or millage rate is an ad valorem tax on the value of a property, usually levied on real estate. The tax is levied by the governing authority of the jurisdiction in which the property is located. This can be a national government, a federated state, a county or geographical region or a municipality. Multiple jurisdictions may tax the same property. This tax can be contrasted to a rent tax which is based on rental income or imputed rent, and a land value tax, which is a levy on the value of land, excluding the value of buildings and other improvements.

23. *Answer choices:*

(see index for correct answer)

- a. Property tax
- b. Conveyancing
- c. Statute of Enrolments
- d. Allodial title

Guidance: level 1

:: Asset ::

In financial accounting, an _____ is any resource owned by the business. Anything tangible or intangible that can be owned or controlled to produce value and that is held by a company to produce positive economic value is an _____ . Simply stated, _____ s represent value of ownership that can be converted into cash . The balance sheet of a firm records the monetary value of the _____ s owned by that firm. It covers money and other valuables belonging to an individual or to a business.

24. *Answer choices:*

(see index for correct answer)

- a. Asset

- b. Fixed asset

Guidance: level 1

:: Management accounting ::

_____ is a professional business study of Accounts and management in which we learn importance of accounts in our management system.

Exam Probability: **Low**

25. *Answer choices:*
(see index for correct answer)

- a. Variable cost
- b. Revenue center
- c. Responsibility center
- d. Certified Management Accountant

Guidance: level 1

:: Accounting ::

_____ are key sources of information and evidence used to prepare, verify and/or audit the financial statements. They also include documentation to prove asset ownership for creation of liabilities and proof of monetary and non monetary transactions.

Exam Probability: **Low**

26. *Answer choices:*

(see index for correct answer)

- a. Professional services networks
- b. Efficiency Based Absorption Costing
- c. Tour accountant
- d. Accounting records

Guidance: level 1

:: ::

A _____ is an organization, usually a group of people or a company, authorized to act as a single entity and recognized as such in law. Early incorporated entities were established by charter . Most jurisdictions now allow the creation of new _____ s through registration.

Exam Probability: **High**

27. *Answer choices:*

(see index for correct answer)

- a. Sarbanes-Oxley act of 2002
- b. deep-level diversity
- c. process perspective
- d. similarity-attraction theory

Guidance: level 1

:: ::

An _____ is an asset that lacks physical substance. It is defined in opposition to physical assets such as machinery and buildings. An _____ is usually very hard to evaluate. Patents, copyrights, franchises, goodwill, trademarks, and trade names. The general interpretation also includes software and other intangible computer based assets are all examples of _____ s. _____ s generally—though not necessarily—suffer from typical market failures of non-rivalry and non-excludability.

Exam Probability: **Low**

28. *Answer choices:*

(see index for correct answer)

- a. process perspective
- b. open system
- c. co-culture
- d. Intangible asset

:: Information systems ::

_____ are formal, sociotechnical, organizational systems designed to collect, process, store, and distribute information. In a sociotechnical perspective, _____ are composed by four components: task, people, structure , and technology.

Exam Probability: **Medium**

29. *Answer choices:*

(see index for correct answer)

- a. Manufacturing execution system
- b. knowledge Pyramid
- c. Big bang adoption
- d. Information systems

:: Stock market ::

A _____ , securities exchange or bourse, is a facility where stock brokers and traders can buy and sell securities, such as shares of stock and bonds and other financial instruments. _____ s may also provide for facilities the issue and redemption of such securities and instruments and capital events including the payment of income and dividends. Securities traded on a _____ include stock issued by listed companies, unit trusts, derivatives, pooled investment products and bonds. _____ s often function as "continuous auction" markets with buyers and sellers consummating transactions via open outcry at a central location such as the floor of the exchange or by using an electronic trading platform.

Exam Probability: **Medium**

30. *Answer choices:*

(see index for correct answer)

- a. Stock Exchange
- b. Relative valuation
- c. High-frequency trading
- d. Shareholders

Guidance: level 1

:: Management accounting ::

In finance, the _____ or net present worth applies to a series of cash flows occurring at different times. The present value of a cash flow depends on the interval of time between now and the cash flow. It also depends on the discount rate. NPV accounts for the time value of money. It provides a method for evaluating and comparing capital projects or financial products with cash flows spread over time, as in loans, investments, payouts from insurance contracts plus many other applications.

31. *Answer choices:*

(see index for correct answer)

- a. Net present value
- b. Cost accounting
- c. Environmental full-cost accounting
- d. Management accounting

Guidance: level 1

:: Accounting terminology ::

In management accounting or _____ , managers use the provisions of accounting information in order to better inform themselves before they decide matters within their organizations, which aids their management and performance of control functions.

32. *Answer choices:*

(see index for correct answer)

- a. Managerial accounting
- b. Fund accounting
- c. Accounts payable
- d. General ledger

Guidance: level 1

:: United States Generally Accepted Accounting Principles ::

In a companies` financial reporting, _____ "includes all changes in equity during a period except those resulting from investments by owners and distributions to owners". Because that use excludes the effects of changing ownership interest, an economic measure of _____ is necessary for financial analysis from the shareholders` point of view

Exam Probability: **Medium**

33. *Answer choices:*

(see index for correct answer)

- a. Permanent fund
- b. Comprehensive income
- c. Available for sale
- d. FIN 46

:: Legal terms ::

A _____ is a gathering of people who have been invited by a host for the purposes of socializing, conversation, recreation, or as part of a festival or other commemoration of a special occasion. A _____ will typically feature food and beverages, and often music and dancing or other forms of entertainment. In many Western countries, parties for teens and adults are associated with drinking alcohol such as beer, wine, or distilled spirits.

Exam Probability: **Medium**

34. *Answer choices:*

(see index for correct answer)

- a. Jurisprudence constante
- b. Injunction
- c. Innominate jury
- d. Factual basis

:: International taxation ::

_____ is the levying of tax by two or more jurisdictions on the same declared income , asset , or financial transaction . Double liability is mitigated in a number of ways, for example.

Exam Probability: **Low**

35. *Answer choices:*

(see index for correct answer)

- a. Tax information exchange agreement
- b. Foreign personal holding company
- c. European Union withholding tax
- d. European Union financial transaction tax

Guidance: level 1

:: Legal terms ::

_____ is a state of prolonged public dispute or debate, usually concerning a matter of conflicting opinion or point of view. The word was coined from the Latin controversia, as a composite of controversus – "turned in an opposite direction," from contra – "against" – and vertere – to turn, or versus , hence, "to turn against."

Exam Probability: **High**

36. *Answer choices:*

(see index for correct answer)

- a. Culprit
- b. Controversy
- c. Forfeiture
- d. Charge

Guidance: level 1

:: Valuation (finance) ::

_____ refers to an assessment of the viability, stability, and profitability of a business, sub-business or project.

Exam Probability: **Low**

37. *Answer choices:*

(see index for correct answer)

- a. Graham number
- b. Financial analysis
- c. Diminution in value
- d. Value date

Guidance: level 1

:: Cash flow ::

In corporate finance, _____ or _____ to firm is a way of looking at a business's cash flow to see what is available for distribution among all the securities holders of a corporate entity. This may be useful to parties such as equity holders, debt holders, preferred stock holders, and convertible security holders when they want to see how much cash can be extracted from a company without causing issues to its operations.

Exam Probability: **Medium**

38. *Answer choices:*

(see index for correct answer)

- a. Free cash flow
- b. Discounted payback period
- c. Cash carrier
- d. Factoring

Guidance: level 1

:: Management ::

Business _____ is a discipline in operations management in which people use various methods to discover, model, analyze, measure, improve, optimize, and automate business processes. BPM focuses on improving corporate performance by managing business processes. Any combination of methods used to manage a company's business processes is BPM. Processes can be structured and repeatable or unstructured and variable. Though not required, enabling technologies are often used with BPM.

Exam Probability: **Low**

39. *Answer choices:*

(see index for correct answer)

- a. Management styles
- b. Process Management
- c. Supply management
- d. Design management

Guidance: level 1

:: ::

The _____ of 1938 29 U.S.C. § 203 is a United States labor law that creates the right to a minimum wage, and "time-and-a-half" overtime pay when people work over forty hours a week. It also prohibits most employment of minors in "oppressive child labor". It applies to employees engaged in interstate commerce or employed by an enterprise engaged in commerce or in the production of goods for commerce, unless the employer can claim an exemption from coverage.

40. *Answer choices:*

(see index for correct answer)

- a. surface-level diversity
- b. process perspective
- c. deep-level diversity
- d. personal values

Guidance: level 1

:: Employment classifications ::

Generally, tax authorities will view a person as self-employed if the person chooses to be recognized as such, or is generating income such that the person is required to file a tax return under legislation in the relevant jurisdiction. In the real world, the critical issue for the taxing authorities is not that the person is trading but is whether the person is profitable and hence potentially taxable. In other words, the activity of trading is likely to be ignored if no profit is present, so occasional and hobby- or enthusiast-based economic activity is generally ignored by authorities.

Exam Probability: **Medium**

41. *Answer choices:*

(see index for correct answer)

- a. Self-employment
- b. Freelancer
- c. Responsible position
- d. Migrant worker

Guidance: level 1

:: Password authentication ::

A _____ , or sometimes redundantly a PIN number, is a numeric or alpha-numeric password used in the process of authenticating a user accessing a system.

Exam Probability: **Medium**

42. *Answer choices:*

(see index for correct answer)

- a. Pre-shared key
- b. Personal identification number
- c. Password-authenticated key agreement
- d. Password authentication protocol

Guidance: level 1

:: ::

The U.S. _____ is an independent agency of the United States federal government. The SEC holds primary responsibility for enforcing the federal securities laws, proposing securities rules, and regulating the securities industry, the nation's stock and options exchanges, and other activities and organizations, including the electronic securities markets in the United States.

Exam Probability: **Low**

43. *Answer choices:*

(see index for correct answer)

- a. Sarbanes-Oxley act of 2002
- b. Character
- c. Securities and Exchange Commission
- d. similarity-attraction theory

Guidance: level 1

:: Financial ratios ::

The _____ is a financial ratio indicating the relative proportion of shareholders' equity and debt used to finance a company's assets. Closely related to leveraging, the ratio is also known as risk, gearing or leverage. The two components are often taken from the firm's balance sheet or statement of financial position , but the ratio may also be calculated using market values for both, if the company's debt and equity are publicly traded, or using a combination of book value for debt and market value for equity financially.

44. *Answer choices:*

(see index for correct answer)

- a. EV/EBITDA
- b. Net interest spread
- c. Financial ratio
- d. Debt-to-equity ratio

Guidance: level 1

:: Accounting source documents ::

An _____ , bill or tab is a commercial document issued by a seller to a buyer, relating to a sale transaction and indicating the products, quantities, and agreed prices for products or services the seller had provided the buyer.

Exam Probability: **High**

45. *Answer choices:*

(see index for correct answer)

- a. Bank statement
- b. Air waybill
- c. Purchase order
- d. Banknote

:: Financial statements ::

In financial accounting, a _____ or statement of financial position or statement of financial condition is a summary of the financial balances of an individual or organization, whether it be a sole proprietorship, a business partnership, a corporation, private limited company or other organization such as Government or not-for-profit entity. Assets, liabilities and ownership equity are listed as of a specific date, such as the end of its financial year. A _____ is often described as a "snapshot of a company's financial condition". Of the four basic financial statements, the _____ is the only statement which applies to a single point in time of a business' calendar year.

Exam Probability: **Low**

46. *Answer choices:*

(see index for correct answer)

- a. Balance sheet
- b. Consolidated financial statement
- c. Government financial statements
- d. Emphasis of matter

:: Capital gains taxes ::

A _____ refers to profit that results from a sale of a capital asset, such as stock, bond or real estate, where the sale price exceeds the purchase price. The gain is the difference between a higher selling price and a lower purchase price. Conversely, a capital loss arises if the proceeds from the sale of a capital asset are less than the purchase price.

Exam Probability: **High**

47. *Answer choices:*

(see index for correct answer)

- a. Capital cost tax factor
- b. Capital gains tax
- c. Capital gain

Guidance: level 1

:: Expense ::

A company`s _____ , or As a result, the computation of the _____ is considerably more complex. Tax law may provide for different treatment of items of income and expenses as a result of tax policy. The differences may be of permanent or temporary nature. Permanent items are in the form of non taxable income and non taxable expenses. Things such as expenses considered not deductible by taxing authorities , the range of tax rates applicable to various levels of income, different tax rates in different jurisdictions, multiple layers of tax on income, and other issues.

48. *Answer choices:*

(see index for correct answer)

- a. Expense account
- b. Freight expense
- c. Corporate travel
- d. Operating expense

Guidance: level 1

:: Tax law ::

_____ or revenue law is an area of legal study which deals with the constitutional, common-law, statutory, tax treaty, and regulatory rules that constitute the law applicable to taxation.

Exam Probability: **High**

49. *Answer choices:*

(see index for correct answer)

- a. Territorial nexus
- b. First-tier Tribunal
- c. Tax law
- d. Tax Law Rewrite Project

:: Finance ::

_____ is the ability of a bank customer in the United States and Canada to deposit a check into a bank account from a remote location, such as an office or home, without having to physically deliver the check to the bank. This is typically accomplished by scanning a digital image of a check into a computer, then transmitting that image to the bank. The practice became legal in the United States in 2004 when the Check Clearing for the 21st Century Act took effect, though not all banks have implemented the system.

Exam Probability: **Low**

50. *Answer choices:*

(see index for correct answer)

- a. Depletion
- b. Remote deposit
- c. Indication of interest
- d. Equity

:: Accounting terminology ::

Accounts are typically defined by an identifier and a caption or header and are coded by account type. In computerized accounting systems with computable quantity accounting, the accounts can have a quantity measure definition.

Exam Probability: **High**

51. *Answer choices:*

(see index for correct answer)

- a. Chart of accounts
- b. Statement of financial position
- c. Double-entry accounting
- d. Share premium

Guidance: level 1

:: Business law ::

An _____ is a natural person, business, or corporation that provides goods or services to another entity under terms specified in a contract or within a verbal agreement. Unlike an employee, an _____ does not work regularly for an employer but works as and when required, during which time they may be subject to law of agency. _____ s are usually paid on a freelance basis. Contractors often work through a limited company or franchise, which they themselves own, or may work through an umbrella company.

Exam Probability: **Medium**

52. *Answer choices:*

(see index for correct answer)

- a. Court auction
- b. Inslaw
- c. United States labor law
- d. Output contract

Guidance: level 1

:: ::

_____ is a costing method that identifies activities in an organization and assigns the cost of each activity to all products and services according to the actual consumption by each. This model assigns more indirect costs into direct costs compared to conventional costing.

Exam Probability: **Medium**

53. *Answer choices:*

(see index for correct answer)

- a. empathy
- b. hierarchical perspective
- c. co-culture
- d. corporate values

:: Legal terms ::

An _____ is an action which is inaccurate or incorrect. In some usages, an _____ is synonymous with a mistake. In statistics, "_____" refers to the difference between the value which has been computed and the correct value. An _____ could result in failure or in a deviation from the intended performance or behaviour.

Exam Probability: **Medium**

54. *Answer choices:*

(see index for correct answer)

- a. Error
- b. Interlocutory injunction
- c. Colour of right
- d. Informed assent

:: Generally Accepted Accounting Principles ::

Expenditure is an outflow of money to another person or group to pay for an item or service, or for a category of costs. For a tenant, rent is an _____ . For students or parents, tuition is an _____ . Buying food, clothing, furniture or an automobile is often referred to as an _____ . An _____ is a cost that is "paid" or "remitted", usually in exchange for something of value. Something that seems to cost a great deal is "expensive". Something that seems to cost little is "inexpensive". " _____ s of the table" are _____ s of dining, refreshments, a feast, etc.

Exam Probability: **Medium**

55. *Answer choices:*

(see index for correct answer)

- a. Pro forma
- b. Expense
- c. Shares outstanding
- d. Net realizable value

Guidance: level 1

:: Corporate crime ::

_____ LLP, based in Chicago, was an American holding company. Formerly one of the "Big Five" accounting firms , the firm had provided auditing, tax, and consulting services to large corporations. By 2001, it had become one of the world's largest multinational companies.

56. *Answer choices:*

(see index for correct answer)

- a. Ovson Egg
- b. Walter Forbes
- c. Titan Corporation
- d. Arthur Andersen

Guidance: level 1

:: ::

A _____ is a fund into which a sum of money is added during an employee's employment years, and from which payments are drawn to support the person's retirement from work in the form of periodic payments. A _____ may be a "defined benefit plan" where a fixed sum is paid regularly to a person, or a "defined contribution plan" under which a fixed sum is invested and then becomes available at retirement age. _____ s should not be confused with severance pay; the former is usually paid in regular installments for life after retirement, while the latter is typically paid as a fixed amount after involuntary termination of employment prior to retirement.

Exam Probability: **Low**

57. *Answer choices:*

(see index for correct answer)

- a. co-culture
- b. hierarchical perspective
- c. empathy
- d. functional perspective

Guidance: level 1

:: Accounting ::

_____ examines how accounting is used by individuals, organizations and government as well as the consequences that these practices have. Starting from the assumption that accounting both measures and makes visible certain economic events, _____ has studied the roles of accounting in organizations and society and the consequences that these practices have for individuals, organizations, governments and capital markets. It encompasses a broad range of topics including financial _____ , management _____ , auditing research, capital market research, accountability research, social responsibility research and taxation research.

Exam Probability: **Low**

58. *Answer choices:*

(see index for correct answer)

- a. Accounting research
- b. Merdiban
- c. Accounting period
- d. Russian GAAP

:: Business law ::

A _____ is an arrangement where parties, known as partners, agree to cooperate to advance their mutual interests. The partners in a _____ may be individuals, businesses, interest-based organizations, schools, governments or combinations. Organizations may partner to increase the likelihood of each achieving their mission and to amplify their reach. A _____ may result in issuing and holding equity or may be only governed by a contract.

Exam Probability: **High**

59. *Answer choices:*

(see index for correct answer)

- a. Partnership
- b. Lien
- c. Fraudulent trading
- d. Business courts

INDEX: Correct Answers

Foundations of Business

1. c: Exchange rate

2. c: Performance

3. : Cultural

4. c: Insurance

5. : Publicity

6. : Availability

7. c: Net income

8. : Focus group

9. d: Customs

10. c: Financial services

11. : Brand

12. d: Debt

13. c: Marketing strategy

14. b: Bribery

15. a: Organizational structure

16. a: Selling

17. d: Policy

18. d: Social security

19. : Six Sigma

20. : Investment

21. c: Political risk

22. b: Budget

23. : Procurement

24. : E-commerce

25. b: Creativity

26. c: Credit card

27. b: Cooperative

28. c: Question

29. d: Analysis

30. b: Firm

31. c: Franchising

32. d: Market segmentation

33. a: Opportunity cost

34. a: Credit

35. b: Accounts receivable

36. a: Tool

37. b: Quality control

38. b: Tariff

39. d: Incentive

40. c: Size

41. a: Bias

42. : Project

43. c: Economic growth

44. a: Specification

45. d: Return on investment

46. c: Business model

47. c: Demand

48. b: Employment

49. b: Economic Development

50. b: Marketing

51. b: Schedule

52. c: Logistics

53. a: Shareholders

54. a: Information

55. : Competitive advantage

56. : Stock

57. : Corporate governance

58. a: Buyer

59. d: Capital market

Management

1. d: Firm

2. : Law

3. : Human capital

4. d: Industrial Revolution

5. d: Customs

6. b: Product life cycle

7. d: European Union

8. : Interview

9. c: Cost

10. a: Chief executive

11. a: Competitive advantage

12. : Patent

13. b: Inventory control

14. c: Distance

15. b: Quality control

16. c: Certification

17. d: Question

18. a: Insurance

19. : Glass ceiling

20. c: Project manager

21. : Leadership development

22. a: Good

23. a: Pension

24. : Board of directors

25. c: Balanced scorecard

26. c: Forecasting

27. c: E-commerce

28. a: Resource management

29. b: Justice

30. a: Assembly line

31. a: Control chart

32. : Reason

33. d: Profit sharing

34. : Quality management

35. d: Threat

36. c: Recruitment

37. a: Problem solving

38. b: Executive officer

39. b: Enabling

40. : Grievance

41. d: Human resource management

42. a: Initiative

43. a: Merger

44. a: Sales

45. : SWOT analysis

46. a: Brand

47. d: Officer

48. c: Affirmative action

49. c: Business model

50. a: Performance appraisal

51. b: Efficiency

52. b: Project management

53. d: Performance management

54. c: Performance

55. a: Training and development

56. d: Export

57. c: Philosophy

58. c: Bottom line

59. b: Job analysis

Business law

1. d: Res ipsa

2. d: Prima facie

3. a: False imprisonment

4. c: Breach of contract

5. c: Employment discrimination

6. b: Constitutional law

7. : Executory contract

8. c: Licensee

9. : Unconscionability

10. a: Purchasing

11. a: Security agreement

12. c: Wire fraud

13. a: Competitor

14. d: Sherman Act

15. b: Arbitration clause

16. d: Voidable contract

17. b: Utility

18. b: Jury

19. c: Undue influence

20. b: Judicial review

21. d: Option contract

22. b: Duty

23. : Parol evidence

24. : Negotiable instrument

25. : Appeal

26. : Garnishment

27. a: Anticipatory repudiation

28. : Substantive law

29. c: Litigation

30. a: Contract law

31. c: Statute of frauds

32. c: Limited partnership

33. c: Incentive

34. d: Wage

35. c: Antitrust

36. : Perfection

37. c: Board of directors

38. d: Income

39. : Exclusionary rule

40. : S corporation

41. a: Trustee

42. c: Copyright

43. : Foreclosure

44. a: Shares

45. a: Commerce

46. b: Labor relations

47. c: Fair use

48. : Personal property

49. : Specific performance

50. d: Independent contractor

51. c: Economy

52. b: Comparative negligence

53. b: Tort

54. : Insurance

55. a: Estoppel

56. b: Federal Arbitration Act

57. d: Holder in due course

58. a: Berne Convention

59. d: Federal Trade Commission

Finance

1. c: Partnership

2. : Generally accepted accounting principles

3. b: Expense

4. : Perpetual inventory

5. c: Bad debt

6. : Variable cost

7. b: Stockholder

8. c: Cash equivalent

9. d: Preference

10. : Cost accounting

11. d: Compounding

12. b: Accounting

13. d: Internal rate of return

14. a: Trial balance

15. b: Journal entry

16. : Accrual

17. b: Mutual fund

18. b: Intangible asset

19. c: Securities and Exchange Commission

20. d: Stock market

21. c: Yield to maturity

22. : Fraud

23. c: Cost of capital

24. d: Capital budgeting

25. a: S corporation

26. d: Income statement

27. a: Opportunity cost

28. a: Equity method

29. c: Strategy

30. c: Risk

31. c: Capital asset pricing model

32. d: Long-term liabilities

33. a: Raw material

34. c: Market risk

35. c: Historical cost

36. : Face

37. c: Asset turnover

38. d: Absorption costing

39. a: Manufacturing cost

40. d: Net worth

41. b: Bank reconciliation

42. d: Net asset

43. : Saving

44. : Choice

45. d: Accountant

46. b: Goldman Sachs

47. d: Secondary market

48. : Rate risk

49. d: Normal balance

50. d: Forecasting

51. c: Financial risk

52. d: Cost object

53. a: Liquidation

54. b: Worksheet

55. c: Chart of accounts

56. d: Current ratio

57. b: Advertising

58. a: Compound interest

59. d: Discounting

Human resource management

1. b: Union shop

2. d: Labor union

3. : Departmentalization

4. c: Onboarding

5. a: Workforce management

6. : Exit interview

7. a: Task force

8. : Information overload

9. d: Global workforce

10. d: Human resources

11. a: Affirmative action

12. c: Performance management

13. b: Cross-functional team

14. : Internal consistency

15. d: Restricted stock

16. : Whistleblower

17. c: Cost leadership

18. : Self-assessment

19. c: Social contract

20. : Employee Free Choice Act

21. d: Executive search

22. a: Family violence

23. b: Asset

24. a: Expert power

25. : Work ethic

26. a: Halo effect

27. b: Phantom stock

28. d: Committee

29. d: Age Discrimination in Employment Act

30. c: National Labor Relations Act

31. b: Flextime

32. c: Pension

33. a: Material safety data sheet

34. d: Agency shop

35. d: Sexual harassment

36. d: Employee assistance program

37. a: Management

38. b: Online assessment

39. d: Realistic job preview

40. b: Local union

41. d: Assessment center

42. a: Outplacement

43. c: Talent management

44. b: Problem solving

45. d: Living wage

46. d: Sick leave

47. a: Minnesota Multiphasic Personality Inventory

48. b: Coaching

49. b: Self-actualization

50. : Evaluation

51. a: Employee referral

52. : UNITE HERE

53. : Unfair labor practice

54. c: Mergers and acquisitions

55. : Externship

56. d: Trainee

57. d: Organizational commitment

58. b: Sweatshop

59. b: Socialization

Information systems

1. d: Expert system

2. : Domain Name System

3. a: Yelp

4. b: Trojan horse

5. : Text mining

6. : Search engine

7. c: Enterprise systems

8. c: Fraud

9. b: Business-to-business

10. b: Content management system

11. a: Phishing

12. b: Data warehouse

13. : ICANN

14. b: Mozy

15. a: Dashboard

16. b: Wide Area Network

17. b: Economies of scale

18. d: Collision

19. a: Microprocessor

20. c: Disintermediation

21. c: Extensible Markup Language

22. : Data

23. c: Innovation

24. d: Artificial intelligence

25. a: Internet

26. c: Groupware

27. a: Mass customization

28. d: Change control

29. b: Authentication protocol

30. d: Edge computing

31. d: Data center

32. b: Strategic planning

33. : Craigslist

34. c: Mobile commerce

35. d: Interoperability

36. : Interview

37. c: COBIT

38. b: Epicor

39. a: Master data

40. c: Chart

41. : Availability

42. c: Web content

43. : Switch

44. b: User interface

45. b: Management information system

46. c: Data link

47. : Telnet

48. d: Government-to-business

49. : Data aggregator

50. d: Google Maps

51. d: American Express

52. c: Information management

53. c: Clickstream

54. a: Social media

55. b: Entity-relationship

56. : Privacy policy

57. b: Database

58. c: Enterprise application

59. a: M-Pesa

Marketing

1. a: Manufacturing

2. : Customer value

3. a: Integrated marketing

4. : Goal

5. b: Innovation

6. d: Household

7. b: Leadership

8. b: Brand extension

9. d: Census

10. : Telemarketing

11. b: Logistics

12. : Mobile marketing

13. a: Health

14. a: Price

15. c: Competitive intelligence

16. b: Business model

17. a: Brand awareness

18. a: Respondent

19. c: Psychographic

20. c: Management

21. c: Early adopter

22. d: Social network

23. : Commercialization

24. a: Competitor

25. : Commerce

26. c: Inventory

27. a: Database marketing

28. : Relationship marketing

29. : Direct selling

30. : Interactive marketing

31. d: Qualitative research

32. a: Entrepreneur

33. : Ford

34. c: Credit

35. : Inflation

36. a: Business marketing

37. d: Logo

38. a: Star

39. d: Life

40. : Microsoft

41. c: Commodity

42. a: Hearing

43. b: Infomercial

44. b: Price war

45. b: Advertising

46. a: Customer experience

47. b: Creativity

48. d: Franchising

49. a: Brand

50. a: Cost

51. a: Marketing mix

52. : Tangible

53. c: Authority

54. d: Mission statement

55. a: Argument

56. d: Distribution channel

57. : Loyalty program

58. b: Small business

59. c: Market share

Manufacturing

1. d: Opportunity cost

2. d: Extended enterprise

3. d: Sales

4. c: Customer

5. : Synergy

6. c: Steel

7. c: Cost reduction

8. : Technical support

9. c: Concurrent engineering

10. : Aggregate planning

11. b: Waste

12. b: Service level

13. b: Material requirements planning

14. : Scientific management

15. c: Purchasing process

16. : Rolling Wave planning

17. b: Quality function deployment

18. c: E-procurement

19. d: Production schedule

20. c: Total cost

21. a: Scope statement

22. d: Pattern

23. c: Water

24. c: Management process

25. : Minitab

26. d: Business process

27. d: Request for quotation

28. d: Total cost of ownership

29. b: Quality by Design

30. b: Economic order quantity

31. c: American Society for Quality

32. : Change management

33. c: Inventory control

34. d: Toshiba

35. : Authority

36. d: Reorder point

37. : Supply chain risk management

38. : Cost

39. : Solution

40. a: Sony

41. : Product differentiation

42. c: Reboiler

43. c: Vendor

44. d: Project manager

45. : Project

46. : METRIC

47. : E-commerce

48. d: Assembly line

49. c: Milestone

50. b: Furnace

51. d: Stakeholder management

52. d: Economies of scope

53. b: Time management

54. d: Total productive maintenance

55. b: Resource allocation

56. d: Heat transfer

57. a: Bullwhip effect

58. b: Sequence

59. a: Asset

Commerce

1. : E-commerce

2. : Authority

3. c: Dutch auction

4. d: Import

5. d: Control system

6. b: Minimum wage

7. c: Purchasing

8. c: Netflix

9. a: Phishing

10. a: Pension

11. a: Boot

12. a: Chief executive officer

13. b: Accounting

14. : Initiative

15. d: Invoice

16. a: Bankruptcy

17. b: Lease

18. b: Vickrey auction

19. c: Expense

20. a: Free market

21. c: Planning

22. c: Revenue management

23. : Bottom line

24. : Manufacturing

25. : Trade

26. b: Inventory control

27. : European Union

28. a: Shopping cart

29. d: DigiCash

30. d: Corporation

31. a: Market segmentation

32. c: Economy

33. c: Tourism

34. b: Inventory

35. b: Marketspace

36. a: Electronic commerce

37. d: Issuing bank

38. a: Vendor

39. c: Goal

40. : Marketing strategy

41. c: Interest

42. b: Contract

43. c: Variable cost

44. : Entrepreneur

45. : Preference

46. c: Permission marketing

47. : Standing

48. b: Electronic funds transfer

49. a: Charter

50. b: Front office

51. c: Yield management

52. c: Productivity

53. a: Aid

54. c: Mobile commerce

55. c: Logistics Management

56. d: Auction

57. c: Information system

58. a: Disintermediation

59. a: Pop-up ad

Business ethics

1. d: Interlocking directorate

2. c: Utilitarianism

3. b: Electronic waste

4. b: Endangered Species Act

5. c: Capitalism

6. a: Corporation

7. a: Petroleum

8. a: Patriot Act

9. a: Habitat

10. c: Stanford Financial Group

11. : Trojan horse

12. c: Fraud

13. c: Fannie Mae

14. d: Hedonism

15. b: Better Business Bureau

16. : Vigilance committee

17. b: Recovery Act

18. d: Toxic waste

19. b: Business model

20. d: Subprime lending

21. a: Invisible hand

22. a: Federal Trade Commission Act

23. b: Wall Street

24. b: Human nature

25. b: Junk bond

26. a: Undue hardship

27. : Auditor independence

28. d: Organizational culture

29. b: Green marketing

30. b: Transocean

31. d: Perception

32. a: Ethics Resource Center

33. : Kyoto Protocol

34. c: Socialism

35. b: Ponzi scheme

36. a: Employee Polygraph Protection Act

37. : Skill

38. d: Consumer Protection

39. c: United Farm Workers

40. d: Marketing

41. d: Lead paint

42. b: Insider trading

43. d: Self-interest

44. a: Organic food

45. c: Clayton Act

46. b: Referent power

47. d: Statutory law

48. b: Corporate social responsibility

49. b: Corporate citizenship

50. d: Consumerism

51. d: Madoff

52. c: Enron

53. c: Community development financial institution

54. a: Tobacco

55. d: Financial Stability Oversight Council

56. d: Volcker Rule

57. b: Planet

58. b: Solar power

59. b: Urban sprawl

Accounting

1. a: Fair value

2. a: Standard deduction

3. b: Contributed capital

4. d: Debtor

5. c: Inventory

6. : Probate

7. a: International Federation of Accountants

8. d: Adjusting entries

9. d: Adverse

10. : Market value

11. d: Certified Public Accountant

12. a: Preferred stock

13. : Return on investment

14. : Gift card

15. : Fraud

16. b: Subsidiary ledger

17. a: Gross profit

18. a: Common stock

19. : Bookkeeping

20. : Loan

21. b: Incentive

22. b: Quick ratio

23. a: Property tax

24. a: Asset

25. : Accounting management

26. d: Accounting records

27. : Corporation

28. d: Intangible asset

29. d: Information systems

30. a: Stock Exchange

31. a: Net present value

32. a: Managerial accounting

33. b: Comprehensive income

34. : Party

35. : Double taxation

36. b: Controversy

37. b: Financial analysis

38. a: Free cash flow

39. b: Process Management

40. : Fair Labor Standards Act

41. a: Self-employment

42. b: Personal identification number

43. c: Securities and Exchange Commission

44. d: Debt-to-equity ratio

45. : Invoice

46. a: Balance sheet

47. c: Capital gain

48. : Tax expense

49. c: Tax law

50. b: Remote deposit

51. a: Chart of accounts

52. : Independent contractor

53. : Activity-based costing

54. a: Error

55. b: Expense

56. d: Arthur Andersen

57. : Pension

58. a: Accounting research

59. a: Partnership

CPSIA information can be obtained
at www.ICGtesting.com
Printed in the USA
LVHW011543301019
635718LV00004B/389/P